A journey to Awakening.
The memoirs of a Dhamma disciple

by
Michael Kewley
Dhammachariya Paññadipa

Nothing proceeds without a cause.
(The Buddha)

Nothing just happens.
(Dhammachariya Paññadipa)

All rights reserved.

No part of this publication may be reproduced, stored in a retrieval system or transmitted, in any form or by any means, electronic, mechanical, photocopying, recording or otherwise, without prior permission of the publishers.

This book is sold subject to the condition that it shall not by way of trade or otherwise, be lent, re-sold, hired out or otherwise circulated without the publishers prior consent in any form of binding cover other than that in which it is published and without similar condition including this condition being imposed on the subsequent purchaser.

Copyright©Michael Kewley 2017

ISBN: 978-1-899417-20-9

Published by:
Panna Dipa Books.

e-mail:
dhammateacher@hotmail.com

The memoirs of a Dhamma disciple

Dedication.

To the world that I serve,
may all beings be happy.

A journey to Awakening

Content

Introduction.   9

- PART 1 -   11
Finding my Path

- PART 2 -   191
The India Years

- PART 3 -   303
My life as a koan

Epilogue.   327

A journey to Awakening

Introduction.

When I was first asked to write these Dhamma memoirs my immediate response was a definite no!
However, the argument was put that should I die soon, my disciples would have my teaching in various books and compact discs, but not my story and perhaps understanding my personal journey would give light to their own path.
Eventually I was convinced that it had value and so I set to work, after all, I had always delighted in hearing the life stories of my own teacher, like the time his mischievous action of secretly smoking the cigars of a recently deceased monk was assumed to have been the return of the monk himself in ghostly form to conclude his final earthly pleasure. When I asked if he had told his fellow monastics exactly what had transpired, he simply shook his head, laughed his impish laugh and said, «No, I just stayed quiet.»
Here then is my account of my Dhamma life and my training, as well as the time spent with my teacher during twenty two years as a disciple, a fully ordained monk and assistant to him, and how I remember it.
I have focused almost entirely on my practice and the influences that led me to that practice and then kept me on my path.
Personal relationships, except when they were influential to my training have been skirted over. This is not to say that they did not have value, only that they do not have a significant relevance to my Dhamma storyline.
I have been as true as my memory would allow, but as I didn't keep notes or any accurate records I'm sure that it is possible for the most pedantic reader to find small errors with dates and specific events in the time line. However, for the most part, everything happened as written and although one or two things may be out of sequence, I do not think it detracts from the narrative.

It was a blessing to meet the people that I met and receive their Dhamma lessons, good or bad, for in the end when our heart is open, everything becomes our teacher.

I put my hands together in Anjali to all who have been a part of my life and say thank you for without your presence and your influence perhaps this journey would not yet be finished.

Michael Kewley
Dhammachariya Paññadipa
France
December 2016

- PART 1 -

FINDING MY PATH

A journey to Awakening

If everything I have been told is correct, I was born at four o'clock in the morning on the thirteenth of December nineteen fifty one, at the Jane Crookhall Maternity Home, Douglas, Isle of Man.

My mother, Violet Catherine Carrier, then a nineteen year old girl from Liverpool, did not tell me very much about the birth except to say that I wanted to arrive whilst we were still in the ambulance, but through sheer determination, closed legs and gritted teeth she held on until she was rolled into the delivery room.

She had left her home and family of father and two brothers, Norman and Billy, to come to the Isle of Man and work in the hotel trade as a low level maid, cleaning rooms and taking care of the thousands of tourists who would visit the island in the summer. It was here that she met my father, then recently discharged from the army, fell in love and married in Saint Ninians Church, in Douglas. Two years later I arrived.

I think that my father was pleased to meet me, having spent the early hours of the morning pacing up and down in the corridor, smoking extra strong untipped Capstan cigarettes and awaiting the sound of the slap from the doctor on a baby's bottom, and the shriek of this new being arriving in his life.

This was also the day my father was laid off work. There was no redundancy in those days, so people really had to endure the shock of no work suddenly appearing in their life.

My father, Thomas Noel Kewley, was a joiner journeyman who unfortunately finished his contract of installing interior doors at Central Drive, a terrace of newly constructed houses in Onchan, in those days, a small village adjoining Douglas.

Now he had a young wife, a new baby and no work. What to do? For the next two years or so we lived in Palatine Road, Douglas, with my father finding work where he could. A little bit of this and a little bit of that was not his recipe for a secure life and so he began to explore the possibility of moving off the island.

It would not be his first time away, having been, at the age of

eighteen, part of the D. Day landings in France.
Like so many men of his generation, he never spoke about the war and only mentioned it to me in passing as we were sitting together on the sofa one Sunday afternoon watching the twenty fifth anniversary of the beginning of the 'final push' on the television. When the commentator mentioned 'gold beach' my father simply said, 'that's the beach I landed on!'
I was shocked. He was a young man, a dispatch rider taking messages on his motor bike to the front line and collecting identification from dead allied soldiers to send home to their families. As I reflect now all those years later, I see that all those horrors of war informed his gentleness, kindness and compassion. In all our time together, he never hit me!
I can say comfortably that my father was a caring, loving and protective man, with incredible humour, whose idea of honor was to take care of those dependent on him, and who now found himself unemployed less than ten years after the end of the war, with a new family to take care of.
With this in mind he contacted an older man he knew in England who owned his own building company, and asked for work.
Percy Proctor, was a small big bellied Yorkshire man who offered my father a job and so the small Kewley family packed everything they could into his Triumph motor bike and sidecar and rode onto the boat to begin our new life in Barnoldswick, Yorkshire, England.
My parents took a house in this small town and began to renovate it. My job was to keep out of the way and to help with that, my father would give me a large piece of wood, a hammer and a bag of nails. The instructions were simple, 'keep your eye on the head of the nail, and don't hit your thumb'. Many happy hours were spent in this activity, and the never ending stream of my father's simple practical advice stood me in good stead in later years when I would work as a husband and father in my own house.

Number twenty two Essex Street became my home for the next few years where I was king of the castle until on the thirty first of December nineteen fifty four at Skipton Hospital, my sister was born.

I have no memory at all of the preceding months of my mothers pregnancy, only that she arrived home like the queen with a little princess. This little princess, my sister, was named Sandra, apparently on my suggestion after the woman who took care of me occasionally and with whom I had fallen in love, and Jane after my grandmother. Now the Kewley family was complete, with no more new arrivals, planned or not!

Things changed again and school began. Rainhall Road primary school opened its doors to me and my education began. We played football or games of army or cowboys and Indians during playtime, had outdoor toilets where as young boys one of our favourite pastimes was to see who could pee highest up the wall. Such fun and such innocence.

I stayed for school lunch which in my mind always was and will be awful. Lumpy, watery mashed potato with a piece of dead animal on a plate was our regular fare, which we ate because there was not always so much at home. Our evening meal, prepared by my mother after her work at Silentnight mattress company came always with a choice of 'take it or leave it,' there was no third option.

'Fill up with bread,' my father would shout if we were still hungry, and to make that offer more interesting on one occasion my mother offered me a sugar butty.

Simply, this is bread and butter liberally sprinkled with granulated sugar.

It was awful, and perhaps because of this I never really developed a 'sweet tooth.'

My father by this time was working for Rolls Royce as a capstan turner on the night shift. He was my hero and my mother was the love of my life.

I became a 'latch key' kid, letting myself in after school as my father slept and stayed quiet in the house. Everything was a great adventure and as we didn't know another way to be, we were quite content with our lot.

Working with my mother at Silentnight, was her younger brother, my uncle Billy. He was recently released from his national service, serving with the army in Egypt.

I thought he was incredibly handsome and film-starish, with his slim body and black brylcreemed hair. He would take me for rides on his motorbike, with me straddling the petrol tank. No helmet for either of us, and no protective clothing. Once again we didn't know another way to be, and I loved it. We were stopped one day by a policeman who thought this was not a good idea, and so that was the end of that.

Uncle Billy drove the big delivery van for Silentnight, taking mattresses to different parts of the country. On shorter journeys he would let me ride along. One time he asked if I would like to ride in the back with the mattresses. For some unknown reason I said yes, and so for the next forty minutes, which seemed like an eternity I sat in the back of this huge van watching the enormous stack of mattresses sway and tilt expecting them to fall on me at any moment. It was terrifying.

If my father was James Stewart, uncle Billy was James Dean, and in accordance with that, was married to auntie Sylvia, a buxom blonde in the style of Marilyn Monroe, wearing tight, low cut dresses and walking with a pronounced wiggle.

Even at such an early age I knew she had a certain, 'je ne sais quoi.'

But uncle Billy and auntie Sylvia had one more quality to attract the attention of a small boy. Their neighbour was a well-known television actor appearing in England's longest running soap opera, Coronation Street. On one occasion when I was staying with them he arrived home from the television studio where he had been filming and waved to me. That was really something. The actor was Bernard Youens and played the character of Stan Ogden, long suffering husband of Hilda. These were popular characters and so to be so close to one of them was truly wonderful.

Even if she worked a full-time job my mother always took a loving care of me. I unconsciously appreciated this and on one occasion when she came to meet me from school, she held my hand as we walked up the small hill to the backstreet where our house was. I couldn't help myself and had to express my deepest feelings for her, «Mum,» I said, «you are the prettiest mother in the whole school.» Such is love.

My mother was a poorly educated young woman whose dream of being an Olympic swimmer died when she became ill with an abscess in her ear, lost her hearing on one side and was no longer allowed in water. Perhaps it was because of this that she held great aspirations for me.

She herself loved to read and encouraged me to follow her example at every opportunity. She could also multitask to an art form and I remember her sitting on the sofa knitting, reading a book and watching television. Of course, the most common question to anyone who was with her was «Who's that?» flashing a glance at the black and white images on the television screen.

Naturally she had her weaknesses. She could be loving, playful and kind, but also angry and sometimes forgetful.

On one occasion I was sitting on the floor in the living room after school watching Popeye on the television. My sister was sleeping in her pram somewhere behind me.

I became aware of something behind the sofa and went to investigate. I couldn't be sure what I had seen so I went to the kitchen where my mother was cooking.

«Mum,» I said, «there's something red coming out of the sofa.»

She came to look and screamed, «My god, the house is on fire!»
Apparently a match had fallen into the springs of the sofa and ignited when someone had sat on it. Nobody noticed until I became aware.

My mother grabbed me and ran out of the house. Neighbours were always available in those days and soon help arrived.

«Where's Sandra?» Someone asked.

«Oh god, I've left her in the house!» cried my mother.

In her shock she had forgotten the sleeping baby. However, no damage was done to either the house or the baby, and all ended well.

On another occasion when my father was working his night shift and I was asleep in bed, I was awakened by a terrific crash from the next room. With sleepy eyes I stumbled into my parents bedroom to find my mother lying on the floor semi-conscious with a huge gash in her head. She had stood upon a chair to fix something at the window and fallen. Happily I was able to comprehend the situation in some way and go next door to get help, and again all ended well.

My sister and I would be put to bed in the evening, often with the threats of the slender, silver, wooden stick above the door that would be used to beat us if we didn't obey immediately. Naturally in such a family as ours, it was never used, even if on occasion it would be taken down and brandished as a last resort to send us upstairs.

However, usually our mother would stand at the foot of the stairs and begin the nightly threats, and then begin to count from one to three slowly and menacingly. At three we would run past her giggling and scramble into our beds. I could then read for half an hour the most wonderful stories of Biggles, the Famous Five, and other children's books, whilst she read to my sister. Then it was time for sleeping, but before that, a song.

My mother had no ability to sing, and she couldn't carry a tune in a bucket as the expression goes, but this was the moment we all loved.

Sitting on my sister's bed she would sing 'Tea for two,' and then a cuddle and a long kiss goodnight.

Now me. My song was 'Lily of Laguna,' and although I didn't like the song at all, I loved her singing it to me. Then for me too, a kiss good night, and as she left the room my sister would shout, 'leave the door open,' and I would follow with my specific instruction, 'leave the landing light on'.

My days at school passed without incident and I remember only three teachers with any clarity. The first was a young Scottish man, Mr McKay, strong, athletic and handsome, memorable because one morning as the school was filing into the hall for assembly he saw a mouse sitting in the middle of the floor. Like a rocket he raced towards it and kicked this little being with all his might and ended its life as it slid motionless across the waxed surface.

The second was I think everybody's favorite, an ancient lady of tiny stature with grey hair tied into a bun and thick knitted stockings. Her name was Miss Ogden, whom we affectionately called 'Oggy Poggy'.

The headmistress of this small school, Mrs Robinson, is memorable for two things. She was a large lady with a huge bosom and I think a caring heart behind it. She taught arithmetic, which was as strange and incomprehensible a subject to me as any subject could be. I can remember sitting in class crying because I could not understand the concept of 'carrying one' or 'pay back one' in subtraction. She was kind and caring to this little boy so upset in class, but was not able to help me comprehend the language and formula of arithmetic. Although I eventually became comfortable with simple mathematics, the difficulty with numbers stayed with me throughout my school life.

This large lady one day announced that something special was to happen that day and that we, the senior class, would walk the short distance to her house to watch this event on her television, so historic was it.

The day was the twelfth of April nineteen sixty one and it was the moment when the first human being would return to earth having orbited our planet three times. Yuri Gagarin was a small Russian cosmonaut and the first man to leave the earth's atmosphere. He was a global hero.

We sat in a crowded parlor watching the event on a small black and white television, wondering what all the fuss was about. It was true that it was time away from the classroom, but none of us as ten year old boys and girls grasped the significance of the debut of space travel.

One of the two most memorable events of my school career in Barnoldswick was the day when our young class teacher said «Today I'm going to read you a story, so sit quietly, fold your arms in front of you and listen.»

The story was Peter Pan by J.M. Barrie. I think it had a huge effect on my life, this story of the boy who never grew up and I carry the memory of this experience with me even today. It opened me to a world of wonder, excitement and a sadness. Such is the power of words.

On Monday mornings we would be allowed to draw on foolscap paper. One morning I drew a simple sail boat and wrote underneath, 'yacht'. Mrs Robinson, our headmistress, sauntered past, looked over my shoulder and stopped in amazement.

«Michael, where did you learn to spell yacht?»

Of course I had no idea. At home we had the full collection of the Encyclopedia Britannica, and I spent many happy hours reading and looking at the pictures. I imagine I had seen the word written there and for some reason, the spelling stuck.

I told her I didn't know, but she was so impressed that she gathered other teachers to come and look. Perhaps she felt that she had a child prodigy in her class - it didn't last. In the end I excelled at being average!

Playtime was always a pleasure with all of us boys dividing into our different groups and playing football or endless games of cowboys and Indians or war.

The rules for war were simple. We were to be an areoplane running around the school yard with our arms outstretched shooting the other side making the famous machine gun noise at the back of our throats. More than that there was nothing to do except occasionally parachute out of our damaged plane and begin a land war making the same machine gun noise but this time using our arms as the gun.

No one ever died and we all emerged heroes.

In winter we would play in the snow until we were so cold and wet we would beg our mothers to let us back in the house.

One favorite story from my father was the day he sent me off to school in mid winter after a big snowfall. I was wearing little red Wellington boots, and apparently I ran around the corner of our backstreet directly into a huge snowdrift. I must have been running quite fast because I became stuck in the snow and it was only after some time that I managed to free myself and slowly walked home again crying and looking like a mobile snowman.

The summer days were long and hot, with the tar melting in the street giving us boys something to make models with and drive our mothers crazy by ruining our clothes. It seems that there was always something to do. Boys arriving at the back door and asking if I could come out to play?

«He's having his dinner,» my mother would say, «wait there, he'll be out in ten minutes.»

In those days it was rare to allow other children into the house, even when it rained.

We played football, rounders and cricket in the street, and even held the street Olympic Games where John Barnes, the biggest, oldest and so senior boy in the group would win everything in sight, and if not him, then his cousin Walter who had a 'pot' leg but could still outrun the rest of us.

We would go out in the morning during the long school holidays with a bottle of water and a packet of sandwiches to King Hill. There we would stay for hours, playing cowboys and Indians, war, African explorers and other boy games. We would eat our sandwiches and share the bottle of water, taking turns to drink from the bottle and not minding at all the breadcrumbs floating in the water after each mouthful.

During one of our long summer holidays my parents announced that we would go to Blackpool for the day. This is a northern seaside town, famous for its one third size copy of the Eiffel Tower in Paris, the Golden Mile, a long street of amusements, fish and chip shops, gambling and penny arcades. In other words, paradise!

We loaded our things into my father's Singer Gazelle car and set off. My mother naturally had made sandwiches with a thermos of tea for them and orange juice for us children and put them in a large picnic basket. This had been placed on the back seat next to my sister.

«Put the basket on the floor,» my mother told my sister. My sister declined to act.

«Put the basket on the floor,» my mother repeated. Still no movement.

Finally she gave up, and the journey continued in peace.

After some time we arrived at a long line of cars stationary in a traffic jam.

We sat there for a few minutes and soon became aware of a sound approaching, getting louder and louder. It was an engine and was roaring. Then, from nowhere, a large object appeared from around the bend where we had stopped.

It hit the car hard with glass being sprayed everywhere accompanied by the sounds of nightmares. Screeching brakes, metal sliding along the road.

It took some moments to realize what had happened, but later we discovered that a motorbike and sidecar had taken the bend too fast, crashed into our immobile car, thrown off the rider and his passenger who then slid up the road until they came to a stop, broken and almost dead.

My father being the truly wonderful man he was immediately jumped out of the car to see if he could help, whilst my mother turned around to see if we children were O.K.

We were fine, shaken of course, but not injured, for all the glass that came flying into the car had been stopped by the picnic basket that my sister had refused to move.

We were taken to our mother's brother's house whilst our parents made statements to the police etc.

The couple on the motor bike survived, but were hospitalized for a long time. My father visited them often.

Although we went to Blackpool many times as children, my mother never again insisted that the picnic basket should be put on the floor!

On the rare occasions when friends of my parents or relatives would visit on a Sunday afternoon, my sister and I were told to perform. We would have to give a small concert in the living room where we would sing together popular songs of the time. The preference of my mother and grandmother who would sit together on the sofa with adoring eyes, was a song by a famous young singer of the time, called Cliff Richard. He was a huge star of those days and the song was called 'Theme for a dream.' I would sing the lead and my sister the backing vocals, to the delighted smiles and appreciation of everyone. Next would be my solo effort, another popular song, this time by a man called Lonnie Donagan. The title, 'My Old Man's a Dustman.' This was my favorite mainly I think for the humour in it. I don't think I needed too much persuasion to perform and perhaps that played a part in preparing me for my quite public life now?

On Friday evening my father would finish work early and I was allowed to wait for him in my pale blue dressing gown with the little teddy bear on the pocket, having just had my bath in front of the open fire in the living room, until he arrived with fish and chips in newspaper to share at nine o'clock.

It was on one of these Friday evenings I heard him make the funniest and cleverest joke I had ever heard.

My mother, father and me sat together in front of the small black and white television, my sister already asleep in bed, watching the classic film, 'The guns of Naverone,' a war time story of heroism starring Gregory Peck, David Niven, Anthony Quinn and a host of others.

The team had arrived at night on the island of Naverone and had to move on.

«We must travel light,» said Gregory Peck.

The scene changed immediately and showed the group in the morning moving into their positions.

«Well,» said my father, «they said they needed to travel light.»

This was the most brilliant thing I had ever heard anyone say, the sheer genius of the manipulation of the word 'light'.

It was a sign of the years to come of clever, stupid and heart-warming jokes from the man who became my first hero.

Soon my little sister joined me at school. It was my job to take care of her and make sure we arrived and left together. Each day my father, just home from his night shift at the factory would cook a traditional breakfast for us of porridge in winter and a fried egg on toast for the rest of the year. Of course he meant well, but really I hated this egg with its runny yolk sticking to my teeth, but forced myself to eat it every morning. What else was there? Then we would clean our teeth and receive one penny each to spend on sweets. My preference was to buy four licorice chews called 'black jacks' at a farthing each after school and so I would carry my penny with me all day and spend it on the way home.

This worked well until my sister would wait for me at the school gate in the afternoon and with a soulful expression tell me, «Mike, I've lost my penny.»

She was my little sister, what could I do except give her mine?

This scenario played out almost every day until we stopped attending Rainhall Road school, and in all that time I never suspected the truth, that she had spent her own penny in the morning and manipulated me into giving her mine. Such is brotherly love.

One of my closest friends in those days was Keith Bateman, a small, thin, pale child with blonde hair and large national health glasses. Each evening after school we would go to his house to play for a while. This was both a blessing and a curse. A blessing because we were 'best friends' and a curse because his father was a baker and his house adjoined the bakery. The aroma of bread and cakes baking in the oven was almost too strong to bear.

The most important thing for my mother was my education, and for my father, my childhood, and so life continued with me joining the Cub Scouts, primarily to own my own knife which would hang from my belt, but also the idea of camping and living in the wild appealed to me very much. Like everything in life the idea is much bigger and more colourful than the reality and after a few weeks I stopped going. My parents, especially my father, were always supportive of decisions like these and I can only presume now, all these years later, that they too were not people always looking to belong to different groups and associations, and although they did not prevent their children from trying things out, they did not insist that we stay with something that they themselves were indifferent about.

The only thing they insisted upon was that we attended Sunday school each Sunday afternoon. This was not really a chore for me because it seems that we all had a nice time with bible stories and game-playing, but there was always a doubt as to why we had to go.

Neither of my parents were religious in any way, and many years later when I asked my father if he believed in God, his surprising answer was a shoulder shrugging, 'yes, I suppose so.'

However, later as an adult I understood the insistence on Sunday school.

My father worked at nights, my mother worked during the day. The only 'special' time they had together was Sunday afternoon. Who would want to deprive them of that?

The Cub Scout leader was our neighbour from the opposite side of our back street, a photographer called Richard Brennan. He and his wife, Hilda had two children, the eldest a girl called Janet, who was my age and her younger brother, Philip. Janet and I were close friends and played together often. She was also, according to my mother, my greatest rival at school, with her and I vying for a better place in class than the other each year. I think that we were both oblivious to this competition until exam time, but even then, neither of us were very interested. It seems that at primary school, at least as far as term results were concerned, we were always next to each other in class.

I learned many years later that as a young woman of perhaps twenty one years of age, Janet had died horrifically in a car crash in the town of Clitheroe. She was a passenger trapped in the back of the car as the vehicle burned.

In those days Christmas and birthdays were always a special family affair.

As children we received a small amount of pocket money and with this we could go to the Saturday afternoon cinema and be thrilled by Tarzan, Captain Marvel and the rest. At some point however there was the requirement to procure a gift for the birthdays of our parents. Both my sister and myself would always share our money and buy between us what we considered to be a very special soap and so a very special gift for my father. Imperial Leather, was a tablet of what we considered to be a high quality soap, beautifully packed in a red box and carrying with it a label actually attached to the centre of the bar itself. It looked so elegant and exquisite that this became the favored gift each year.

On the final year of this particular birthday present my father opened the now familiar packet to find the now very familiar gift. He held the soap in his hand and looked so lovingly at us with his mischievous twinkle in his eye and said, «You must think I'm a dirty bugger?»

I think he was the funniest man I ever knew.

Many months before Christmas the big catalogue would come out and we would be allowed to choose our main gift. On Christmas Eve pillow cases would be put at the end of our beds and miraculously and magically filled in the morning. Our principal gift with smaller presents, an orange, dates and a box of Turkish delight.

Christmas lunch was also magical with my grandmother often visiting and a table filled with food. A true feast day. After the main course of turkey and all the trimmings would come the Christmas pudding. It was always a magical moment when both my sister and I would find each year a small silver coin, a sixpence in our pudding.

So much did I believe in the magic of this that it took me well into my adult years before I realized the my mother had deliberately put these coins into her children's pudding before she carried it from the kitchen.

Time passed and occasionally our family would visit my mother's father in Prescott, a small town close to Liverpool. He owned a bar and unknown to my sister and myself, my parents were interested in taking a bar for themselves. As with everything in life, who you know means something and as my grandfather was well respected in this business it was good to be close to him. For myself, I cannot remember anything special about this man except he was small and dapper and allowed us children to play darts when the pub was closed and listen to Freddie and the Dreamers singing 'If You Gotta Make A Fool Of Somebody' but we never really had a relationship to speak of.

He had married for a second time, his first wife, my grandmother having died many years before of diphtheria. I never knew her. On one Saturday afternoon we sat together in his lounge whilst he smoked his cigarettes, drank a beer and tried to interest me in horse racing on the television. It didn't work and quickly I was outside playing in the garden with their dog. Meanwhile my mother and father were learning the bar trade and soon had their name on the list for a pub in Liverpool.

We children were blissfully unaware of the things to come and so it was a shock when one day, sometime in the long summer holidays, they announced that we were going to live in Liverpool, and more than that, we had our own pub.

Of course, we didn't want to leave our school and our friends, but what choice did we have? First, though, we had as a family to go and see this pub where we were going to spend the next years of our lives.

My first impression of the Goat Hotel was not favorable. It was dark, gloomy and of course smelt of beer and cigarettes. It was a working man's pub in the docklands area of Liverpool located on the corner of Great Howard Street and Regent Street. Regent Street joined the Dock road which ran parallel to Great Howard Street, so on one side were the docks and the other was Silcocks corn business, Tate and Lyle, Bents Brewery and more pubs of course.

This was Liverpool in the 'sixties, at that time ready to become the greatest place in the world. The city was just giving birth to the Beatles, the Swinging Blue Jeans, Gerry and the Pacemakers, and the whole Mersey Sound and to be there and see in the street famous group members and pop stars became quite normal. However, that was a year or two in the future. First there was the subject of a new school.

My sister and I attended the primary school together. It was a street off the now famous Scotland Road, where Cilla Black lived, called Penrhyn Street. It was impressive for me in as much as the playground was on the roof and the boys could wear jeans.

After the initial shock of being the new boy and having to face the first day interrogation I was quite well received.

I was asked if I supported Liverpool or Everton football teams? I have never supported a football team as much as I enjoyed playing it at school and even in the school football team in Barnoldswick where I was given the nickname, 'the terror of the pitch'. A title I enjoyed though never understood what it meant.

So there I was, standing in front of a group of boys all claiming that I spoke with a posh accent (flat Yorkshire rather than the more nasal Scouse) and demanding to know which team I supported. I had to think fast and so I said, 'Manchester United.' Big mistake. Better to have played stupid than to give a response like that.

My reply was met with a silence and then the production of a pair of scissors and the removal of a piece of my hair. The reality was that only an answer of either Liverpool or Everton would have been accepted, with a further possibility of Tranmere Rovers. The other important question to be answered was if I was a Catholic or Protestant? I had no idea what either of these two terms meant, such was the blessing of belonging to a family where religion was not seen as important at all. I said that I didn't know and so it was assumed that I was a Protestant - a proddy doggy.

After that all went well except for the time one boy told me he would meet me after school and kill me. I had never heard a threat like that and I believed it to be literal, so I spent many days avoiding him and finding new ways home in the evenings.

My father used to take my sister and me to school in the morning in his new car and this became one of my saddest memories at Penrhyn Street. We would stop outside the gate and he would kiss my sister and me lovingly on the cheek as we left the car.

One morning my classmates saw us and being boys, made fun of me all day.

'Bye darling, bye love, bye treasure,' and so on, followed by endless kissing noises.

The next day I asked my father not to kiss me. He understood of course, but now when I think of it there is a sense of regret. Such is growing up and the reality of peer pressure.

At the age of eleven I and the rest of my class, were obliged to take a special examination called the eleven plus, to decide whether we would attend a secondary modern school or be selected for a grammar school.

I think I just managed to sneak through and much to my mother's delight was accepted at the John Hamilton high school for boys. This was located in Everton and taking two or three busses to go and return each day was not considered exceptional, and certainly nothing to complain about. On top of that we were given three hours of homework each day, and excuses were not accepted.

These were different days and as children we were given and accepted high degrees of self responsibility.

The pride of my mother showed in her face and when the day arrived that we had to go into the city proper to be measured for my school uniform she almost exploded.

The uniform was very specific from cap to shoes, but because I was so small I had to wear short trousers. This of course I hated, but it was only for one year and I was certainly not the only one.

The first day was something quite military with the new influx of boys standing stiffly in long rows in the school yard wearing our caps and awaiting inspection of our uniforms and hair length. The headmaster, Mister Baxter, immediately known as 'baldy Baxter', because of his incredibly shiny bald head, arrived wearing his long black flowing robes and mortar board, followed by the deputy headmaster, Mr. Hall. They were very different with Mr Baxter, quite military, erect with a very upper class accent and a way of speaking that was very unfamiliar. One day some years later I was called into his office to be told that my hair, just touching my collar at the back was too long.

«Tell your people, boy,» he lectured, «that we don't allow long hair at this institution.»

'My people?' I thought, 'who does he think we are?'

Mr Hall was much more relaxed, funny and easier to relate to. He caught a group of us smoking one day some years later and compassionately lectured us about the danger of cigarettes. So loving was he that we just giggled throughout the whole thing, and continued smoking of course.

We formed our different groups in class, and I became one of those boys sitting quite close to the back, joking and fooling around.

The discipline was quite strict and military style. Whenever a teacher would arrive in the classroom we all had to stand and wait to be told to sit again. If we were ever asked our name, we would have to jump up with arms by our side and speak loudly and clearly, 'Sir, Kewley, Sir.'

Nicknames became the bane of our lives, some of them being very unpleasant.

My favourite one for me was 'Spike', and least favourite was 'Fuzz', because of my very curly hair. Oh how I wanted straight hair. I even slept in a tight hat very often to flatten and straighten it for the next day. The effect was short lived and within hours it would spring up again. My mother and grandmother of course thought it was lovely, and kept telling me how they wished they had hair like mine. I would have happily swapped!

Even in later years when I wore my hair long it grew out before it grew down. Happily I was a fan of Jimi Hendrix so I didn't feel awkward. Love and peace, man.

We played our games, selected our favorite teachers and tortured the rest.

Through one accidental moment a new, young and inexperienced teacher immediately became our hero. He was short, wore glasses and taught French, three things working against him until the magic moment arrived. His name was Mr Sneath.

He had given our class (the B stream, always the middle of the middle for me) a test to asses our understanding and arrived the next day for the forty minute period with the results. His arms were full of our exercise books when he pushed open the door with one hand. The spring on the door was strong and the door began to close on him. To save himself he extended his leg to push the door open, and that is what a collection of thirty, twelve year old boys at a grammar school in Liverpool saw: a teacher really angry kicking open the door to our classroom. It was fantastic and he soared in our estimation. He arrived at his desk, slammed down our books and glared at the class, «I'm not satisfied with your puny efforts,» he yelled. But we were more than satisfied with him. He became our hero and I'm sure he received more respect and admiration than any other teacher in the school.

One of my favourite memories in French class was when Michael Dever, one of our back of the class gang was asked to translate a paragraph from French to English.

He had no idea of course and desperately looked around for help, and we, as his closest and best friends, were ready to assist in any way possible.

The first sentence began with the words, 'le lendemain' meaning 'the next day'. I knew the true meaning but whispered, 'the laundryman' to which Michael gratefully accepted and said aloud. There was a pause, Mr Sneath pointed at him, then the door and uttered with an exasperated sigh, the beautiful words, «Out Dever, out.»

Learning a second language at school was compulsory and the first French lesson was a revelation to all of us. Although we knew that there were other languages in the world, as far as our social information was concerned, gathered from many Hollywood films, everbody spoke English.

'This is ridiculous,' I thought, 'when will I ever need to speak French?'

Who knew that thirty five years later I would fall in love, marry a French woman and live in France? Such is the beautiful uncertainty of life.

Naturally we had names for all our teachers, but my preferred one was for our gym teacher. He was tall, muscular with a thick black beard. He was called 'Gillette'. He broke many health and safety rules by making gym class entertaining and fun. Coastguards and pirates was our preferred game with one group of boys chasing another group of boys on every piece of equipment in the gymnasium. The rules were simple, we were not allowed to touch the floor, and although we only needed to touch the other for them to join the 'coastguards' team, in reality we were often dragged to the floor and jumped on. Such great boys fun!

Cross country running days was a different affair as I was one of the group of boys who would run out of the field at the beginning, and once out of sight immediately stop, gather with my little gang of friends and stroll the rest of the way of our route to the finishing line ready to get changed and go home.

Perhaps we thought of it as a protest against the school institution, but mostly I think we felt it was pointless just to run for no purpose. Our English teacher Mr Cross, was the most miserable man I think I have ever met, but he liked and encouraged me and the lessons were enjoyable.

Surprisingly my very favorite teacher was Mr Evans, the maths teacher. Although I still could not understand the subject at all, he was always kind and playful, taking his pipe in and out of his mouth as he made the most incomprehensible mathematical points. I even had private lessons with him at lunch time towards the end of my school career in Liverpool, but all to no avail.

In the end these extra maths lessons didn't really help me but happily anything more than simple addition and subtraction, multiplication and division, has never been really necessary for me. I think I had a form of number dyslexia, something that I could only accept and move on.

One day came the announcement that a supply teacher would be taking us for a week or two as our form master was ill. We were told it was a lady and we should be courteous to her.

We naturally expected a woman 'of a certain age' possibly with blue hair and thick knitted stockings and sensible shoes, but this was not the case.

Miss Rogers was young, blonde and very attractive. She wore a tangerine knitted mini dress with a gold linked belt hanging from her hip. We followed every sentence she uttered, but could not remember a single word she said. It is a testament to her beauty to a class of thirty two fourteen year old boys that I have no memory of the subject she taught.

Education is important, but playing the guitar is importanter!

The Beatles and the Mersey Sound were sweeping the country and they influenced all of us. The first thing was to dress as much like them as we could. This was difficult for me as my hair was curly and more in the style of Jimi Hendrix rather than John Lennon, but my now best friend, Peter Early, really looked the part. I was envious of his height and his straight black hair which he would wear in the Beatle fashion, and that he had a Beatle jacket. He looked so cool, trendy and fashionable in my eyes. We also smoked in those days, which was not so outrageous. In fact, it was almost a rite of passage.

My father had found cigarettes (stolen from the bar) in my bedroom and asked me if I smoked. I was caught red handed so I could only say 'yes'.

«I don't want you smoking in secret,» he said and offered me a cigarette. Soon it became completely natural to share a cigarette together, often joined by my grandmother.

Peter and I were best friends and played football endlessly. His father Joe owned the pub nearest to us and we would practically live in each other's house.

I encouraged my parents to buy me a guitar so I could form a group. I wanted an electric one of course as acoustic guitars were only for folk singers and the remnants of the skiffle era. My father, being the generous and in this case naive man that he was agreed and bought me a beautiful red Burns Trisonic solid, three pick up guitar, similar to the one Hank Marvin of the Shadows played. That and a small but powerful Selmer amplifier were the perfect gift and I was ready to form my first group. Of course the problem was that neither I nor Peter nor anyone else we knew could play a note. Never mind, we can all practice in my bedroom.

The noise was horrible and the constant shouts of, 'turn it down!' from both my mother and father stay with me forever.

One evening my father, now exhausted by his work and the noise of four teenagers lost in the imagination that the sound they were making would one day threaten the Beatles, threw open the door of my bedroom and made an ultimatum, «You either learn to play that thing properly or I'm throwing it on the fire!»

My father had taken to the publican's life with a passion and had already started to offer sandwiches at lunchtime in the bar, a completely new innovation, and in the morning before I would find my mother often accompanied by my grandmother, slicing demi baguettes, or nujjers as they were called in Liverpool and filling them with either cheese or ham. The idea of combining these two fillings was still some years away.

These nujjers would be wrapped in tin foil and sold at lunchtime to the dockers who would arrive at the doors for opening time by the dozens.

Later came hot pies. The bar filled every lunch time and evening and for the weekend three semi professional musicians would arrive to perform. Together they were called 'The Magestics' and they were incredibly popular. There was a drummer, a pianist and a very competent guitarist. Friday, Saturday and Sunday evening the bar was heaving with people singing together accompanied by The Magestics and soon the highlight of each evening would be when Lily, the pub cleaner, a very large lady with an equally large voice, would sing Ave Maria. People would cry at the beauty of her rendition.

So, my father asked the guitarist of The Magestics if he would give me a few guitar lessons. He said yes, and so I was taken, reluctantly to his house one evening for the first one.

We sat down together and he asked me what my favorite Beatles song was. I couldn't think which it was in that moment, so he said, 'how about this?' and played, 'If I Fell', truly a great song taken from their first film, 'A Hard Day's Night'.

So that's what we played and what I learned. I went home to where Peter was waiting for me in my bedroom with his guitar at the ready and I showed him what I had learned, and we practiced and practiced.

Every week there was a new song, and every week we played until our fingers could no longer press down the strings. I continued my lessons until after six weeks he said, 'now you're on your own', and taught me no more. But it was enough and I was addicted. Peter and I would watch Top of the Pops each Thursday evening to see if you could spot the chords being played in our favorite songs.

On one occasion I was standing at the bus stop with my guitar close to my father's bar when a man approached slightly under the

influence of alcohol. As we were waiting for the bus he noticed my guitar and spoke to me.
«Can you play that thing?» he asked.
«Yes, a bit,» I modestly replied.
«If you can play 'A Hard Day's Night', I'll give you a pound,» he continued.
A pound! That was a fortune, and even better, I could play it, and so I did.
I stood with my guitar at the bus stop as people passed and played and sang the most popular song of the moment by the most popular group of the moment.
This drunken stranger was as good as his word, and as the bus approached he patted me on the shoulder and gave me the pound. As we mounted the bus he said to everyone, «Hey everyone, pay attention, we've got one of the Beatles here.»
It was nice, and I felt good.

On Saturday afternoons we would simply hang out in Frank Hesseys music shop in town and play the guitars there, buy sheet music and stand in admiration as Gerry Marsden from Gerry and the Pacemakers would pop in, or other pop idols of the time.
Peter and I began to write our own songs. Of course three chord amateur attempts but fun and creative anyway.
At this time my sister decided with her best friend Moira MacKenna to form a singing duo and so wrote her own song.
This song still in my mind equals many of the so called hits of today and before. I remember the lyrics completely.

If your baby ever leaves you (yeah, yeah)
Don't call him back (oh no)
'Cause he's been untrue (yeah, yeah)
And you don't know what to do...
Everyday I'm sad loosing you

But in a way I'm glad loosing you...
If your baby ever leaves you (yeah, yeah)...,

It looses something without the music, but I still love it.

In retrospect my own songs were often about loneliness and isolation but these seem to be the thoughts of the evolving teenager.
However, loneliness or not, these were some of the happiest days of my adolescence.
Football in the street, guitars and music in my bedroom, and no idea at all how to meet girls. Everything seemed fine.
However, soon this simple and unconfused life would have to change.

Although as children we were oblivious to the reality, the bar and its demands put a strain on the marriage of our parents, perhaps not helped by the fact that my father loved the work and the innovations and saw the whole thing as his raison d'être, my mother saw it more as a means to an end, a way to establish a more comfortable life, and waited for the time when my father would slow down. It didn't happen and the marriage struggled.
My father became more and more preoccupied with his vocation and intention to create one of the best bars in Liverpool, whilst my mother felt pushed away and perhaps ignored and no longer the full partner she needed to be.
It was at this time George arrived.
George Bellis was a rough and in my mind a poorly educated man, who came to drink in the Goat Hotel.
He began to flirt with my mother, and she, tired of being ignored and pushed to one side, responded favorably to his advances.
In the evening in one of the side rooms of the pub I was allowed to play on the pin ball machine at which I became quite a star.

The juke box played such wonderful music of the time, 'Good vibrations' by the Beach Boys, anything and everything by the Beatles, and many, many more. As I think every generation will say, we just had the best music!

However, sitting in the corner, too close to each other for my comfort, would be my mother and George. As a young boy I can say in all honesty, I hated this man.

Not only because he was stealing the woman I loved, but perhaps even more his hard and unsophisticated way to speak and his rough and unshaven appearance. I suppose the shock was how my mother could be attracted to such a man when my lovely father was just a few feet away.

Whether my father realized what was happening is not sure, but in some way he must have been suspicious.

So, the relationship continued and deepened and naturally my mother wanted me to like this interloper into the family, but it never happened. I disliked everything about him, and that never changed.

School continued, music continued and the questioning of life continued. It was well understood that the world would end quite soon with a nuclear war between the Soviet Union and America. I was terrified of this. Just the idea to be blown apart or worse, to die horribly of radiation sickness terrified me. This deep and profound fear, coupled with the situation with my mother, whose loving and motherly behavior towards us children had dissipated somewhat, became the foundation of my horrible behavior. My fear fuelled in part by my galloping hormones, manifested as anger and constant irritation and apart from my best friend no one could bear to be close to me.

This became apparent one morning and was the first true life changing moment that I can remember.

I slept late and grumpily arrived in the kitchen wearing my 'I hate everyone face'. My father was there with my sister and as I entered he protectively but jokingly put his arms around her and said, «Look out, here he comes.»

I knew he was joking, but I saw the significance of his gesture.

My presence, established as it was in easily justifiable fear and anger brought nothing of value to any situation. I was difficult to be with and others always had to be very careful around me and treat me with an unnatural degree of consideration, if only to protect themselves from my caustic comments.

I saw that in an instant and vowed to change something.

I think that moment defined the whole of my Dhamma life, that I should endeavour in every situation that my presence should bring something worthy, and something of value.

But how could I change it? How could I end my fear?

It seemed that there were two possibilities, the first was that I could bring peace to the whole world, but in honesty, as a fifteen year old boy this didn't seem likely.

The second was that I could become enlightened!

The fear consumed and compromised my whole life and so affected every relationship I found myself in. Although I never followed the crowd I was absolutely afraid of being left behind. This paradox inside my social and familial group brought only ever more confusion and frustration. Sometimes it felt as though my head would explode, but enlightenment........

Wasn't that the way of peace, joy and understanding? Wouldn't that be the solution to my difficulties? I would have to try, after all so many people were talking about it now.

Indian spirituality had arrived in the west thanks to the early hippies and I was naturally attracted by their long hair, exotic clothes and as it seemed, their knowledge of meditation.

Like the Buddha when he was a young man and whose presence was just making headway into 'sixties British youth culture, I was wondering what was the point of anything if in the end we would never be able to find perfection. Books about Zen teachings and Theravada meditation were surfacing and I was always interested, but much more important was the fact that the Beatles had discovered and now made popular and easily accessible Transcendental Meditation under the guidance of Maharishi Mahesh Yogi. Of course there was an intuitive recognition to the importance of this on my part, but in reality their influence opened the door to the rest of my life.

Although it would be three more years and another city before my meditation life would begin, the seeds were sown, and I read and consumed as much as I could about Indian, Japanese and Tibetan teachings, and formulated my own, very often completely wrong ideas.

The relationship between my mother and George continued and deepened. She stopped taking care of me in her usual loving way and her unhappiness in our home became apparent. No more questions about my day at school, no more dinner on the table. No more interest in the family or her life.

One evening, in the depth of despair she decided to end everything. I was slumped down on the sofa unseen from behind, watching something on television when she came into the room and picked up the telephone. It was obvious that she hadn't seen me, and she sat down at the then fashionable 'telephone table', pushed the living room door closed and dialed.

Unknown to me or anyone else, she had taken a huge amount of tablets from her medicine cabinet, mixed them with some alcohol and waited for the combination to take effect.

I was certainly not paying attention but I could hear her voice and that she was speaking to George. What I noticed was that her words were becoming more slurred until finally there was a huge crash and she fell unconscious onto the floor. Of course now I looked and saw the situation. I needed help and so I ran to the intercom next to the telephone and called my father in the bar, first hanging up the telephone thus destroying the latest evidence of infidelity.

«Dad,» I cried, «come quick, mum's collapsed.»

He left the bar immediately and ran up the stairs. Unfortunately my mother had fallen directly in front of the closed door and needed to be moved. I tried as much as I could but it was not easy. She was a slight woman, but her dead weight was difficult to maneuver. Finally there was enough space for my father to enter and he in his anger and fear grabbed her and half carried and half dragged her into the kitchen. I heard him slapping her and, I imagine, putting his fingers into her throat. She vomited and coughed, cried and cursed and vomited some more. I'm sure that he saved her life that night. I suppose the doctor was called later, but I cannot say for certain. I only know that my father never spoke of it after the event.

The marriage could not survive after that and one Friday evening as I was sitting on the stairs between our bedrooms and the living quarters, she left. There was a huge row in the kitchen between my parents, lots of slamming things and stamping around until finally my mother emerged from the living room with a huge, obviously very heavy suitcase, and dragged it with both hands down the second flight of stairs to the street. Half-way down the suitcase flew open and out poured the best china, the traditional wedding gift and smashed into a thousand pieces on the hard stairs.

My heart broke, this poor sad woman couldn't even leave with dignity.

The story didn't end there of course and they tried a reconciliation but to no avail. The trust was gone, the love was gone, and all that remained was resentment and suspicion.

Because the marriage had ended and divorce proceeding had begun, citing infidelity and desertion, my father lost the bar. It was the love of his life but the conditions of keeping a bar with the brewery of Greenhall Whitley in those days was that the tenets had to be a married couple.

The only thing to do was to return home, back to the Isle of Man. It was a hard time for my father, but there was still one more thing he could lose!

One day my sister and me were called to the living room to meet a judge. He was a very pleasant man but needed to ask one important question, and I had to answer for both of us.

«Now Michael,» he began, «you know that your mother and father no longer live together, and I have to ask you to think for a minute and tell me who you and Sandra (my sister) want to stay with?»

I loved my mother and wanted to be with her forever, but it seemed important that Sandra and I stay together, and in any case my mother had already begun a new life with the hated George, and perhaps the most valuable thing was that I knew my father would always take care of us. The decision made itself.

«We want to stay with dad,» I said.

So it was fixed. Some time later we packed our things, said goodbye to our friends and went to begin another new life on the Isle of Man.

I didn't see my mother again for many, many years.

My father, my sister and I arrived on the Isle of Man again in a cloud of unhappiness. Sandra and I had lost our friends and my father had lost his marriage, his bar and the life he loved. Now, back to where he started from all those years before he began his new life.

I remember the unhappiness he arrived home with after his first day at his new job working at the Ronaldsway Aircraft Compay, a factory that produced components for Martin Baker ejector seats for fighter aircraft.

He hated it and felt he had lost everything. Of course this quickly changed as my father's natural disposition was to be quite joyful and humourous, and soon he accepted this work and became more and more popular in the 'inspection pen' and had many new

people lined up to be trained by him. He had a way to be with everyone, but especially women that was playful and innocent. I heard him say things to women that other men would have had their face slapped for, but with him they just giggled and touched his arm.
I always wondered why it should be like this until many years later I realized the truth.
He didn't want something from them. He never flirted, he only played with an overwhelming innocence, and treated everyone equally and the same. At some unconscious level the women around him understood this and so always felt safe and secure in his company.
Many years later whilst teaching in India I had the same experience.

At one time during my early days in Budh Gaya, I became friendly with a young German man. Even now I cannot remember his name, but it is not important because he was known to everyone throughout the town as 'that lucky German'. This nickname arrived because of an accident on the road to Kathmandu some weeks before we met.
He was travelling on a full bus of Indian and Nepalese people when the bus careered off the narrow, winding road and plunged into a deep valley.
Any of us who have made this journey know how dangerous these long roads to Nepal can be and so cannot be surprised to hear of accidents.
The bus tumbled and turned until it finally came to a halt on its side. Many people died, but he survived.
Some months later whilst taking the same route to Kathmandu, we passed this place on the road, and there was the bus of 'the lucky German,' lying on its side as witness to his story.
He was pulled out of the crashed vehicle and taken to hospital in Kathmandu. Seeing his nationality on his passport the hospital

staff knew him as a German man who had survived a terrible accident, hence the nickname.

When he arrived in Budha Gaya some time later he came to learn meditation with me and we became travelling friends.

One day sitting in a local café he spoke to me.

«You know,» he began, «every time we see you in the street you are accompanied by a beautiful woman.»

I had not thought of this before, but it was true. My preconception of female travelers being strong, sturdy women in mountain boots and calf length trousers had been completely demolished, and I had met young, attractive women, independent and happily traveling alone in a strange land.

I was quite well known in Budh Gaya by this time and the small town itself was a very social place, so often I would be accompanied as I walked along the single road to the stupa or back to the Burmese Vihar.

Of course, I was very happy to think that beautiful women were attracted to me and so I left the café with a slight ego based smile on my lips.

Some time later I met 'the lucky German' again and he was excited to tell me that he now knew exactly why these young women were always happy to walk with me.

«It's because they feel safe with you,» he said smiling.

At first this was not the reason I wanted to hear, but when the disappointment of not being likened to Robert Redford or some other handsome movie star of those days passed, I experienced an enormous joy in my heart.

Is this how others really perceive me? That I want nothing from them and so they are safe with me?

Without realising, after so many years of sitting and applying love and awareness to my life, the results could be experienced by others. The true manifestation of the loving Dhamma heart became apparent, with each aspect of every relationship based in

integrity and love for all living beings.
Not to exploit or maneuver, but to serve and support.
It is said that true Dhamma practice is like walking in the mist or fog, and that slowly, slowly without realizing it, we become soaking wet.
Our Dhamma heart opens and love becomes the gift in our life, first for ourselves and then for all beings.
To be in a relationship, no matter how short-lived, with someone who does not make demands on you is a great gift in your life. To be with someone who is not, even at a very subtle level, trying to manipulate you creates an environment of safety. In this environment you can find the space to be foolish and not be judged. Here you can be relaxed knowing that the other will not mock or humiliate you. This is the highest relationship in life, and when you struggle with your relationships it only means that you are not moving from this place of peace and balance. Now perhaps you will see that the moment and the situation you are experiencing is conditional and you are making demands. Let go of that and all the difficulties just fall away.
Even if others cannot do this for you, you are always able to do this for them.
Simple, but not easy.
To cultivate a life based on how everyone should or should not be can only be a life filled with frustration. Look at the world. Look at its diversity, and look how people struggle to control others so that they themselves can feel secure in their view of how things should be.
Beings are the way they are, that is their choice. You are the way you are and that is your choice.
Live with love and be aware and let all your demands on the universe for you to be happy be seen as the manipulative devices they really are.
When this happens, happiness is already there.

Pure Dhamma works in a beautiful and consistent way provided that we stay on the path. Slowly, slowly the fear we have always justified and explained falls away and we are left with a simple purity of being.

If we let go a little, there is a little peace.
If we let go a lot, there is a lot of peace.
If we let go completely, complete peace.
This is the way of Dhamma.

Back on the Isle of Man as an unhappy teenager, I began St Ninian's High School in Douglas, the capital town. We lived at 54 Royal Avenue, Onchan, almost directly across the road from my grandmother, and I began by taking the school bus in the morning. This was often a pleasurable experience as the girls had to ride on the top deck with the boys on the lower deck. This meant that as we all boarded together there would often be a glimpse of stocking top (tights had not yet become the convenient fashion for women) as the girls mounted the stairs. I was now fourteen years old with hair on my body and more than ready for romance.
But hormones of course, bring their own difficulties.
My behavior at home was not very pleasant. As most adolescents I was self obsessed and blamed everyone and everything for my unhappiness. I had lost my life in Liverpool, my friends, my school and especially my mother. I don't think I ever blamed my father for any of those things but it seemed obvious that he didn't understand my pain.
Of course I didn't see or understand his pain either. Whatever I felt I had lost he had lost many times over. His wife, his free life doing the one thing he loved and his friends and colleagues. Now he was alone with two children, doing the very best he could and yet having to meet at the end of a day's work, a brooding, sulking teenager who would verbally attack and criticise him at

every opportunity.

These were the most difficult times between us. I was becoming an adult in the nineteen sixties and the notion that I would simply follow his instructions was completely outdated.

I wanted to wear my hair long as was the fashion of the social group I identified with and so one day when he told me to get my hair cut I asked why.

«Because I tell you,» was the response.

«That's not good enough,» I shouted as I stormed out of the room. On another occasion I was able to follow every unhappy adolescent in the world when I retorted to what I am sure was a well deserved criticism of my conduct, «Well, I didn't ask to be born!»

And it's true, I didn't ask to be born, but when I was born my parents took care of me. They fed me, clothed me, educated me and did the best they could according to their understanding. To say that neither my mother nor my father were enlightened is superfluous, but they were kind people, and in all my tantrums and uncooperative behavior, my father never, not once in all our years together hit me.

It took me many years to appreciate that he was my first teacher, and that I was blessed to know this man.

My father, slowly passing through the shame and embarrassment of his broken marriage, and as he perceived, his broken life, as he explained it to me many years later, was also ready for romance and met an old flame from his youth and the sun once again began to shine in his life.

Eileen Quiggin was two years younger than my father, but the moment they re-met their love story began. It was a love that lasted all of the rest of their lives and truly is the stuff that stories are made of.

As their romance developed, my father took my sister and me to one side and told us he would like to marry Eileen, and what did we think?

For myself I didn't mind a bit. I was already thinking about the days when I could leave home and so would not want to deny my father happiness after his recent unhappy times with my mother. I don't think it was quite the same for my sister, being her daddy's little girl, who would now have to relinquish this coveted position. However, we both said yes. My father proposed and Eileen said yes. The day was set, the ceremony was conducted and Eileen moved in.

This did not go so smoothly at the beginning due to the conflict between two women fighting for the attention of one man. Now things were different again at home, from moments of tension around the table when Sandra could not decide quickly enough if she wanted Eileen to pour tea into her cup or not, to the joy of seeing my father dressed and ready to go out with Eileen on a Saturday evening, sitting on the sofa, with his newly acquired piano accordion. He told us that he learned playing piano in the local church when he was a boy, for which he would be given two cigarettes as a bribe from his mother. The sheer pleasure in his eyes as this music filled the house was beautiful to see. Of course we 'children' made our sarcastic remarks as he played, but he continued undisturbed, and actually I think we both enjoyed seeing him so happy.

For myself, I liked Eileen and we became and remained friends all her life, but then, I didn't consider her as the enemy!

Eileen's mother however was a different story.

She was a short, round, snobbish and basically an unpleasant woman who I think looked down on Eileen for marrying a man with two teenage children. She would come for lunch on Sunday afternoon and Sandra and I would hate her presence, until the day when all that changed.

Lunch was finished and Mrs Quiggin, this is how she was known, was ushered to the easy chair close to the table. It was the place of honor after the meal. However, as she lowered herself into the sitting position she let out the loudest and longest passage of wind that we had ever heard. Eileen shouted, «Mother!» Mrs Quiggin went red and my sister and I laughed and laughed. My father, as always being the lovely man he was rushed to her side and said, «Don't worry Mrs Quiggin, it took me years before I could do that.» It didn't help.

He was referring to a huge bowel operation he had endured when he was a young man, and it had taken time for his internal organs to settle again.

After that we didn't mind if Mrs Quiggin came for lunch again just in case there would be a repeat of the above incident - there never was.

Such a delightful moment of joy passed, and it was back to ordinary life again.

As school continued I stopped taking the bus and began to cycle the two miles, I think principally for my own independence. This is a feature that has stayed with me forever: not to be dependent on others for my convenience or comfort.

Being the new boy at such a late stage in my school career brought its own misery. The subjects I had studied at grammar school in Liverpool were not the same as on the Isle of Man, mathematics still eluded me and I felt alone and isolated. I began to play truant and sit in the park across the road from school, smoking cigarettes and day dreaming about a future happiness.

On one occasion I was called to the headmaster's office to explain my absence from so many classes. I stayed calm, straight-faced and lied. I told him I had numerous hospital appointments because of a broken toe. This was partially true as my sisters pony had stepped on my foot quite recently, but the truth was that although it had been painful, no real damage was done.

So this was my story. We both knew it was a lie, but for convenience it was accepted.

One of the few lessons I attended was swimming. I had been a good swimmer in Liverpool and gained all my life saving and distance certificates and enjoyed the water, so the swimming baths was always a glimpse of sunshine in my grey and cold life. One day I noticed, standing at the pool side, a skinny ginger haired boy, shoulders hunched up around his ears, shivering in the cool air. I don't know what attracted me to him, maybe it was because he looked as miserable as I felt, but I approached him and spoke. We immediately became friends and I think that friendship in this moment was the beginning of the sun shining in my teenage years.

Donald Duggan had a dry, merciless wit and a catalogue of choice expressions. One of his greatest pleasures was to run past butcher's shops shouting, «Dealers in death!»

He bought a bass guitar and later we formed the first group I was ever in.

We were called, 'The Breed,' and played covers of pop songs.

I was the singer and rhythm guitarist, Donald the bass player, Philip Bottomly was the lead guitarist and Nigel Johnson the drummer.

Philip was the youngest and smallest and so picked on quiet a lot. He complained about this often and so Donald created his new nickname, 'Acher,' because as he explained, he was always 'belly aching.'

We practiced in the empty ballroom off season in Nigel's father's hotel, the Westlakes, on the promenade in Douglas.

Another friend, Jim Caine became our manager, but that was really in name only and his job was to help us with our equipment and provide a manic high pitched laugh for the beginning of our opening song, 'Let's breed!'

This was an instrumental and simply repeated the same verse three times. These were of course much more innocent and naive times and guitar skills were still quite rare with adolescents. This meant that 'The Breed' were surprisingly popular and played at school, youth club dances and the like. It was the days of 'flower power' and we dressed accordingly with huge flared trousers, patterned shirts and chiffon scarves around our necks. For myself, I had acquired a large floppy hat which added to the hippy image. It also meant that girls were quite interested, but none of us really knew what to do, and in any case Donald kept reminding us that they were not really interested in us as people, it was just a 'guitar touch'.

I still struggled at school and spent many hours each day sitting in the park opposite smoking cigarettes instead of attending lessons, and wishing for something to happen. It did, I was called into the headmaster's office and confronted with my truancy.

I lied again and told him I had a series of hospital appointments because my sister's pony had stepped on my foot and damaged a toe. We both knew this was a lie, but the headmaster played the game so he didn't have to take any action.

School report cards arrived at the house and they were not good, how could they be, I was never there! I was now fifteen as my father read the final report of my school career.

«This is not very good,» he said, «do you want to leave?»

I immediately replied, «Yes,» and so quit school at the end of that week.

This was a time of full employment and I immediately began an apprenticeship at Headquarters, an ultra modern salon as a ladies hairdresser, inspired by comments from Ringo Starr, and a desire to meet women!

I learned my trade, to wash, cut, perm and colour hair, stood close to women and flirted for all I was worth. My boss, a young, slim handsome man was not only the first gay man I had ever met, but an inspiration as to how tight trousers could be worn. This introduction into more adult fashion stood me in good stead in the summer months on the Isle of Man as every two weeks thousands of new tourists would arrive on packed boats from the Isle of Man Steam Packet Company, and young girls ready for summer romance would present themselves for us local boys. Actually, it was always very innocent, but as I reflect now, a happy time in my life.

Late evening walks through Summer Hill Glen, whispering romantic promises and kissing until our lips were swollen.

Time went on and the group evolved. We changed our name and our line up, and were now called the Raspberry Caddilac, playing much more psychedelic music. We grew our hair, got girls in to help with special songs such as 'I am the Walrus' and others. We were young and everything was changing.

One of the highlights of this time was a meeting with a cousin of mine. Actually, it was so brief that I cannot even remember her name, but it was an important moment for me. She was home from university and we met by chance, whereby she immediately recognized me and informed me that we were distant cousins. This was the Isle of Man in the nineteen sixties so it was not unusual to find yourself related to someone that you would just meet in the street.

What I remember about her was that she was very attractive and quite large, reminiscent of Mama Cass, from the folk rock group the Mamas and the Papas.

She was dressed in the hippy style of the time, a flowing flowery dress, strange boots that seemed not to match the rest of her clothes and a large floppy hat. She was so mature by comparison to this babbling teenager in front of her that I immediately fell in love. We talked together for a while about music and life, and she kept calling me 'man.' It was so cool.

I don't think that we ever met again.

My father was married again, my sister had met Ian, the man who is still the love of her life and I had left home and taken a small apartment in another town close to where I was working.

Donald went to live in Nottingham, but only stayed for three days as he didn't like it.

We were growing up and beginning to become adults.

When I was eighteen years old I left the Isle of Man to travel the world. Actually, I arrived in Jersey at the beginning of spring in my eighteenth year and took a job as an electricians mate, helping build the new prison. The work was hard, back-breaking in fact, but I liked the masculine camaraderie and playfulness which reminded me of school days in Liverpool. This was such an obvious change from being a ladies hairdresser where the client always had to be pampered in exchange for a tip. Here it was honest labour and no excuses. This raw honesty fitted me very well. It matched my father's life teachings of 'do or don't do - but don't mess around!'

I rented a small room in someone's house and wrote songs with an old beat up guitar.

I think it was a coming of age time.

I earned only slightly more money than the rent I had to pay for the room, and so I smoked lots of cigarettes, very cheap in those days, to curb my appetite, and survived on 'Jersey bean soup' a cheap and tasty working man's lunch at a local bar.

I also ate ravioli in the evening. This was quite devisive as even the thought of it would make me feel nauseous. I would heat a small tin in the kettle in my room and after two possibly three small mouthfuls I would feel so sick I could not face any more. Perhaps I stumbled upon a new weight loss regime but the only intention was not to feel hungry at night, and this objective was satisfied.

As always things changed and I became friends with a young man a year younger than me, working for the same company. He had long hair, good, good humour and we fitted very well. His name was Paul.

We spent all our free time together, and as I was the older and in his eyes a world traveler, I was given to deciding what we should do. Listening to music and talking about the meaning of life featured very highly.

The room I stayed in was close to the airport and often the planes could be heard taking off and landing. Inspired by this I wrote my very first real song. A twelve bar blues attempt called, 'Airport blues.' This opened the door for many such efforts and some of them stay with me even to this day.

The summer in Jersey wore on. It was hot and heady and a wonderful experience.

One day a letter arrived from a former girlfriend of mine, now living in Cardiff, South Wales, inviting me to visit. She had obtained my address during a chance meeting with my father when she was visiting her family back on the Isle of Man.

We had experienced an adolescent romantic relationship some years before, swore everlasting love to each other and immediately separated. Now we were grown, and each still interested in the development of the other. It seemed like a good idea, and I could stay for a few days in Wales and then go back to the Isle of Man, so I packed my few things, said goodbye to Paul and the other friends I had made on the wonderful island of Jersey, and left.

I took a flight to Rhoose airport, where I was stopped and searched for an unknown reason, perhaps my long hair indicated an attraction to drugs? It wasn't true, but we never really know what other people see when they look at us.

I arrived in Cardiff and took a lodging room for a few days. My plan was clear, I would visit my friend, stay for a week or so, and head back to the Isle of Man to invest in my new song writing career.

My stay in Cardiff lasted five years and was the beautiful spiritual environment that informed the rest of my life.

My girlfriend, a lovely young woman called Louise, and I rekindled our romance and took a small apartment together, and so now we were a couple. This meant I should take a job which in those days was not so difficult to do. I scanned the newspapers and settled on a job as an electricians mate, having had some experience in Jersey with this sort of employment. I telephoned the company and arranged an interview.

I arrived on time and sat in front of the boss, Ken Bateman, who was kind and fatherly and prepared to offer me employment provided I could answer one question favorably: «Will you cut your hair?»

These were the days when long hair was more than a fashion, it was a statement of rebellion against the 'establishment' and a larger group identity. I was just too young to have been a true hippie, but prided myself in aligning with a long haired group of individuals called 'freaks' as opposed to more conventional people known as 'straights'. The lines were drawn and there was no going back.

Simply I replied, «No!»

«Well, I can't have you arriving at people's houses looking like that.»

«O.K.» I replied, and stood to leave.

«Wait a minute,» he said, «I can't have you arriving at people's houses like that, but I can offer you a job in our stores. What do you say to that?»

I was delighted and some days later I began.

The job itself was not in any way interesting, finding components and the like for the electricians to use in their work, but I received a wage every week and that supported my life.

Once I was established in my job and our apartment I bought a new guitar. It was an Echo Jumbo acoustic six string, with a curved back, smooth action and beautiful tone. It cost £50.00, a fortune in those days, but I could pay £1.00 a week for a year and that seemed reasonable. Actually this guitar was a very good investment as it was the key to the most significant part of my life, and in fact, I still have it and play it often almost fifty years later! I was writing songs and dreaming of being a singer, song-writer in the style of Cat Stevens, Neil Young, Paul Simon etc, and so on a whim entered the Double Diamond (a famous beer of the time) Search for a Star talent competition.

I successfully passed through the first round and even got my name in the local paper. Now came the second round. More intensive where I had to perform three songs on a stage of a local working men's club to a mixed audience and the panel of judges. Of course I chose three songs that I had written myself as a long haired 'freak'. The first was a protest song against the war in Vietnam, the second highlighted the angst of being young and misunderstood and the third I think was a simple love song. There was a splattering of applause after the set and I knew I had not done so well, but of course, the audience consisting entirely of 'straights' didn't 'get me'. I sat down next to a fellow competitor, a rather eccentric woman who had played a small Welsh harp and sung three traditional folk songs. The audience didn't 'get her' either, so we sat together in each other's good company.

We began to speak and she introduced herself as Jo, an art teacher at a college in Cardiff. I liked her eccentricity and her light-hearted humour and so we got on well. Then, from nowhere came her revelation.

«You know, I've given my house over to the Transcendental Meditation people. They teach there and it's all really cool and far out. You should come along.»

This is really how we spoke in those days.

Of course I was immediately interested, and by this time T.M. was quite well known in the U.K. having been made popular by the Beatles in 1966. They had met Maharishi Mahesh Yogi a Hindu monk and the promoter of this simple practice, at a lecture in London and been impressed by what he presented. They immediately went to a meditation session in Wales followed by several weeks amongst other famous celebrities at a meditation camp in Rishikesh, northern India.

This was well documented and was where many of the songs for the Beatles 'White Album' were written.

My ears pricked up, 'meditation,' I thought, that's exactly what I need!'

However, Cardiff is a big place and although I didn't really want to take lots of busses from one place to another, I reluctantly asked for the location.

She gave me the address, and I questioned it.

«Are you sure?» I foolishly asked.

«Yes, of course,» she answered.

«Then I will come tomorrow evening if that's O.K. for you? It's no problem at all. You live in the next street to me!»

And so the next evening at the prearranged time I arrived with my girlfriend to meet Jo who would introduce me to Morgan, the T.M. instructor.

Jo was right, it was cool and far out and there was no pressure at all. We drank tea and I was able to ask as many questions as I liked. Morgan was a thirty something handsome Welsh man with a lilting accent and good humour. In time we became friends and I consider him to be one of the greatest blessings in my life.

After several social visits my girlfriend and I decided to become Transcendental Meditators and so arranged initiation. It was the summer of my nineteenth year.

We arrived at the prescribed time bringing with us the necessary gifts to the simple ceremony, plus of course the fee required to become part of this 'two hundred percent life'.

Once again as I recall these events I feel blessed to have met the kindnesses of people who in one way or another have supported and encouraged me on my Dhamma path. The fee, which was ordinarily very high was reduced for us as we came as a couple and were both low earners. This meant that we only had to pay the students rate. It was still quite a lot for us, but as with everything that has value, worth every penny.

We were taken upstairs to the meditation room. The atmosphere was still and silent and we ceremoniously handed over our symbolic gifts. A white cloth (handkerchief), a bunch of flowers and fruit. Then we sat in the armchairs and Morgan explained the technique that applied to this style of (samatha) meditation. When we said that we had understood he came close to us individually and whispered the secret mantra in our ear. We were told that we must never reveal this mantra to anyone and that it is special and unique to us. In all the years that followed, I never asked my girlfriend to reveal her mantra and she never asked me. We honored our commitment to the tradition and I have always though that it was the perfect opening into my Dhamma life.

The mantra is a mental device used gently but consistently to allow thoughts and other internal disturbances to fall away. It is not a word that has meaning as this would simply create another train of thought, but rather a sound of two syllables (in my case at least) lightly resting on the breath.

The three of us sat together for twenty minutes, which seemed to pass very quickly, until Morgan ended the session by saying 'in his soft Welsh accent, Jai guru Dev', to honor the Indian Hindu monk who had originally formulated this style of practice before sending his disciple, now known as Maharishi Mahesh Yogi into the world.

This was the beginning of the latest and what became the most important part of my life.

A group of us newly trained meditators would assemble every Wednesday evening at the home of Jo, meet with Morgan and sit together for twenty minutes in the meditation room before listening to a teaching or receiving further instruction on the practice itself. However, because the session and the whole environment was so relaxed many people fell asleep during the meditation period. This concerned me and touched a part of my being that I later recognized as my ascetic direction in meditation and the whole of Dhamma practice. 'Why are people sleeping and snoring when they should be focusing on their mantra?'

As much as I loved the simple practice of Transcendental Meditation, I was disappointed by the behavior of others. If meditation was considered to be essential for enlightenment, why did others not recognize its value?

This troubled me and although I never expressed my views, they became a barrier between us.

One day whilst in the city centre I saw a poster advertising a course of Zen meditation. This was fantastic, and if everything I had read about Zen was correct, it was exactly what I had been looking for.

I telephoned the number given and spoke to the Zen Master. He gave me the information I needed and so I arrived at his house one Sunday afternoon to begin a new form of meditation with a small group of others.

The door was opened by a small but impressive bespectacled, balding middle aged man with a double pointed black beard and wearing a black robe, not dissimilar from the ones worn by our teachers at grammar school in Liverpool five years before. Once we had assembled in his living room he presented himself formally. His name was Stanley Rosenthal, a university lecturer in Cardiff, but his Zen name was Tekisui, meaning 'drop of water'. He told us he was a disciple of the world famous D.T. Suzuki, the Japanese scholar responsible for introducing Zen to the west, but was disappointed that he had not been given his rightful place as his successor in the United Kingdom. This apparently had gone to the high court judge, Christmas Humphries.

Of course none of us knew anything about this and being so young and naive, alarm bells did not sound.

When you are looking for a Master, it is not surprising that someone will present themselves as exactly the thing you are looking for. Then of course comes the endless compromising to make this person fit with your fantasies of the perfect being. In the end everything is teaching us, but often it takes time to understand the lesson.

So began my time with Tekisui and even very early on in our relationship I had to fight internally to give him his place as Master.

I had always been impressed by the love and kindness of the Buddha and so when Tekisui began making discreet racist remarks about the young black man in our group, I immediately felt uncomfortable. This was followed by a distinct favoritism towards the young and very attractive woman, praising everything she said and did. The maneuvering of Tekisui became apparent very soon, and quite quickly we discovered he had seduced this young woman and that they were involved in a romantic relationship, even to the point of writing a book together called, 'Zen in the art of love.' These were the heady days of spiritual understanding, and coming with that, teachers ready to exploit the young and naive.

He explained that there was an initiation test before we could be fully accepted as disciples. This suited me perfectly being young and filled with spiritual energy, and he explained what we had to do.

In principle it was simple, all that was required was that at sometime within the next two weeks we would sit in our meditation posture for three hours without moving.

We would do this in our own homes, so the honor system was in force, and simply tell the teacher when it was completed.

I wondered how I would do it, and then hit upon the solution. I chose an evening when my partner was out of the house and a good film was on the television. I prepared my food, took it to my cushion in front of the T.V, assumed my posture and ate. When I had finished I stayed still and waited for the film to begin. In this way the three hours passed fairly quickly and I didn't experience any depth of discomfort.

Of course, it's cheating, but I didn't know that. I simply sat still for three hours as instructed. The distraction of eating and then watching television helped the time pass quickly. In the end it's how we spend our life, being distracted from the moment and missing the true connection with ourselves.

It seems that I was the first student to accomplish this small task and as a reward was given a small book.

Tekisui had written and self published a small booklet with physical and mental exercises and filled with deep and profound spiritual teachings. The problem was that these deep and profound spiritual teachings were simply the often incoherent ramblings of a confused mind. It was the attempt to be and sound wise, but for me at least it was completely incomprehensible. Please remember that I was still wanting this man to be my Master and so I tried and tried to understand the words, wanting and even needing them to make sense.

I struggled with this book for weeks and always felt that the fault was with me. I was just not wise or intelligent enough to grasp the hidden meaning.

This internal wrestling came to its conclusion one Saturday afternoon as I lay in a bath of hot water.

During this period of my life I had become almost obsessed with Japanese culture and as well as training in zen meditation, I had begun learning the martial art of karate, in the style of Kykushinkai. These days of Bruce Lee and the film 'Enter the Dragon' and also David Caradine in the television show, 'Kung Fu,' were inspirational and so considered as real as any documentary. Joyful, magic times and I wanted to be a part of that fantasy.

The first thing was to stop eating meat. I have always abhorred any kind of cruelty and violence and having spent many of my childhood summer holidays on my uncle's farm on the Isle of Man, was completely aware that the smiling cow, the laughing pig and the joyful little lamb of publicity illustrations, was never the reality, and so to extrapolate myself from this situation, I stopped eating any kind of flesh. These were the days long before Paul and Linda McCartney introduced simple vegetarian food into supermarkets and so my lifestyle choice created some difficulties for me, but truly I feel, and perhaps especially now, what is a little inconvenience in my life compared to the torture, humiliation and finally death of a fellow living being?

So I became a vegetarian. I have never struggled with this decision nor weakened from its application. Intuitive and spontaneous connection with the life of all beings is the way of Dhamma.

A friend made a kimono for me and I would arrive home from work in the evening, put on my kimono, eat a bowl of noodles with chopsticks and pretend to be a Japanese samurai. I even made a pair of geta, the Japanese wooden shoes that I would wear in the house. Part of this ritual was the hot bath every day.

To fill the bath with plain very hot water, bow to it and climb in to soak was the best I could do to imitate this cultural practice and this is what had happened the Saturday afternoon when I had the life changing realization about Tekisui.

The hot water was around my armpits and I held the small booklet in front of me once again desperately trying to understand the somewhat hidden message of truth when it suddenly hit me. There was an incredible rush of relief and pure understanding as I realized fully and without doubt, 'this book is absolute rubbish!' I almost laughed out loud and without any intention other than to release this book from my hands, threw it across the bathroom where it hit the wall and ricocheted into the open toilet. A fitting end for such nonsense.

This moment heralded the end of my association with Tekisui and although I still heard about him from time to time, we had no more contact.

However, as much as a charlatan Tekisui was, I remember two pieces of Dhammic advice he gave me and that I have incorporated into my life.

I was practicing karate once a week and I hated it!

One evening I told Tekisui that I would stop going to karate lessons. He asked why, and I simply shrugged and said, 'I don't know, I just don't like it.'

He replied, «Don't stop just because you don't like it, find the real reason. Then you will continue or stop as you like, but you will at least know why.»

This is pure Dhamma advice which I now impart to my own disciples.

I took this advice and continued with karate for a full year more until one Saturday afternoon when I was in Cardiff city centre with a friend, I saw by chance a demonstration of aikido. In that moment I knew completely why I didn't want to continue with karate. The graceful elegant movements suited my temperament much more than the hard straight lines of karate.

I took to aikido immediately and used this beautiful martial art as an important part of my own spiritual practice for more than eleven years.

The second piece of Dhammic advice from Tekisui was to ignore the voices in my head.

I had mentioned to him that often if I spontaneously did something that could be considered kind or generous it would be accompanied by a small voice which would tell me how good I was to have performed such an action. I hated this voice because it took away the pure intention from the act itself, but by following his advice and allowing the voices to be there but not interacting with them, they finally fell away by themselves.

And as for the attraction to Japanese culture, that also ended in a blinding flash of realization. I was clumping around our apartment wearing my kimono and geta having eaten a bowl of noodles with my chopsticks when everything stopped and the small voice inside my head yelled, 'what are you doing? You're from the Isle of Man and on the Isle of Man we don't dress or act like this, so stop right now. You are enough as you are, no need to try to become something else.'

I took off my kimono, folded it and never wore it again.

I have understood in all these years of putting down different ideas and identities that in the end nothing tastes so sweet as the flavor of liberation.

However, the path to liberation is not always smooth and many difficulties arise to challenge us and our opinions as to what a spiritual life is, or at least should be.

It was at this time that an official letter arrived in the post. It was an invitation to take part in jury duty at the high court of Cardiff, and as the invitation did not accept refusal except for the most serious reasons, I met a great confusion. I already felt myself to be something of a Buddhist and so not equipped to sit in judgement on a fellow human being. My mind moved in many directions and I thought I could write to Christmas Humphries, the leader of the Buddhist Society in London. Of course, he was also a high court judge and so probably unsympathetic to my confusion. After that I had exhausted all my limited ideas on how to avoid something which at that point I did not understand and had formulated only a confused fantasy about.

The day of the trial arrived and I still had not found a way to avoid my civic responsibility and so I found myself with a large group of people waiting to be called and either accepted or rejected by the defense and prosecution barristers. I was selected and so now had no option but to take my place on the jury. The trail was for a man who was charged with three offenses, the third one of assault being the most serious.

The high court judge entered in his wig and ermine trimmed red gown, bowed to the court, and we began.

Actually immediately it was fascinating and educational. It is not the jury who will pass a judgement on another person, it is the judge who will do that.

The responsibility of the members of the jury is to listen to two presentations of a situation and decide which we accept as being the most likely. The curious thing I found was after the prosecution offered his version of events I accepted it completely. Then came the defense version and I accepted that completely. I sat in the jury believing both the defense and prosecution equally at the same time.

Happily we had to debate and discuss the case in the jury room and although the other eleven members were happy to decide guilty, because I superficially disagreed we had to discuss it.

Although the trial lasted three days our deliberations were reasonably short and when the verdict was given to the judge by the foreman I felt quite comfortable and the sentence handed down was suspended for two years, and so prison was not necessary.

I now began the next part of my Dhamma training.

I was alone. I had the practice of Zazen, but no teacher so what could I do?

The answer was simple, just continue. I made the spare room in our apartment into my meditation hall and sat every day. I had found several books that really helped and encouraged me, 'Zen Mind, Beginners Mind' by Shunryu Suzuki, 'The Empty Mirror' by Janwillem van de Wetering, and 'Zen Flesh, Zen Bones' by Paul Reps. The first two encouraged me in my solitary practice whilst the third book introduced me to the classic short Zen stories and perhaps more importantly, the study of koans.

I had become familiar with koans only through reading and naturally had no understanding of the tradition behind them or their illogical nature but for some reason they began to stick in my mind. They were ever present, but I never struggled to understand them, and perhaps in the end, that was the secret.

One evening whilst sitting quietly in meditation I suddenly and intuitively understood a particular koan. It was the one about the water vase:

Master Hyakujo decided to found a new monastery, but he had the difficult task of selecting from among his disciples the right person to be the new monastery's abbot. Then he came upon a solution.

Hyakujo called all his disciples together and told them that the person who best answered his question would be named the new abbot. Hyakujo filled a vase with water and set it on the ground before the assembled monks. «Who can tell me what this is without naming it?» he challenged.

The senior disciple stepped forward and answered accurately, «No one can call it a wooden shoe.»

Then Isan, the lowly cook, stepped forward and knocked the vase over with his foot, and walked out of the room.

Master Hyakujo smiled and declared, «My senior disciple has been bested.» Isan the cook was named the new abbot.

I spontaneously realized that the 'label we put on something is not the thing itself,' it is only what we call it!

Vase is a concept, not a reality.

The understanding of koans would arise without warning bringing with it an opening of the heart and a simpler and more beautiful relationship with life.

There was however one koan that I could not grasp. One of the big ones and famous for its place in Zen literature.

It was the great koan of Bankai about one hand clapping, considered perfect and a classic by other Masters from the moment of its creation.

I reflected upon this koan for a very long time and read and listened to many explanations.

'It's the sound of the deepest meditation,' was the most familiar conclusion from less informed spiritual voyagers. However, I did not feel that was the correct understanding and so I made a space in my life for this koan to live and stay with me.

Many, many years later I heard the full koan and only then did the understanding arise, and this really is the point.

If we don't have all the information we cannot fully comprehend what is in front of us.

If we don't have the full practice we are likely to miss something important.

In Dhamma training people are less and less inclined to be patient and want to be the teacher before they have been the disciple.

However, it is only by being the disciple that the Master has the opportunity to share their wisdom with us.

It is only by being the disciple that we have the opportunity to surrender to the practice of liberation.

It seems to me that Awakening rarely happens by chance, and that it takes a long time of unraveling the complexities of 'self' before it is completed.

Where there is fear and desire, there is self, and as fears and desires can be subtle and often easily defended and explained, we need the whole Dhamma practice to train ourselves to live free from their influence.

Bankai's koan is only a gift if we have all of it.

We all know the sound that two hands make when they clap together, but what is the sound of one hand clapping?'
Before we have everything, we actually have nothing.

Dhamma is the same. Taking the parts we like and thinking we have everything is not a complete practice and it is sure that something will be missed on our path.
There are no answers to koans, only the understanding of them. With this understanding, the light of liberation enters our life.

Added to my growing fascination with my spiritual practice was my developing musical career.
I was home alone on Saturday afternoon when our apartment bell rang. I went downstairs to find a long-haired young man standing there.
«Are you Michael Kewley?» he asked.
I didn't know him at all so I nervously answered that I was.
«My name is Trevor Wright, and I'm a musician. I play bass guitar and write songs and I wondered if you wanted to get together and jam a bit?»
This sounded wonderful and was uplifting after my recent talent competition episode.
«Yes,» I said, and so as he had his equipment in the car we went upstairs, set up and created the beginning of the singing, song writing duo, 'Sparrow'.
By this time I had changed my job from being a store-man at Bayntons, having asked for a raise and been refused, and more than that, being told that I was lucky not to be sacked as I wasn't very good at what I was supposed to do and had applied and been accepted as a life guard at the Wales Empire Pool.
It seems that I was highly qualified and actually in demand as I had gained many life saving awards whilst at school in Liverpool. Swimming in pajamas and diving for rubber bricks became more than fun, it was now a career move.

Trevor and I wrote individually but arranged our songs together. He really was the musician and I almost always took advice from him. He knew how to present the best harmonies and had almost made it in the pop world several times. He had even mimed bass guitar to a song that was in the end not a hit, on Top of the Pops. To an eighteen or nineteen year old man, that was quite impressive.

However, Trevor was quiet and modest and wrote songs about escaping to the countryside to smell the freshly cut grass and raise his children - of which he had none. These were the post hippie themes of the time.

When we had six songs completed and arranged we decided to try them out to a bigger audience than Christine, his wife and Louise, my girlfriend.

We arrived at Chapter Arts Centre, the place where I had seen by chance the aikido demonstration that had saved me from the hell which was karate on a Sunday evening for what is now called, an 'open mike' night. Trevor and I were very nervous waiting for our turn and full of judgement watched the acts before us. The first was a traditional folk couple, the man with a beard and finger in his ear and the woman in a heavy knitted sweater playing a guitar. They seemed to be very good, if you like that sort of thing, was my feeling.

There was a smattering of applause as they finished and the organizer and master of ceremonies, a young woman called Bea, thanked them and introduced the next act. They were a couple of young men like us, writing songs and playing guitars. They had the wonderful name of Red Blood Sun. They performed three or four songs and I thought they were excellent, much better than we could ever be, and because of that I became even more nervous. There was much more applause this time and even some cheering. Next it was us.

Bea took the microphone and announced us. She reminded people that it was our first time here and for them to be kind to us.

«And so, without further ado, let me present Trevor and Michael, also known as Sparrow.»

There was polite support and we began.

We had only the six songs that we had written and arranged ourselves, and certainly would not entertain the idea of cover versions, even from our favorite artists, but by the time we had finished the first, with our simple lyrics and close harmony, we were already the hit of the evening. People were enthusiastically cheering and applauding and waiting for the next one, and then the next and then the next.

It felt incredible and when I announced that this song was to be our last there was already the shout for more!

We left the stage to thunderous applause and sat at our table. Bea came running over and gave a handful of coins to each of us.

«That was fantastic,» she said, «will you come and be the support act next month for the Brigitte St John concert?»

Brigitte St John was a minor though popular folk style singer and songwriter of those days and this obviously was our chance to upgrade our possibilities for fame and success.

By this time, with applause and cheers still ringing in our ears we were high on adrenaline and so without thinking further we simultaneously said, «Yes!»

It was a wonderful moment in my life if only for the relief from so much anxiety before we began.

Later in the evening I saw Red Blood Sun sitting together mumbling to themselves. I approached to say how much I had enjoyed their set, but they were suffering the disappointment of not being the best and were not really interested in my support or comments. I'm sure they thought that next time they would be better than us, but in honesty and without any arrogance, they never were! We made our place on Sunday evenings at Chapter Arts Centre as the act to see, and maintained that position as long as we continued to play.

The concert with Brigitte St John was to be the highlight of our musical career, and although we performed often to an appreciative audience nothing matched the presentation and feeling behind our opening set at the Chapter Arts Centre that evening.

The room was full and this time we were in the concert hall with professional lighting and sound system, and we ourselves were presented as a professional duo, writing and singing our own songs under the name Sparrow.

We were very well received and later congratulated by the organizers and audience alike.

Brigitte St John was excellent as one would expect, but was not so interested in meeting Trevor and me, but no matter, the evening and the whole event was a fantastic success.

So, now I had my long hair, a meditation practice, my own place to live with my girlfriend, a certain minor celebrity because of Sparrow and a deepening interest in Buddhism.

By this time in Europe the teachings of Buddhism were becoming very popular and it was considered to be the fastest growing religion in the west.

This of course led to a deluge of books by writers whose understanding was simplistic and therefore inaccurate to say the least, a trend that continues even today all these years later.

I do not remember the title of the terrible book I procured but the stunning absence of true comprehension stays with me still.

The Four Noble Truths are the foundation of all Buddhist schools, and the deep, profound and intuitive grasping of their deepest meaning is essential for Awakening - Buddhist or not. Truth does not belong to any one group or organization and the liberation that we seek must transcend all limitations of religion and gender. Therefore it is necessary to have a good teacher with clear understanding to help the student develop. If it was so easy to understand this fundamental teaching, everyone would be enlightened!

So, to open the page at this section and find the following words

was confusing to me. The author had presented the Four Noble Truths as:
Life is suffering
Suffering is caused by desire
Desire can be broken
The way to do it - The Eightfold Path

Life is suffering
I was a young man in the best part of my life. Nowhere could I see suffering. 'Did the Buddha, this great man really say that?' I immediately began to search for suffering in my life - still nothing. I carried this doubt with me for many years until I began to understand the Buddhist word, 'Dukkha'.
Our earliest understanding of Buddhism came from Christian missionaries in Asia and naturally they interpreted what they saw and met according to their own cultural and religious understanding.
Christianity is established around the suffering of Jesus on the cross and his sacrifice for us so that we can be saved. Buddhism is not like that. Although it is true that life can contain moments that we can call suffering it is not the essential quality of life.
'Suffering' is the totally inadequate and overly simplistic translation of Dukkha.
A much more accurate understanding of this word is 'unsatisfactory.'
Therefore the nature of life as we meet it is to be unsatisfactory and whatever we experience can always be improved upon in one way or another. Whatever we have is never enough and so we spend our time chasing the illusion of a permanent and ever lasting happiness.

Suffering is caused by desire
It is true that unfulfilled desire can often be a form of suffering, but

once again the Second Noble Truth does not state so emphatically that this is the case.

The mind seeks perfection, happiness and peace through its desires, aversions and endless negotiations with life. However, no matter how intelligent we are, we always arrive back at the First Noble Truth, that everything leaves us disappointed and so is intrinsically unsatisfactory.

Desire can be broken
When we understand properly we will recognize the Third Noble Truth as the gift that it truly is, that we are not trapped in a life of unsatisfactoriness, and that we can transcend the limitations of the mind that is habitually based in greed, hatred and delusion, desires and aversions.

So, 'desire can be broken' is a violent interpretation of the the Third Noble Truth, whereas a more loving and realistic version is that desires and the act of reaching for something in the future to bring happiness to our life can be transcended.

The way to do it - The Eightfold Path
The Eightfold Path is usually understood as follows.
Right Understanding,
Right Intention,
Right Speech,
Right Action,
Right Livelihood,
Right Effort,
Right Mindfulness,
Right Concentration.

The eight aspects of the path are divided into the three categories of Sila, Samadhi, Pañña, translated from the Pali language as morality, mental development and wisdom.

Sila means to live in a way that brings no harm to ourselves or others. Samadhi means to develop the faculties of concentration, awareness and acceptance so that we are no longer deceived by what the mind presents as reality, and wisdom is the culmination of these two things.

As a young man in Cardiff I wrestled with this inadequate interpretation as I had done with the writings of Tekisui but could not find a comfortable solution to the conflict between this presentation and my own life experience.

In the end I thought I would leave the book alone and continue my own private meditation. This is what I did. Now however I added one more thing to my flowering late adolescent life.

Arriving at Trevor's house one evening to sit and talk, play and listen to music, we were introduced to marijuana.

We already smoked cigarettes as did the overwhelming majority of people in those days, and to be handed one very thick one with a fragrant odor and told to inhale and hold it in our lungs for a few seconds before exhaling was new and different. And wonderful! Things were changing again.

Now we were listening to different music, Pink Floyd, Frank Zappa and The Mothers of Invention, Traffic and others. Sitting around talking and laughing under the influence of friendship and marijuana, feeling creative and exactly in the place where I wanted to be. I enjoyed my time as an adolescent. I liked my meditation practice, I liked making and writing music, I liked listening to music and I enjoyed the company of more mature people who treated me as an equal, and I enjoyed being stoned.

These were truly wonderful times. What could possibly go wrong? However, the first Noble Truth was always waiting...*

As this is not a book about Buddhist teaching I will not go further here.
For a complete introduction to the life of the Buddha and his teachings as they apply to modern life please see: Walking the Path by Michael Kewley. Published by Panna Dipa Books.

Trevor, now at the grand old age of twenty six and under pressure from his wife to find a real career before it was too late, decided that his dream to make his life in music would not happen, and that he would quit performing and apply to a teacher training college. He did and was accepted. Sadly it was the end of Sparrow.

During this time my relationship with my girlfriend also began to deteriorate as I would spend more time in my so called spiritual and hippie life and less time with her.
After five years together we separated in a dramatic lover's row and now, with nowhere to go, I thought I would return to the Isle of Man.
The evening before my departure I went to say goodbye to two special friends. They were a married couple known as Sugar and Pace, and with their dog Van, had befriended me as I began my meditation life. They continued with Transcendental Meditation as I had drifted away into Zen and music. My plan was to quickly say goodbye to these two lovely people, go back to the friend's house where I was spending my final evening in Cardiff, meditate and sleep ready for the long journey home the next day.
This is not what happened, and led to a life defining moment.
It is true that I arrived to say goodbye and was welcomed with a cup of tea and a biscuit. Then came the joint (marijuana not beef), good and wonderful laughter and joy until the time to leave.

I walked through the quiet residential streets of Roath, the district of Cardiff where I had lived for five years and knew I was stoned. I also knew now that I could not possibly meditate in this condition and so I made my vow, 'from this moment I will never allow anything to interfere with my meditation practice.' In that moment I renounced quite easily the use of marijuana and never turned to it again.
I consider my years in Cardiff perhaps the most important in my

life, principally because of meditation, but there were other things too of course.

My minor celebrity as part of a singing songwriting duo, my evolution in music and my experience with marijuana.

Also I was able to see some of the greatest live bands of the time; Led Zeppelin, Paul MacCartney and Wings, the Strawbs, 10cc, King Crimson and many others.

I arrived back on my home island in December 1975, to receive an unjustified heroes welcome from my father. He took his wife Eileen, my sister and myself out for a meal and I felt comfortable. According to my slightly revolutionary nature I was still wearing my hair long and hippie style clothes, but more than that, in a dramatic moment after the separation from Louise, I had encouraged a friend to make a hole in my ear lobe with a sewing needle so I could wear an earring. Of course this is absolutely nothing these days, but all those years ago it was something quite dramatic, as was the public wearing of it, and so its place in my life as a non-conformist became very important.

The idea of living at home horrified me and so with the help of my father, who knew everyone it seemed, I found a tiny apartment and a job as a delivery van driver at a big 'do it yourself' store called the Home Improvement Centre, in Onchan.

For the next seven years, still committed to my meditation practice, I sat every day and trained alone.

However, now I had other books to help and support me and this time they were written by a Master in Buddhism, a venerable monk from Sri Lanka called Hamalawa Saddhatissa.

There were three that I read in rotation. The first being a simple but beautiful account of the life of the Buddha, revealing his kindness and generosity in his presence and teachings. The second was more practical, explaining clearly and expertly the Four Noble truths and what they meant in daily life, and the third book was more scholarly exploring Buddhist ethics.

My life went on. I heard about a man who could teach aikido and so I contacted him.

His name was Alan Ruddock and he had trained in Japan with the founder of aikido, Morihei Ueshiba. He said we should meet and so I arrived at his house in the town of Laxey about twenty minutes from where I was living and we began. At first it was Sunday afternoons in his garden but soon it developed and we found a place with mats to rent each week. Even if Alan is now dead, his influence for the purity of this art form still holds on the island, with classes still meeting in his name.

I trained with Alan and eventually understood it as moving meditation. I became quite proficient and on Sunday mornings was appointed the instructor to the group. I stayed with Alan and aikido for many years until an injury occurred and I could no longer practice, but that would be some time in the future.

The large store where I worked was located under an equally large supermarket called Celtic Trader, and as I would be loading or unloading my van I would notice a young and very attractive blonde woman at the till next to the window. We began to steal glances at each other, then smiles and eventually a smile combined with the wave of a hand.

This went on for a long time until finally I found the courage to ask her out on a date.

It was a nervous moment for both of us but having told me that she would think about it (needing time to end her current relationship) she said yes.

So began my relationship with Fiona, the woman I married and who became the mother of our two children.

We were young and very different from each other. Perhaps this was the attraction, I don't know, but our relationship was not always easy. Fiona was an ordinary young woman who wanted ordinary things in her life. I was the odd one, pursuing Dhamma and searching for someone, anyone that I could share my ideas with.

When I was still a teenager in Liverpool I remember my father in a moment of frustration with me exclaiming, «Michael, you're odd!»

This disturbed me a little and so I went to my sister. «Sandra, do you think I'm odd?»

«Michael,» she replied, «we all think you're odd!»

Strangely this answer satisfied me. At least I was not doing something outrageous simply to irritate my father. This oddness, this being out of step with the world, stayed with me always, and so in my married life who could blame Fiona for struggling against it, or me when I tried to conform?

We married on 26th June 1978 at St Peters Church in Onchan. The marriage almost never happened because I became very ill a few weeks before and was taken to hospital. It took a long time to diagnose my illness until the need for hospitalisation was considered necessary as I deteriorated visibly with my energy and vitality evaporating almost by the hour.

I was living at home again by this time and my father as always was taking care of me. Fiona was very concerned and thought I would die, and finally an ambulance was called on a Sunday morning two weeks before the wedding and I was taken to Nobles Hospital in Douglas. My father rode with me in the ambulance and when we arrived I was immediately taken to an isolation ward, and my father told to put on a gown, hat and mask by the nurse on duty.

«Don't be ridiculous love,» he said, «I've been taking care of him for the past two weeks. If anything he has is contagious it's sure I have it also.»

He was allowed then to come with me into the isolation ward without protective clothing.

After endless blood tests that went through the night I was

diagnosed with glandular fever, the honeymooners disease. There were also complications as my throat had almost closed, but in the end, as uncomfortable as it was, it was not life-threatening.

The next day the specialist, Mr Bourdillon, came to see me with the test results and told me that there was no treatment for what I had but if I needed two aspirin they would provide that. There was relief all around but I thought that if there was no treatment the best thing I could do would be to heal myself. This I did and two days later I was home again. Although it took many months to regain my health completely, the wedding went ahead on schedule with me now wearing a suit that was one size too big.

One disappointment around my wedding was that my very best friend Ian had refused to be my best man. He and his wife Jeanette had been a wonderful discovery for me on the Isle of Man and although they had no interest whatsoever in meditation or Buddhism, they were kind, generous and above all, funny.

However, Ian is very tall, and I am not. «We'll look ridiculous on the photographs,» he said. «I'll be an usher, but if we are photographed together you will have to stand on a step.» I had to concede that he knew what he was talking about. Jeanette was part Chinese, petite and dainty, and that as he said, was the long and the short of it!

Fiona's older brother David agreed to be my best man and took care of everything and did everything he was supposed to do. His speech was wonderful.

I also had to give a speech to thank and toast the bridesmaids, as is the tradition and surprisingly I enjoyed it. Perhaps it was a foretelling of my public speaking to come?

So began married life, first in an apartment in Douglas and later buying a house in Oakhill Close, a new small private estate in upper Douglas. Of course, when I say buying a house I really mean going into a tremendous amount of debt to the bank for our mortgage, and working really hard to pay for everything and yet never having enough money to enjoy it.

After fourteen months of married life and whilst we were still living in our apartment our first son was born.

The whole pregnancy was an exciting time and Fiona was enormous. These were the days when permission had to be given to the father to attend the birth and I am grateful to say that it was given. Being present at the birth of both my sons I consider to be two of the greatest moments of my life. Fiona was wonderful, and delivered both our boys in a quiet and natural way - nothing like in the movies. I was with her all day until the long awaited moment arrived and then was given the responsibility to wipe her forehead with a damp cloth and encourage her to 'push'. This seemed foolish to me as I felt that in her present condition of giving birth she would know herself what needed to be done without me yelling instructions in her ear.

All went well and Michael was born at ten past six on the twenty fifth of October 1979, at the Jane Crookall Maternity home, just like his father and mother many years earlier. I cried and immediately loved him, and that of course has not changed. He was slightly jaundiced and so was placed in an incubator, however, not before murmuring his first word of 'mioux'.

I went to the phone to tell my father and then Fiona's parents of the news. More tears from me.

I arrived in the private room to find my son asleep and Fiona sitting up in bed drinking a cup of tea. We had already chosen his names with care, which were to be Aaron Michael, but as I walked through the door she said, 'his name is Michael Aaron'. I thought that might be confusing for the world, but actually it never was.

We took him home to our apartment and he was lovely, sleeping quietly so much of the time. Before we went to sleep at night Michael would be in his cot at the end of the bed hardly breathing. Fiona would watch over him lovingly unable to resist the urge to gently poke him into wakefulness, just in case he had died.

It was at this point that I suffered the injury from aikido that would polarize my meditation life.

My instructor and friend Alan had been asked to give a demonstration of aikido at a large sports centre on the island. He naturally agreed and asked me to be his partner to show the power, grace and beauty of aikido. I was equally excited at the possibility to share this wonderful martial art, as presented by someone who really understood it at its deepest level, to people on the Isle of Man, and so naturally said yes.

The evening arrived and we were told everything is ready, and so we began.

Aikido is an elegant and extremely powerful art and as the senior student I committed completely to the attacks I was asked to give. This meant that Alan, a man filled with 'ki,' his inner energy, would have something to work with and therefore be able to throw me a great distance on the mats. I was experienced in receiving his power and so we worked together in harmony. However, the mats had not been secured properly and as I rolled out of one throw, they slipped out of position. Spontaneously my body tried to right itself and I felt something 'click' in my back. Never mind, I had to continue with the demonstration, and so I bravely continued, saying nothing.

The demonstration ended and I went home. A hot bath, some methyl salicylate cream, sold under its slightly easier to remember name of 'Deep Heat' rubbed into the injured part and all will be well, after all, there is another demonstration tomorrow.

I felt better the next day and by the time the evening arrived I was ready. I was still aware that all was not completely correct in my upper back, but I didn't want to refuse to continue, so I changed my clothes and arrived on the mat. After the first throw I was in agony. I still hadn't told Alan, so he was merciless.

Finally it was over and I was able to hobble home. Another hot bath, more Deep Heat, and a good nights sleep. Nothing more is needed.

The next morning I awoke unable to move. From the neck down I was paralyzed and in absolute agony. I struggled to move, accompanied by Fiona's laughter until she realised the seriousness of the situation.

A doctor was called, pain killers issued and a long series of hospital visits to have my neck stretched to release the trapped nerve, the cause of the problem.

Eventually I recovered some mobility and could walk slowly and carefully, but had lost all feeling in my left arm. Work was out of the question and so for six weeks I sat, mostly on the floor, almost immobile either meditating with my newly born son lying across my unfeeling arm, or listening to 'The Wall,' by Pink Floyd.

It was a turning point in my life, as intuitively I recognized the infinite value of what we call meditation. Sitting still without intention, being one with the mind and accepting the reality of the moment. However, like the Buddha in his early life, this clarity would fall away until the perfect conditions would arise to reignite the fire of the Dhamma heart.

Although I tried I could never return to aikido. Something had changed and that chapter of my life had ended.

As always, I put my hands together in Anjali to say thank you for all the blessings and people this beautiful martial art brought.

It was also about this time that my mother re-entered my life.

I had not seen or had any contact with my mother for almost twenty years. It is sure that I carried the pain of our separation but I had pushed it deep down inside me. It influenced me and my behavior in many subtle ways but of course I wasn't aware of it. It would take another ten years and an interesting encounter with an Indian guru for the conditions to be perfect to expel completely the emotional pain and its consequent, often unkind behavior to leave me completely. My mother's younger brother Billy telephoned me one morning completely out of the blue. Finding Kewleys on the Isle of Man is not so difficult and so a simple trial and error series of telephone calls would not take a particularly long time.

The message was simple: your mother is in hospital in Liverpool dying of cancer. Please go to see her before it's too late.

I contacted my sister and we immediately made arrangements to go across on the ferry the next morning to Liverpool. In our minds, based on the information from uncle Billy we had mentally constructed a horrifying image of a skeleton woman, old before her time, with dry and wrinkled yellow skin, lying on a hospital bed waiting to die. It wasn't the case at all.

We arrived at the hospital and looked for the ward where uncle Billy had told us to go. Just as we arrived we met a doctor and more or less asked him how many more hours did our mother have to live. He looked surprised and pointed to a woman walking around the ward laughing and joking with the other patients.

«She's fine,» he said, «and her treatment is going very well.»

Nevertheless she had been very ill and had undergone extreme surgery because of severe cancer. She had endured a double mastectomy and a large part of her abdomen had been removed. This, I think would have been tragic enough, but later she told us that George, the man she had abandoned my father for, had arrived in her room after the operation and told her that because of her condition she was no longer a woman to him. He left, never to return.

Everybody has their own life story of course and perhaps this in some way was part of his, but it is a hard thing to say and do to someone we have lived with for twenty years.

In the ward it was a grand reunion for my mother and my sister, with tears and gentle embraces, but for me, in the meeting with the woman I had loved so much when I was a child, something was missing.

Even if she looked as I remembered her, she was a stranger to me.

She did not know me and I did not know her. She was not present for the most important moments in my life, my first girlfriend, my first performance with Sparrow, my excitement at discovering meditation, my marriage and the birth of my children. When she left our home in Liverpool I was a little boy, now I was a man with a family of my own and she had not been part of any of that. Perhaps in a romantic Hollywood movie violins would have played and we would have cried in each other's arms together, but real life is different and the space between us was too great.

She herself had lived a very different life to me, sinking lower into a style of life that revolved around bars and alcohol. She was not an alcoholic, not at all, but the culture she and George had been part of certainly revolved around those things.

We said good bye and there was a sad sense of relief, and the hope that perhaps we would never have to meet again. The memory was much sweeter than the reality.

My sister and I took our place on the ferry and returned to the Isle of Man where I immediately resumed my Dhamma life.

Now I worked with my father in the factory making components for Martin Baker ejector seats. I had taken this job when Fiona first discovered she was pregnant and so by the birth, I was well-established there. I was a store-man and working in a small department known as the 'finished parts store' with about eight other people.

When speaking about my Dhamma training I will often say that I have lived in a monastery and worked in a factory, I wouldn't want to say which was the better teacher as both showed different aspects of myself. For me, factory life was pointless and empty of any kind of job satisfaction. I was there, as were the majority of people, to earn enough money to take care of my family. I got used to it of course, and in fact stayed for eleven years, but there were many days when I just couldn't face being there and I would find a reason not to go.

The job I had before this was very different. I was employed by Sayles the drapers, a very old and time honored business. My job was to install curtain and other window fittings in people's homes before the careful hanging of expensive and exclusive curtains and things like roller blinds, Venetian blinds, louvre blinds and the like. I really loved this job, not only because of Tom, the man I worked with who was an educated person, intelligent, funny and introduced me to the music of Beethoven, but also because when I would arrive at a house to begin my preparatory work, I would be greeted like a king.

I would ring the door bell and wait. The lady of the house would open the door and I would say who I was and why I had arrived.

«Oh, wonderful,» they would say, «come in love, do you want a cup of tea before you start, and how about a piece of cake?»

These were very happy times. Driving the works van, talking with Tom and being welcomed so wonderfully into people's homes. Unfortunately the pay was not so high, and with a baby on the way I had to leave and join my father.

Soon Fiona, baby Michael and I left our apartment and moved into our new small house in upper Douglas. There is a perceived prestige in buying your own home, but the reality, at least in our case, did not live up to the fantasy.

As soon as we took the mortgage all the overtime at the factory stopped. This was simply because peace had broken out and other countries were not ordering so many ejectors seats. The problem for me was that our mortgage repayments had been calculated on a percentage of weekly overtime. We had no savings, and so we began to struggle financially.

I took a Saturday job in the warehouse at a large store where later I would work full time, and helped with renovation work of friends houses. It was exhausting. I was still sitting for half an hour each day, but it didn't seem to help, and now Fiona was pregnant again.

Actually we were very pleased with this, and looked forward to a new arrival sometime in the future. Also, I need to say that both my parents and Fiona's parents were always offering help and support in one way and another.

Still ... it wasn't easy!

I had had no further contact with my mother since the day we met in the hospital ward in Liverpool, but now that was to change. In a moment of compassion, generosity and love she was invited by my sister to live with her and her family on the Isle of Man. As I was not involved I did not have any real interest one way or the other.

So, it was done and she arrived in time for summer.

This was an uncomfortable period for my father, to have the woman he felt had betrayed and humiliated him back in his life. He deliberately avoided her and so stayed away from my sister's house. This feeling lasted until he and Eileen met her by chance one afternoon sitting in the sun on a bench in Onchan park. They spoke a little bit but in the reality of this meeting the anger was finished and the painful memories fell away. Too many good things had happened for my father since their separation, and too many bad things for my mother. He no longer saw an enemy in front of him, but a sad, tired victim. Standing by his side was Eileen, his strength, his partner, his woman. Who could hurt him now?

For myself, I felt it was my duty to visit her and so made a huge effort to include her in my life and the life of my family. The reality was that I didn't know her and as I met her more and more I didn't like her. She was a stranger to me and I realized that if she was not my mother I would not spend any time with her at all. She came to our small house to meet baby Michael and Fiona, who was now fully pregnant and the size of a house, but there was no connection - how could there be? She was just a stranger visiting us. I never felt it correct to introduce her as granny or nana, but just to say, 'this is my mum.'

The summer passed and autumn began. Life continued as always. When December arrived I received a 'phone call from my father to say that my mother was in hospital.

She had gone to visit an aunt and slipped on the step and broken her hip. Her bones were brittle so even the slightest knock would cause an injury.

It was here that finally we began to make our connection again.

She was an avid reader still and when we were alone we would talk about the books we had read. I was still studying Buddhism, reading the sutras and stories about the lives of great Masters, but there was one book, though not Buddhist, which was one of the greatest inspirations in my life. I related to the main character, Larry Darrell, and felt that if my mother read this book she would begin to know me, after all, if she was a stranger to me, I was also a stranger to her.

The book, by W. Somerset Maugham was called the Razors Edge, and I had read it so many times and each time finding new inspiration to continue with my Dhamma life, often so demanding. I bought a copy especially for her and wrote on the inside cover rather romantically, 'to mum, when you know who Larry is, you will know who I am,' and signed it Michael.

It was Christmas so it was the perfect time to pass this special book. I arrived at the hospital and sat with her. We talked and I gave her my gift and the clue to who I was.

She apologized for not having something for me but handed me the book she had just finished. It was The Stand by Stephen King.

We said goodbye and she died two days later.

There was a brain tumor and nothing could be done. She had not mentioned it to me but it was a ticking time bomb. She died on 27th December 1981. She was 49.

At the funeral a few days later I sat at the back of the church with my father. I think we both felt a bit lost and not really sure of our place. I placed one single rose at the grave with a verse from the Tao te Ching;

Returning is the motion of the Tao.
Surrendering is the way of the Tao.
All things are born from something.
Something is born from no – thing.

Tao te Ching: verse 40.

The new year was about to begin. We look ahead and leave the past behind. I was thirty.

Adam, our second son was born on the sixth of November 1981, six weeks before the death of my mother around one o'clock in the afternoon, although not without some difficulty.
I received a 'phone call from the maternity home where Fiona had already been installed the evening before about eight o'clock in the morning.
«Come quickly, Mr Kewley, the birth is about to happen.»
This meant a sudden change of plan regarding the caring for Michael, and so I called my sister to ask if she would take care of him for a couple of hours. Naturally she agreed and I deposited him at her house before speeding to the maternity home.
Later she told me that as her own children were quite grown, there was nothing for him to play with in the house, and all she could offer for a two year old boy for his entertainment were the rubber toys of her little dog, Sofie. She gathered them together and gave them to Michael. He looked at them for a moment and asked, «Has Sofie got any cars?»
So sweet.
Meanwhile I was arriving to be with Fiona. Actually, it was a relief that the birth had not begun, and so we waited together with the midwife timing the contractions.

Once again Fiona was inspiring and apart from an occasional long sigh made no fuss at all. She lay back in the bed with her knees bent and I rested my arms on one leg and the midwife rested her arms on the other and we waited.

Soon it was time for the delivery room and once again, this time by Fiona's request I was present. However, quickly we had the feeling that something was wrong and that the baby was not coming as it should. The mid-wife and nurses had a whispered discussion and it was announced that the best thing to do was to call Mr Townshend, the specialist.

I remember him as being a very pleasant and highly professional man, approachable and caring for his staff and patients. He entered the delivery room, quickly assessed the situation and asked to speak to me outside. It sounded ominous, and it was.

«The baby is facedown in the womb,» he said, «and cannot be born this way. We must turn him so that he faces up.»

'O.K,' I thought, 'doesn't sound so bad.'

«Is it dangerous?» I asked.

«Yes,» Mr Townshend answered, «very. You see, we have to turn him with forceps around his head, this means that the pressure on his neck is enormous. I'm sorry to tell you but we cannot guarantee complete success.»

I asked him about other options but he said there were none. It was a fraught moment.

We both went back into the delivery room, Mr Townshend to scrub up and me to be with my wife. «Is everything O.K?» she asked.

«Oh yes, fine.» I lied.

Suddenly one of the nurses called out, «Mr Townshend!» He turned immediately, gave an enormous smile and shouted in a 'eureka' voice, «He's turned!»

On the final contraction Adam turned and was later categorized as a spontaneous birth.

He came sliding out, so much of him. It is true that I am certainly no expert in child birth, I could never have imagined a baby so long, so blue, and so heavy. He weighted ten pounds and was in full health. After he was cleaned and had his fingers and toes counted, he was handed to me as there was a problem with the placenta breaking. I held him in my arms next to Fiona's head and welcomed him into the world.

Later I went outside to make the many 'phone calls necessary to share this wonderful news. More tears, more celebration and another being to love.

It was a stressful time for me with a job I didn't like very much, never enough money, a family to support and a deep sense of isolation. I felt as though I had missed an opportunity to be free in my life and instead imprisoned myself in convention and debt. I needed someone to talk to. Fiona was not interested in my strange ideas about life, but was mostly tolerant and patient as I tried to convince her that there could be another way to live. She didn't see it and I could not produce it, so it stayed as a barrier between us.

I was desperate to share my blossoming Buddhist understanding and so I placed a small line advert in the local free paper. It read something like, 'If anyone is interested in forming a regular meditation meeting group, pease call, and then the telephone number was added.

These were the days when meditation was still not completely in the public domain so a simple advertisement like this was enough. Three people responded, two men and a woman. We met at my house on the evenings when Fiona went to her target rifle shooting club in Castletown. For some inexplicable reason she was an incredibly accurate shot and could place the small bullet in the dead centre of the target almost every time. When I asked how she could do that she replied that she didn't know. «It's just that when

I lie there, strapped into my rifle, everything falls quiet inside me and then suddenly it seems as though the gun fires itself. When this happens I don't need to check the target, I know precisely where the bullet has gone.»

This is exactly as the highest level of Japanese martial arts is understood, the emptiness of a self who tries, and simply the selfless action. Beautiful. She was the island woman's champion for many years. So, whilst she was experiencing momentary emptiness of self, I was still only talking about it!

Although I do not remember the name of the woman who regularly came to our small meetings, I do remember her influence and a moment we had between us when having wrestled with a point of understanding for many weeks, I suddenly had the insight into it as I was explaining to her just how I couldn't understand it.

One of the other two men was interested in Bhagwan Shree Rajneesh, an Indian guru who my teacher later said had done more to damage the purity of meditation than any person alive. Of course I didn't know that then but I had heard of him for his use of sex and hippie style freedom in his training of thousands of westerners traveling in India. Many scandals followed this man throughout his life, and he polarized people's opinion - he was either a true Master or a charlatan. However, he had already written many books by this time and these teachings were also presented and gratefully received.

The third, and most influential person in my life at that time was a retired psychologist called Praben Scott. He was of Scandinavian origin and slightly morose as he should have been according to his stereotype. The moment he discovered my interest in Buddhism he invited me to his beautiful home in the Manx countryside to discuss it privately, but more, send me on my way both literally and figuratively with many, many copies of 'The Middle Way,' the Buddhist Society of England's quarterly journal.

The founder and leader of this very middle class Buddhist

organization was Christmas Humphries, the arch enemy of Tekisui in Cardiff all those years before.

It was because of these magazines that I was first introduced to the writings and later the recorded Dhamma talks of the American monk, Ajahn Sumedo who had just arrived in England to establish the Chithurst Buddhist Monastery, and his teacher, the Thai Master, Ajahn Chah. Ajahn is a Thai word meaning teacher, and the flowering of my true Dhamma life began with these two men. However, even more important than the discovery of these two great Buddhist teachers was the correspondence and later meeting with Marjorie Lamont, a lady of a 'certain age' in Scotland.

Based upon my natural empathy and acceptance of the importance of harmlessness in my life I already considered myself to be a Buddhist, but I needed to be sure that I had really understood the teachings that so far I had only read about. In one of the collection of Middle Way magazines there was an advertisement for a correspondence course in Buddhist practice and I eagerly applied for a place. I can't remember if there was a fee involved but if there was it didn't seem to be unreasonable, so I sent off my letter and waited for a reply. Soon it came and I began my postal relationship with Marjorie Lamont. The course would arrive in weekly parts and explain clearly and in detail a much more accurate account of the Buddha's teaching than I had received in books all those years ago in Cardiff. I was also more than pleased to recognize that I had intuitively arrived at the same level of understanding as was being presented by the Buddhist Society.

This relationship lasted for some time and on one occasion I mentioned in a letter to Marjorie that I would like to meet a Master to teach me. She replied immediately telling me about a Buddhist Master who had just been invited and so arrived in England to share the Dhamma. He was in Birmingham and I should contact the monastery.

This was exciting news and was exactly what I did, eventually.

Although the spiritual side of my life seemed to be going well, the regular daily part with work, home and family was a different story. The financial pressure mounted and in the stress of my perception of trying to hold everything together, I developed an ulcer. This was horrendous and took huge amounts of my energy with doctors appointments and dealing with the pain with every mouthful of food.

I was told to stop drinking coffee and tea and basically stop eating anything that wasn't salad. Everything became difficult and life became the paradox of feeling hungry and dreading eating anything.

I was put on a course of Ranitidine, a strong antacid drug known as Zantac. These and over the counter alkaline medication became part of my staple diet.

In time I was sent for an X-ray at the local hospital. This in itself was not so easy as I had to swallow in rapid succession two paper cups of material to allow the ulcer to be photographed. It was agony and not helped by the rather unsympathetic nurse yelling, «Come on Mr Kewley, it doesn't hurt that much.» Actually it did but I didn't have time for an argument.

I lay down on the table and the process began. Painless of course and later when I saw the X-rays I could easily see the growling red abscess which was my ulcer. Of course, X-ray images are in black and white, but in my mind I saw the colour of pain, and it was red!

And so I struggled. There seemed to be no end in sight until I plucked up courage to contact the monastery in Birmingham as Marjorie Lamont had advised.

This has almost been a theme and a blessing of my life, that the universe would often painfully steer me into a position where I felt there was nothing left to do but surrender.

I wrote a letter saying that I was interested in visiting them and received a rapid reply from someone called Peter Ridley telling me I was welcome to visit, but if I was coming from so far, why not stay and sit a Vipassana retreat?

I organized everything with work and Fiona. Although I know she never approved of my Buddhist and meditation activity, it was her presence in my life that allowed me to do it.

The Friday when the retreat would begin finally arrived and I set off early in the morning. Finding enough money to pay for my fist visit to what was to become my spiritual base was not so easy, but in the end I was able to sell some of my favourite, hence most valuable possessions, including my cherished Beatles and Beethoven cassettes. In the end we must give our attention to that which has real value against that with lesser value, no matter how comforting and familiar that thing is.

The ferry gently eased itself away from the quayside, and headed out to an empty horizon and an open and unknown sea. The symbolism did not escape me. However, it was on this four hour sailing from Douglas to Heysham where I met my first crisis. There is a Buddhist precept which states that we will not take drugs, but here was I consuming so many Zantac tablets to help relieve the pain from my ulcer (although my feeling was that they were fairly ineffective) that I didn't know what I should do. I didn't realize then that the rule is not about medicinal compounds but rather any sort of recreational drugs. However, the problem was in my mind, what should I do? I felt I needed to continue with my medication and so I decided to be discreet and continue my daily dosage, if not how would I ever eat anything?

After the ferry journey was a train to Lancaster, then another train to Birmingham and finally a taxi to the monastery. This I assumed would be quite remote, somewhere close to nature, a large building with a long tree lined drive. As with so many things in life, the reality did not match the imagination.

I had already sat simple retreats, first with Transcendental Meditation and later with Zen. Although they were very different from each other, neither compared with the demands I felt in Vipassana practice.

Vipassana is a word from the Theravada Buddhist tradition meaning to 'see things as they are'. The teaching is simple, deep and profound and I took it to heart immediately.

If we truly want to see, know and comprehend reality, we must meditate. The meditation practice established in awareness and love is traditionally called Satipatthana, but in modern language we use the name Vipassana. This word does not describe a technique of meditation, but rather the purpose of that meditation - to see things as they really are.

There are many different schools, styles and forms of Vipassana practice, but in truth, anything that cultivates clear and unclouded vision of each moment can be called Vipassana. The Buddha himself did not prescribe a certain meditation technique for the development of awareness, rather he recommended that his followers (bhikkhus) be aware in every moment and in every action, both physical and mental. This practice of course, should be cultivated, not only in the formal sitting and walking practice, but in each moment of daily life.

I arrived at the monastery tired from my travel and was surprised to see that it was a large terraced house in Carlyle Road, a residential area of Birmingham in the district of Edgbaston, famous for its international cricket ground.

As the taxi pulled up at number forty seven, I wondered if I had the correct address.

I mounted the few steps up to the front door and saw the small sign, Birmingham Buddhist Vihara, I disappointedly knew I was in the right place.

I rang the bell and the door opened. I found myself standing in front of Peter Ridley, a slight, friendly balding man who welcomed me, made me a cup of tea and told me of the retreat programme.

It was horrific, but as my nature is, 'I've come here to do this,' I resigned myself to it and hoped the days would pass quickly and that my ulcer would not give me too much trouble.

Peter mentioned many times a lady who lived in the house and it seemed managed most of the affairs. She was known as Mama, and she would be home soon.

«Mama will do this,» he said, «Mama will do that,» and so it went on. Finally we heard the front door open and close and he said, «Oh that's Mama, come on, I'll introduce you to her.»

To a person brought up on nineteen fifties television and many racist stereotypes I imagined Mama to be a large black lady as in the Tom and Jerry cartoons, speaking with southern American drawl and offering me fried chicken and grits.

However, this was not the case.

Dr Mar Mar Lwin, was a small, slim and elegant Burmese lady and apart from saying hello as she stood at the sink washing cups, she pretty much ignored me on that first evening, me, I'm sure being seen, as just another westerner coming to test Buddhism. However, we became close in time and during all the years we knew each other I found her to be warm and friendly and I can honestly say that she helped me in many ways, even to the point of being my principal supporter when I took later the robes and became a monk. In fact it was her suggestion that I do it. It seems apparent now that she too could see the sincerity in my heart.

She was a research doctor by profession and my teacher's personal assistant and so served the monastery tirelessly. She had her own private room in the monastery and perhaps that was why many of the western students who came with their own very fixed ideas of what Buddhism was and how it should be practiced, didn't like her. Those close to the teacher are often resented by others.

Possibly they saw her as an obstacle to the teacher, whereas I always felt her to be a link to him. It is true that for me she was simply another beautiful gift in my life.

If she was always helpful to me, often sharing her meals and giving her time, she could on occasion be ferocious in her anger, and I experienced this on one occasion whilst staying at the monastery some years later. At that time a young German man had ordained and come to the monastery to be trained. However, the training with my teacher depended deeply on self-reliance. Although he was always available for Dhamma, as the disciple you were expected to remember why you were here, living a life supported by the generosity of others, and so practice in accordance with that. As a monk and layman this idea always fitted me very well, but it did not work for everyone, this young German monk being a good example of that.

A small group of us were sitting in meditation in the Dhamma Hall one evening, I as a visiting lay disciple and by this time, very close to my teacher, and the group sitting quietly behind the young German monk.

My teacher was absent from the monastery at this time but the daily routine continued of course.

The doorbell rang and it was answered by Mar Mar Lwin. The unseen guests entered the monastery and were installed in a small anteroom close to the Dhamma Hall. It was the duty and responsibility of Mar Mar to entertain these unseen people who we later found out were special and quite important visitors, and so they fell deep into conversation. Sounds which could be heard in the Dhamma Hall.

The essence of Vipassana meditation is to make the space where life can continue around you without necessarily being disturbed by it. The sounds that exist in the monastery are not much different from the sounds that exist outside, and so by surrendering to the many things we cannot control, everything is training us to be at peace with things as they are.

However, as simple as it is to say these few words the practice of them is not always so easy, and this is what the German monk found that evening.

After some time he stood up and left the Dhamma Hall and went to the anteroom where the conversation was originating. I intuitively knew what he was going to do and the whispering voice inside my head was yelling to him, 'don't do it, don't do it!'

But too late.

His voice was louder than the guests and he told them quite clearly that this was a monastery and people were trying to meditate, and so would they please have some respect for others making an effort to practice and be quiet.

My heart sank and I waited.

He entered the Dhamma hall again and took his place. In my head I counted the seconds. There weren't very many until the door burst open and there was Mar Mar Lwin. Not so small, elegant and refined in this moment, but consumed by anger and humiliation and truly having taken on the countenance of a demon. She screamed into the silence and told this young monk exactly what she though of him, and how she was serving Bhante by taking care of these special guests until he arrived back at the monastery. As a matter of simplicity, all Buddhist monks can be called Bhante, which means Venerable sir. This is convenient and sometimes confusing as long Pali names do not need to be remembered.

I sat still and looked straight ahead. She was completely right, and he was completely wrong, but actually it was not his fault as no one was training him. Monasteries are not quiet places. There are the sounds from the kitchen, from visitors, telephones and everything else. This is what we must live and practice with.

It became a good lesson for me in my later days as a teacher. If students do not know what they are supposed to do or not to do, how can we blame them when they break the rules?

Two days later when the evening meditation had ended and Bhante was leaving the Dhamma Hall he stopped at me and asked if I would come to his room. Naturally I said yes and a few minutes later arrived in front of him and sat down. He looked serious and possibly a little uncomfortable but as soon as he was ready he spoke.

«Michael, after the incident with Mar Mar and the visitors recently this young monk must be disciplined and told to leave the monastery.»

I replied that I could not be part of this, after all I was no longer a monk and monastery discipline was not my business.

«No,» he said, «I want you here and I want you to speak.» He was insistent so I resigned to what was about to happen.

Soon two more monks arrived in the room, one of them the young German one, the other a very friendly monk from Bangladesh. We sat together and Bhante explained the situation and asked me to begin by giving my opinion of this young monk.

I was able to say honestly that I had no problems with him and I always found his behavior sincere and friendly towards me. The problem in my mind, was that no one was taking care of him, and so he does not know what is acceptable or not as a man in monks robes.

Next the monk from Bangladesh spoke. He was not so friendly towards him as me, but I realized that part of what was happening was cultural. We may arrive at Buddhism with many romantic ideas, but so much of what is taught is cultural. There is an enormous difference between Buddhism and Buddha Dhamma.

Buddhism is a religion that exists in the world. It is cultural and traditional, and can be found in most Asian countries.

Buddha Dhamma is the teachings of an enlightened being that are shared and freely offered to disciples everywhere in the world to help them realise their own Awakening.

The difference between the two is enormous! Picking up a new identity, as exciting as that can be, is not important; Awakening is. The conclusion of this disciplinary meeting was that the young

German monk must find another monastery where he can stay.
The two monks were told to leave and I was once again asked to stay.
When we were alone Bhante asked me what I thought. I told him I thought it was a bit hard and who would train him if he didn't?
He thought for a moment and said, «I will allow him to stay, on the condition that he apologizes to me first. Please go and tell him.»
I left the room and went downstairs. We met in the kitchen where he was making a drink for himself.
I asked him how he was feeling and I'm happy to say that he was able to confide in me. I passed on Bhante's condition for staying, and he replied, «I certainly will apologize, but I won't stay.» I understood.
Soon I left the monastery and did not meet this monk again. I heard he had gone to train with Venerable Khemadhammo who had a small monastery quite close and was known as an exacting disciplinarian. Perfect, now he would receive the training he needed.
Also living at the monastery in those days was a huge cat, aptly named Hercules. We met in my room as he was sleeping on my bed. His position in the monastery was secured by the Chinese platitude, 'it is better to feed one cat than many mice,' although in reality his food was left in a bowl in the kitchen as with all domestic cats and if he ever did catch a mouse it was rescued as quickly as possible and set free.
My first Vipassana retreat began at seven o' clock in the evening. I was apprehensive but something wonderful had just happened and for a moment I felt more at ease, simply because I no longer felt alone. Marjorie Lamont, my Buddhist tutor had also signed on for this retreat and we met in the kitchen like two old friends.
«This is wonderful,» I said, «what are you doing here?» I stupidly asked.

«I wanted to surprise you,» she replied. She had.

We assembled in the Dhamma hall and the silence began.
Silence is an integral part of all Vipassana retreats, simply because it is the perfect environment for the arising of awareness. We spend so much time verbalizing every thought, mood, feeling and emotion that we miss the opportunity to see their origin. Once the habit of speaking about everything falls away, we can hear so much more.
Another level of silence is the instruction not to look at each other, but to put our full attention on ourselves. The world that we experience is the one that we create for ourselves moment after moment, and so it is better once again to turn our attention inwards. The third aspect of silence is make all our movements slow and elegant. This unhurried and deliberate attitude towards our conduct also has the function of creating the perfect environment for awareness.
The last and we may say, the highest manifestation of silence is called in Buddhist teaching, the 'citta viveka', the silent mind. This then is the internal environment where all our thoughts, moods, feelings and emotions can be seen and experienced, but not attached to as being me or mine, or belonging to us. This non attached relationship to the mind is the very essence of Vipassana practice, and so the very essence of peace.

As we sat in the half-light of the Dhamma hall, the beautiful marble Burmese Buddha gently smiling down on us and the fragrance of incense filling the air, the door opened and the man who would become my teacher, guide and source of great discomfort, at least for the first part of our twenty two year relationship, entered the room.
He took his seat on the left side of the Buddha Statue and began to speak. His husky voice was quiet and his accent thick. We really

had to 'tune in' to catch everything, but the first words that I fully understood from him arrived like an arrow in my heart and I knew the universe had brought me to the right place.

«If you want to be happy in your life, you have to cultivate a loving heart,» he said.

I had been practicing meditation for more than ten years, first Transcendental Meditation, then Zen, then sitting alone, but always I felt something was missing. With these few words my practice was complete.

It was love.

I almost yelled out a great 'YES' but of course did not. However, something changed on that first meeting and I knew I had found my Path.

I have no memory of the rest of his first Dhamma talk, but no matter, I heard what I had come for.

As a group we were instructed in one of the principal techniques of Vipassana known as Mahasi.

Mahasi was the Burmese Master who had made popular this particular style of practice which included moving very slowly and mentally identifying each movement of mind. The starting point is the breath in the abdomen where it would be acknowledged as 'rising, rising, rising' on the in breath and, 'falling, falling, falling' on the out breath. Any mental activity would be noted similarly as, 'thinking, thinking, thinking,' or 'planning, planning, planning,' as the attention was steered back to the abdomen.

I trained in this practice for many retreats during those first years, but I can say that I didn't really enjoy it very much. What I really sought out was time with my teacher. He quickly became the guiding light in my life.

The first evening over, it was time for bed ready to begin again the next morning at four thirty.

That day was a nightmare of sleepiness, pain and cold.

We awoke at four o'clock and slowly stumbled our way to our cushions to begin the first of many one hour meditation sittings. The whole monastery was very cold and the only heating in the Dhamma hall was a small gas fire built into the far wall. Over the days this gas fire became everybody's personal koan. There would be the initial slow walking rush as we entered to arrange ourself nearest to enjoy the heat, but very soon the whole left side of our body would be uncomfortably hot whilst the right side stayed cold. Now what to do? Moving, though not prohibited, was frowned upon, and so we struggled as the mind shouted insults and complaints about the situation.

You don't need to go to Japan or study Zen to engage in koan study, simply look at your own life.

This sitting led to the first walking meditation and that led to the next sitting, and so on and so on. Breakfast came and went and I found myself back in the Dhamma hall.

By this time my mind was really in rebellion and seeking sleep as an escape from the situation from hell, and the physical pain and the low temperature didn't help at all.

In that moment I would have given anything for my wife to telephone the monastery with an urgent message that there was a crisis at home and I must come back immediately. Then I could leave whilst still 'saving face.' I could apologize and say to everyone, «I'm sorry, I really want to stay but an emergency has arisen and I must take care of my wife and children.»

Who would not sacrifice their own pleasure of a retreat for the well-being of their family?

Of course, the 'phone call never came and I sat there in my misery blaming the whole universe for how I felt.

The time passed slowly, the only respite from the pain, boredom and cold was the two Dhamma talks from the monk whose name I still did not know. To listen to his words meant that all the discomfort fell away if only for a short time.

Finally it was time for bed and I was ready. I wrote in my journal, 'too sore to sit, too tired to stand.'

The following day began in the same way and had all the marks of being simply a repetition of the day before, with no hope anywhere.

Then it happened.

Suddenly and without any warning everything stopped. There was no more pain, no more cold, no more criticism, no more complaining, no more sleepiness, only peace. A floating peace that was so deep and so profound that its brilliance was equally physical and mental. There was a tranquility never before experienced and time ceased to exist. My body felt as though it was almost made of light and was hovering above my cushion and later, when I walked it did not seem as though my feet made contact with the floor. This was beautiful. Empty and full in the same moment, something never known before. I sat there aware but not involved, simply being present with the moment. There were no assumptions being made, no internal voices or comments, the mind itself was quiet, it too simply enjoying this incredible experience. Somewhere in the distance the bell rang to end the meditation, but I did not move, not because I was afraid to lose what was happening, but only that I didn't know what to do with it!

A voice in my head finally spoke and said, 'Maybe you should go and tell the monk?' At this point I was still not sure of his name, but I asked the retreat manager, Peter, if I had permission to speak with the teacher. He told me just to go to his room and knock on the door jamb.

I almost floated up the stairs and arrived outside his room. There was no door, only a curtain, hence the instruction to knock upon the jamb. In ancient times the disciple would simply cough or clear their throat to announce their presence. The lack of a door was to ensure that nothing untoward would ever take place in this room.

I knocked gently and the same quiet husky voice I had heard the night before said, «Come in.»

It was in this moment that I realized that I didn't know the correct procedure in approaching a Buddhist monk and so I said from the doorway, «Excuse me Bhante, I don't know how to approach you.»

«Oh, you just walk,» he said beckoning me with his arm.

I knelt down in front of him and shared my experience, which was still ongoing.

He listened, asked pertinent questions and finally gave his conclusion.

«This is Piti,» he said, «it is a Jhanic state.» He explained the mechanism of it and shared with me the pleasure of it. Then came the Dhamma teaching, «but just watch it because it will pass.»

This was the moment when I knew I was in front of a real Master.

«Just watch it because it will pass.»

This experience was fantastic. It was wonderful, perhaps even mystical, but it's not IT.

This is not what my practice is about - feeling good in the meditation.

This experience like everything else arises and passes away, to mistake it for something more profound than that is to misunderstand completely the teaching of the Buddha and all the Masters ever since.

'Whatever arises passes away and is not what you are.'

Chasing after profound meditation experiences will take us only to more suffering as we continually try to re-create a unique event in time.

The retreat continued and the experience gently began to fade, but leaving in its trail an understanding now of what Dhamma really is accompanied by an acceptance into the necessity to practice without intention. Just do what you're supposed to do and forget about a goal. Sit as well as you can, move as slowly and deliberately as you can and allow the understanding to come to you.

As the clarity of training became stronger I also had a shocking realization. I hadn't been taking my medication, in fact until that moment I had forgotten all about it. What had happened? I was taking my breakfast and lunch, (no dinner on retreat) without difficulty or pain in swallowing. Of course I didn't understand what had changed, but I didn't try to figure it out either. My body felt in balance again and my ulcer was one less thing to worry about.

The retreat finally finished on a Sunday afternoon, and there was the usual photographs and exchanging of telephone numbers and postal addresses. By three o' clock the monastery was empty, except for me!

My boat back to the island was not until the afternoon of the next day, and so I had asked permission to stay one extra evening in the monastery. Of course my request was accepted and I prepared myself to sit alone until I could take a taxi to the station the next morning.

This didn't happen, and I consider now the once a day ferry services to the Isle of Man to be another blessing in my life.

I sat alone on the sofa in the small anteroom next to the Dhamma hall, the place where some years in the future Mar Mar Lwin would loudly entertain the guests of Bhante, when he came and sat next to me.

This was the moment when due to external circumstances or perhaps our kammic dispositions we truly met.

We spoke for a long time, he asking many questions about my life, and me nervously perhaps, asking about his.

Now I learned his name and title which was Sayadaw Rewata Dhamma. Sayadaw is a Burmese honorific title for a senior monk or abbot of a monastery. He had ordained as a child, following his kammic disposition towards the spiritual life and had studied and trained in the two Buddhist disciplines of meditation and academic study. He held a doctorate in Abhidhamma, the third basket of the Buddhist Cannon and the most intellectual of the three.

It is understood that the whole of the Buddha's teachings are contained in three parts, or baskets (pitakas).

The first is the Vinaya Pitaka, the training rules for monks and their origin. The Buddha was not someone to make rules lightly and so only when there was an incident of unworthy behavior would he instruct the community that this was conduct unbecoming to someone training in a spiritual life. Then a fixed rule would be made. In total there are two hundred and twenty seven rules for monks, and more if we include rules specific to a particular monastery. However, such was the greatness of this man that he also reminded us that the lesser rules are appropriate only to time and place.

One example of this is the rule that monks should bathe every day. This is a good and clear rule as bathing revitalizes the body and mind and helps limit the spread of disease. However, there is a story about two monks living in an area where there was a drought and so they immediately let go of this rule as water then became a precious commodity for the preservation of life. This is how to understand rules as being appropriate to time and place.

The second basket of the Cannon is the Suttanta Pitaka, the teachings and stories of the life of the Buddha. This is by far the biggest basket and according to tradition was recounted with word perfect accuracy by Ananda, the Buddhas attendant for twenty five years at the great council of elders three months after the death of the Buddha.

The third basket is the Abhidhamma Pitaka. This is the analysis of mind and matter, and does not speak of a person, only a collection of elements and mind states (Nama Rupa) that give the appearance of a living being.

This Bhante, although born and educated from childhood as a monk in Burma, had lived in Varanasi, India for twenty five years and taught Abhidhamma at the university, going so far as to write the university book of year some years before.

He was an academic and a meditation Master, and as we sat together on the evening after the retreat I mentally bowed at his feet and gave myself to his instruction.

He made sure I ate dinner, even though he himself, because of his monks vows would not take food in the afternoon, and loaded me with free Dhamma books to take home with me the next day.

«What time do you leave in the morning?» he asked.

«I will take a taxi to the station about nine thirty,» I answered.

«No,» he said, «I will take you in my car.»

I protested but to no avail. It was decided.

I joined him in meditation the next morning, ate a simple breakfast and allowed him to take me to the station. It was the first of many such occasions and for a long, long time I honestly assumed that he did this for everyone. Only all those years later did I discover that it was only for me.

I arrived home excited to share my experiences but once again found myself alone in my life. Meditation, as well as being the vehicle to enlightenment, can also be devisive and become the very thing to separate couples. Without support from the other it can often be interpreted as, 'I would rather be alone than be with you.'

In all my relationship with Fiona I had always been a meditator, but only ever for half an hour in the morning or evening, but never for ten days away from home. Of course she had given her consent for me to go but I am certain that she thought that it would be a one time event.

I had found my new life, complete and perfect for me. From that moment to now, this is where I would put my attention.

Naturally I returned to work and family life and one day received a card from the hospital to check again on my ulcer. This has almost slipped my memory as since the retreat there had been no recurrence of difficulty with it and I had stopped all medication.

I arrived at the X-ray department as before and took the first paper cup of crystals and the second of the barium meal. However, as with everything else passing through my gullet at this time there was no problem and no unnecessary encouragement from the hospital staff. I climbed onto the X-ray table and the examination began.

After a few minutes of searching with something like an ultrasound device, rolling it around over the whole of my solar plexus and looking hard into the monitor, the doctor announced quite sheepishly, «I'm sorry Mr Kewley, we can't find your ulcer!»

It had dissolved in the loving environment of my first Vipassana retreat.

This was not the first time I had experienced something significant with meditation. As I child and teenager, I had suffered from asthma and related respiratory difficulties. These faded and finally disappeared completely with the introduction of meditation in my life. Coincidence, possibly, I only know that the results of a consistent meditation practice are manifold.

Dhamma is the Buddhist word that means 'ultimate truth', the 'reality of things', and 'that which is behind the appearance of things,' and to commit humbly to this beautiful investigation and so reconnect with this 'ultimate truth,' is the function of Vipassana practice. The practice is not to get something, but to see something, namely the very cause of our difficulties and unhappiness in life. However, this practice of perfect awareness does not stand alone and is dependent upon the cultivation of an internal loving environment, called in Buddhist language Metta

Bhavana, usually translated into English as, Loving Kindness.
You are not broken and so you don't need to be fixed, is a theme of mine in the Dhamma hall as I teach now. What we must do in order to be happy is cultivate a loving heart. The beginning of this is to stop criticizing and blaming ourself and the other for the situation we find ourselves in and put our loving attention, embodied by a gentle and unconditional acceptance, onto ourselves. Only in this way will we release ourselves from our emotional relationship to the past. This past arises and colours everything we meet and then naturally influences our reaction to it.

We do not see the world as it is, we only see the world as we are, and so the more fear we carry the more it colours our view and experience of the world. The more loving acceptance we manifest the less this old story will influence our life and the happier and more peaceful we will be. This is also known as 'the way of letting go.'

If we let go a little there is a little peace, if we let go a lot there is a lot of peace, if we let go completely - complete peace.

Time passed and my sitting practice at home increased to one hour daily sittings. Now I had real direction and the feeling of not walking alone. I made another retreat, then another and another. I worked my three jobs, sold as many of my cassettes as I could and used every aspect of my work and home life as a part of my training.

As I look back I see that Fiona was a great gift for me, not that she made things easy, but rather the opposite. She continually threw me back upon myself. On the rare occasions when we would dispute I would just be at the point of closing the argument with an absolutely cast iron conclusion, standing in front of her, so proud of my intellect, when she would softly look at me and in a quiet, calm voice simply inform me that, «That's not a very Buddhist thing to say?»

This comment would stop me in my tracks and I would have to question myself and my arrogance. The true value of teachings like this is rarely realized in the moment, but when we give ourselves to Dhamma we can see that in every way everything is leading us on the path to freedom.

Sayadaw Rewata Dhamma had given me many books to read and I read all of them with enthusiasm. Of course, so much of the significance of what I read eluded me, but I continued and felt that understanding would come with time.

Because of my association with the Buddhist Society in London I was able to buy audio cassettes of different teachers, particularly Buddhist monks. My preferred teacher on cassette was Ajahn Sumedo whose way of sharing Dhamma was light, joyful and directly related to everyday life. This suited me perfectly and harmonized exactly with my relationship to my own teacher.

The very first cassette I bought of an Ajahn Sumedo Dhamma talk opened my eyes to the correct attitude for training. He had recounted his early days as a monk in Thailand where during one difficult period he had met frustration upon frustration. The tension had built up inside him and no matter how hard or intelligently he tried to sidestep the difficulties nothing changed until a powerful realization from the intuitive wise part of him spoke, it said in a clear voice, 'I have to deal with this sometime - it may as well be now.'

When we know how to apply ourselves to real Dhamma training, difficulties are seen as gifts in our life, the things to transcend, to let go of and so realize peace and ultimately liberation for ourselves.

As it is said in Buddhist teaching, 'If it wasn't for our suffering, how could we end our suffering?'

I would play these Dhamma talks on my Walkman at home and at work and lose myself in Dhamma. I used every occasion to apply my limited understanding of how to flow with life and use the situation I found myself in as my teacher. Not always easy, but always available.

I also began to take care of myself a little better and some days when I would ride to work on my little motorbike I would arrive at the roundabout close to the factory, drive all the way around and go home again. This too was part of my training.

After some time of training in and becoming familiar with the Mahasi style of Vipassana practice I arrived at the monastery one Friday evening for another ten day retreat to be handed a box of audio cassettes containing the instructions and Dhamma talks from Goenkaji.

He and my teacher had been boyhood friends in Burma and S.N. Goenka now was famous in the world for his presentation of a 'body sweep' style of meditation given to him by his teacher, a Burmese government official called U Ba Khin.

In this style there is no walking meditation, only the sitting and then slowly and precisely directing the awareness to the soles of the feet having begun at the crown of the head.

Here once again I was more than blessed. After the instruction cassette and the day spent practicing there was the full one hour Dhamma talk from Goenkaji, 'Ji' being another respectful term for teacher. This was interesting and it was a pleasure to listen to those deep Indian tones of the teacher. However, after another sitting session my teacher would arrive in the Dhamma hall and give his evening Dhamma talk. Such joy, to be in the presence of these two beings both living a life of Dhamma.

Once again I trained like this for many retreats and at home, sitting for one hour a day, passing the awareness down through the body and experiencing the subtle sensations of matter arising and passing away.

My relationship to pain began to change, and it was no longer experienced as the enemy, something that came along to destroy the pleasure of meditation, but merely shifting sensations in an endless flow. Eventually the identification with pain ended and siting was now just sitting. The suffering had passed.

Many years later I had a similar experience with sleepiness.
At that time I was still working a lot, overtime at the factory when it was available plus my new Saturday job at Newsons. This was a clothing store on the quayside in Douglas that needed a part time storeman, and as Eileen my stepmother, worked there, I was given the opportunity. Of course I would much rather stay at home on my day off from the factory, but once again it was an opportunity to earn some extra money for my family and pay for my retreats.
It was no surprise then that occasionally I would sleep during my meditation. Of course being the ascetic disciple that I was, I didn't want to and so became frustrated when it happened.
Also sleeping whilst in the Dhamma hall can be an uncomfortable situation as I experienced for myself on retreat with my teacher some years before.
It was the first sitting after lunch, always a difficult one as the energy it seems wants to stay on the bed in our room and not join us in the Dhamma hall.
This being the case my body began to slump and I did nothing to correct it. I stayed in this comfortable 'no place' and gently rocked backwards and forwards. In the distance I could hear a grunting sound like pigs far away, and then I realized it was me and I was snoring.
I awoke with a start, had a quick look around to see if anyone had noticed, and suddenly found the energy to sit with concentration.
I felt uncomfortable but my response was not so extreme as Bodhidhamma, the founder of what became known as Zen Buddhism, who at one time was meditating in his cave when he fell asleep. He was so angry with himself for his lack of focus that he took out his knife and cut off his eyelids. He threw them

on the ground and where they landed there grew the fist tea plant in China, hence now the happy relationship between tea and meditation. A story of course, but meditation is meditation and sleeping is sleeping, they are not the same thing.

One Saturday evening when Fiona and our sons were safely in bed, I sat to make my one hour meditation. I was exhausted and immediately fell into a doze. I awoke quickly, adjusted my posture and began again. The same thing happened. I adjusted once more my posture and began again.

When this happened for the third time I realized that I was so tired I could not continue but I would give myself one more chance and if I dozed off again I would end my meditation and go to bed.

I corrected my posture for the last time, gathered my determination and sat.

Then everything changed.

I found myself immediately in a different world and in a mental image in my mind I was flying unhindered in the sky, passing through grey and white swirls of cloud. This image had my attention and I did nothing to correct it. Then suddenly and without warning, the clouds parted and I was in a clear blue sky with a brilliant sun shining in the distance. I was completely awake and energized, my mind as bright as this sun and as clear as the sky.

Since that moment, no matter how tired I have felt myself to be, I have never slept or dozed in the meditation.

Another two years passed and I, having committed as always to the meditation instruction from my teacher, continued my practice. I continued sitting for an hour a day at home, passing the awareness through the body in the Goenka style and was still making retreats for ten days and weekends.

Then it was time for the meditation to change again, this time for the final time. On this occasion I arrived at the monastery on a Friday evening as usual, tired from my long travel and having met and spent time with my usual traveling companions on the boat to England of doubt and fear. I put down my back pack and went to Bhantes room to pay my respects.

Some time before I had asked if I could be a disciple with him and he had accepted me. In his usual playful way he replied to my request of, «Bhante, is it possible that I could be accepted as a disciple with you?» with, «Well, it's not impossible.»

And so it was fixed. I had the honor and the privilege then to be a disciple of Sayadaw Rewata Dhamma, and so I asked him to demonstrate to me how to bow at his feet, Asian style.

He was reluctant to show me, saying it's not necessary, but I wanted an external form of respect to be evident between us, and so I insisted and he grudgingly agreed, lifting himself out of his chair, kneeling on the floor and demonstrating the five pointed Buddhist bow.

This then became my privilege before and after each retreat, to honestly and humbly show my respect and love for such a human being.

After the bow came the small talk. «How are you?»

«I'm fine, and you?»

«Yes, I'm fine too,» and so it went on.

After our friendly polite conversation our positions reverted to Master and disciple. I knelt on the floor in a respectful attitude and waited.

«So, now Michael, I will show you what we believe the Buddha really taught.»

Wow, what?

«It is the practice that is beyond technique, the Way of Letting Go.»

We sat together and he explained the practice to me. There was no one else on the retreat and so it was just the two of us together for ten days. Another incredible blessing.

Each word, each sentence opened my heart a little bit more. Intuitively I knew this was right and that the Buddha could not have devised a technique for enlightenment, this would really go against what enlightenment actually is. However, simply to sit and be with the endless arising and passing of mind and everything it contains is the way to peace. To let go of our constant involvement and so identification with it as being who and what we are brings a peace and a spaciousness that cannot be explained. The way of letting go, simple, but not easy.

This began the final part of my meditation tuition and although I always continued to deepen other aspects of my path such as my Metta practice (loving kindness) and Maranusati (reflection on death) I have never deviated from this perfect form of Vipassana. In the end, however we may make distinctions between various parts of practice, it is all Vipassana, expressed in the simple yet profound teaching of, 'live with love and be aware.'

Of course it was what the Buddha taught, how could it be different? I had often reflected that the Mahasi style of Vipassana and the Goenka style were very good for retreat conditions but difficult if not impossible to apply moment to moment in daily life. Without that final aspect of anytime, anyplace, anywhere, there would always be something missing and the living practice of Dhamma could not be complete.

So now I had the full and complete practice, to simply sit and allow the mind and all it contained to present itself in an environment of awareness and love. Beautiful.

The retreat itself came and went and I felt more and more connected to my teacher.

He was the guiding light in my life and asked for nothing in return. Any question asked by me would receive a Dhamma answer, no politics, no gender inequality only a wise and loving response based in his own practice of letting go, letting go, letting go.

He was a senior Buddhist monk, but presented himself in front of me as a kindly loving father. He expected me to make my effort and for that he would always serve me. This blessed relationship, although ever evolving and changing, in the end lasted for twenty two years.

Back on the Isle of Man family and work life continued. My sons were growing up and Fiona and I were growing apart. I think we did the best we could but our separate interests were deepening, and financial strains did not help. However, we did have some nice times together, evenings with friends, laughing so hard we almost cried, award ceremonies for her rifle club where we would get dressed up and play our parts and holidays in Majorca. Although these came later when a little bit of money arrived in our life, I remember them with great affection.

Fiona had taken a night shift job at a retirement home in Douglas three days a week. The hours were long and the pay exploitative, but it was money in rather than money out and so it had some value.

Her mother would always be available to take care of our boys when I was working and Fiona was sleeping, but my favorite memory is of Sundays when I would take Michael and Adam to a small wooded area in Douglas called Summer Hill Glen, known to children as the Fairy Glen.

As we would leave the house Fiona would shout her instructions to Michael and Adam before falling asleep, 'don't get dirty,' and we would leave.

As soon as we were installed in the car I would turn around to my two boys and tell them that they can get as dirty and wet as they like. We had a bath, a washing machine and even a tumble dryer, so cleaning them and their clothes was no problem.

Once we arrived at the entrance of the Glen they would run off into the trees shouting and squealing, using their fingers for guns and their imagination as a playground.

For myself, I would walk slowly and mindfully reflecting always on Dhamma and how perhaps one day I would have my life established in a forest like the monks of Ajahn Chah. I tossed my dream into the universe like a pebble skimming on the water in a pond and many years later my desire was fulfilled due to the powerful presence of another one of the most precious beings in my life.

Summer Hill Glen was a special place from my own childhood where in the long summer evenings whole families would walk through the trees and bushes on the paths next to the small stream. There were coloured lights above to show our way and particular areas where tradition and custom said the special magical little beings lived.

In the hushed forest atmosphere synchronized lights in the shape of fairies and forest animals would appear before us and thrill our children's minds. The illuminated squirrels would run up the trees in an well devised pattern, the fairies would sit around on large brightly coloured toadstools and the ornamental baby deer with their dark round eyes and large white spots on their backs would gaze lovingly at us.

Even if we understood clearly that this was only a simple light show, somewhere in our mind we knew that fairies were real and in control.

Fairies form a part of our Manx Celtic culture, and there is a small bridge on the way to the airport known as the Fairy Bridge. It is customary to greet the invisible beings who live there by saying 'Hello fairies,' each time we pass whether by car, bus, bicycle or any other form of transport.

Of course occasionally someone not from the Isle of Man will ridicule our local tradition and shout something offensive - and then meet the consequence of such poor behavior.

Our fairies insist upon politeness and good manners, those who go against this meet with a small misfortune such as a puncture or a minor accident or mishap.

I don't really know if this is true or not, but I always greet these little beings respectfully when I pass. At one time when somebody asked me if I really believed in fairies, I could only answer that I may not believe in them, but certainly I do not not believe in them. According to Theravada Buddhist teaching, there are thirty one realms of existence and as fairies seem to appear in all cultures in one form or another it may be best to keep an open mind about things we have not experienced for ourselves.

Retreat followed retreat, followed by work, family and more retreat. It was my life now and accepted by family and friends alike. It was me, always me who was out of step with the world, and perhaps especially Fiona. She was an ordinary young woman who wanted ordinary things, me, I wanted to live in a hut in the forest! How would this ever work?

At the end of the next ten day retreat in Birmingham I went to my teacher's room to bow, offer my grateful thanks and ask my usual end of retreat question.

I knelt in front of him with my hands together as in the attitude of prayer. This is known as 'Anjali' in Theravada Buddhism and is a gesture of gratitude and respect.

«Bhante, how can I improve my daily practice?»

«Ah Michael,» he answered, «now you must teach.»

This was a shock and certainly not the response I had expected.

The idea of teaching others was something that had never entered my mind and I considered myself only to be a disciple of a teacher, never the teacher himself.

It occurred to me that I had misheard the answer and so I repeated my question.

The response was the same, «Ah, Michael, now you must teach.»

No, no, no, no, this is not what I want!

With all the humility I could gather, I explained as clearly and precisely as I could exactly why I could not be the teacher.

I enjoyed my place as the disciple, to hear the Dhamma not to expound it, to serve my teacher and symbolically carry his spare robes and bowl as Ananda had done for the Buddha, to sit facing the teacher, not the group, and anyway, most importantly, I don't think that I have enough understanding.

He listened for a moment and then replied, «I do not ask you for you. I ask you for the people who live on your island, so that they too might hear and receive the Dhamma.»

With such a response how could I refuse? As with all things from my teacher it was in the service of others. This was not about me, it was only about the continuation of Dhamma. This understanding of service took its rightful place in my life. Dhamma is to be served like a beautiful meal. It is to be shared with others and so should not be used as a business opportunity. Integrity is everything and without it we simply show that we too are lost on the path.

Sayadaw Rewata Dhamma had now lived in England for some years and so he had developed an understanding of British mentality. Based upon this he told me what I should do. These were the days long before the Internet, and so advertising was still a manual affair.

«You make posters and put them in the health food shops on your island. People who are interested in their food may also be interested in meditation.»

This sounded like a good idea but I knew immediately that I would not do it.

The scenario already played out in my mind; I would arrive at the health food shop with my poster and offer it to the person working there, they would open it and see the words Buddhist meditation and spontaneously be interested and comment, «Oh Buddhist meditation, who is teaching that?»

In an embarrassed voice I would answer, «I am.»

They would look at me with a shocked expression and exclaim in a loud voice, «You?» and hand back the posters to me. No, I

thought, I'm not going to do that.
The next morning Bhante loaded me into his car and drove me to the station to begin my long journey home.
By this time I had arrived at my plan and it was simple. The crucial thing was to show an attempt to bring Buddhist meditation to the Isle of Man, but that attempt must fail. Then I would be able to say that I tried, but it didn't work. Simple, what could go wrong?

I placed a classified line advert in our local free newspaper. I deliberately made it vague and obscure. It read:

Vipassana Bhavana now being taught. Call Douglas 28999.

I was happy with that. Who on the Isle of Man knew what Vipassana Bhavana could possibly be?
I relaxed and continued my practice. Now all I had to do was to wait until I could tell Bhante that the plan to bring people to Buddhist meditation had not succeeded.
Then, one evening a few days after the all island delivery of the newspaper the telephone rang. A man's voice said, «Hello, I'm calling about the advert in the paper.»
Immediately I thought he had the wrong number. I'm not the one selling a washing machine or advertising a window cleaning service, so what could he possibly mean?
«It's about the VIP-PA-SA-NA BHAV-A-NA-NA. What is it?» he continued.
«Oh,» I said still in shock, «it's a kind of a meditation, but I don't think you really want to do it.»
«Yes, I think I'd like to,» he replied.
My heart sank, but even with the poorest of intention, I had opened that door, so now I had to let him enter. We spoke a little bit longer and I told him he should come on Monday evening for our first session of meditation called Anapanasati - awareness of breath.

Jack Firth arrived at my house punctually on the Monday evening at the agreed time. He was a middle aged man who had experienced some health problems hence his interest in meditation. Still it remains a mystery as to why he would contact me having seen a simple advertisement in the local paper containing two words in a dead language (Pali) that he did not understand. Perhaps the universe had sent him?

Anyway, he was here now and would be a part of my life for the next twelve or more years.

We spoke together of course and I explained simply the first part of the practice. As this is the foundation practice for everything we do it is important to have a clear idea of what is necessary. After the explanation I asked if he had understood and he told me that he had. The next thing to do then was to sit together. I felt twenty minutes would be enough for a first session and so we began.

The time passed and when the twenty minutes was completed I asked some simple questions about the sitting. He said that it was a good experience but I, still not wanting to take on the role of teacher, made one last attempt to discourage him.

«So, that's it,» I said, «you don't want to come back do you?» hopeful that he would say no, and that once was enough.

However, his reply was, «Yes, I'd like to come back.»

Again my heart sank, but that was that. Now I have my first student and I am obliged to share my limited understanding - and that is how I became an internationally acclaimed Dhamma teacher.

Jack was married and his wife Doreen was interested in learning meditation, so now there were two. Doreen had a friend who was also interested, so now there were three, and so it went on. Soon we had a group arriving at my house each Monday evening, and gradually I began to enjoy it if only because it pushed me deeper in my own practice and understanding.

The meditation group was growing quickly and organically and people were more and more interested in the Buddhist aspect. They asked me to chant in Pali a little before the meditation and I was pleased to do so. Then they asked me to give some small Buddhist teachings, and again, I was pleased to do so. Then Jack suggested that we should go public and advertise ourselves as the Isle of Man Buddhist Group. I was not the most enthusiastic person to receive this idea mostly based on the fact that I would be the teacher and that felt like great responsibility, but nevertheless, I agreed. This time we did design posters for the health food shops around the island to promote a public talk that I would give to explain the foundations of Buddhism, but more, I wrote a small article for the local newspaper explaining who we were and what we wanted to do. A colleague of mine from the factory read it before I submitted it for publication and happily pointed out, «They'll never publish that,» but they did.

The next exciting thing to present itself in the life of the teacher of the newly arisen Isle of Man Buddhist Group was an invitation from the local radio station, Manx Radio, to be interviewed about our project. We had sent handwritten information to them to help publicize our forthcoming public talk, never dreaming even for a moment that they would be interested. But they were. Buddhism was still new and exotic in the west at this time, and that it should arrive on the Isle of Man was truly a news story.

A day and time was arranged and I arrived at Douglas Head, the highest part of Douglas that looks out across the bay and the location of the radio station and the place where a huge and popular bar was where I had played rock and roll many years before.

After Sparrow and my return to the Isle of Man I had been invited on separate occasions to join two different rock bands. In the moment that seemed like a good idea and so I became the singer without guitar for both. It was a good time for me. Mediation

and rock and roll may seem to be a strange combination but as one was solitary and the other not, it balanced well in my life. The first band was called 'Loud and Proud' because of the noise we made. The other was a more sophisticated 'progressive' rock band, called ,'A Nasty Piece of Work,' although none of us were, playing covers of Cream, Deep Purple and others in that style. I sang loud and hard, lost my voice occasionally and enjoyed myself immensely for a couple of years until a moment arose where I felt that I had to make a choice. Meditation or rock and roll.
Singing with the band although good fun was actually empty of any real value, whilst meditation and a more peaceful life was a worthwhile endeavor and perhaps the only thing in my life that I felt had real substance.

I arrived at the reception desk of Manx Radio to be greeted in a friendly way by a very pleasant young woman. I gave my name and explained why I had come. She told me to take a seat and she would call someone to take care of me. After a few minutes a bearded man arrived and introduced himself as the producer of the show that would host the interview. He too was very pleasant and friendly and told me not to be nervous although it was far too late for that particular piece of advice. He escorted me to the small studio where the interview would take place and introduced me to Suzy Richardson, the young and very attractive woman who would ask the questions. We sat facing each other and were 'miked up' whilst she thumbed through some of the literature we had submitted. I waited in silent anticipation until the moment when she threw the switch, the red light came on and she said, «Right, we're on the air.»
She then made her introduction of me and the subject by saying that one of the things she had always been interested in, although never found out anything about, was Buddhism.
'Wait, what?' my mind yelled, 'that's a contradiction isn't it.

Being interested means that we do find out something about it.'
I held on to this spinning thought until I heard her first question.
«So Michael, what has meditation done for you?» Such a simple question, only six words, and although I may have appeared calm and composed on the outside, my mind was in turmoil. How could I answer such a thing, she has no idea of the variety of answers I could give, and actually, no one had ever asked me that before. My mind stopped and I heard myself say, «Well, it has made me calm and peaceful,» an outright lie at that moment.

The interview continued with Suzy thumbing through the literature as I answered one question, and she found another. I realized that she had not prepared at all and so the questions were often unrelated and chosen simply at random as my previous answer was finished.

Finally she publicized the talk to be held some days later. «And whose giving that?» she asked.

«I am,» I replied, all the while thinking, 'that's why I'm here!'

The interview finished and we said goodbye. Surprisingly it was an enormous success as was the public talk when it arrived.

In the years that followed I was interviewed many times by Manx Radio and often by the lovely Suzy Richardson. She became a very popular radio presenter with her own long running afternoon show.

The last time we met in the studio we greeted each other like old friends and she asked me if I remembered the time we met.

«Oh yes,» I said, «that was my very first radio interview.»

«Mine too,» she replied.

So lovely I thought, we grew together.

I prepared for the public talk, entitled Basic Buddhism, which was held at the local youth and community centre in Onchan on November 8th 1984. They were simpler times in those days and microphone, slides and expensive light show presentation was not expected.

Also not expected was the number of people interested enough to come out and listen to an unknown Manxman speak about the Buddha, the Four Noble Truths and an alternative view of life. The audience assembled, fell quiet and waited for the star of the show to arrive in front of them. Jack was sitting in the audience with his wife and as I passed him he touched my arm and said, «Mike, if you need any help, you're on your own!» I continued walking thinking to myself, 'why did he tell me that?'

I took my place at the front, smiled at the assembled crowd and began. I do not remember very much about that evening except once again it was a great success.

Praben Scott was there silently approving and supporting me even to the point where when I announced a short break he took my place and continued the talk. However, the audience mostly followed me to the kitchen for a cup of tea. As I said, simpler times.

At the end of the evening information about the formation of the Isle of Man Buddhist group was given and when and where the next meeting would be held. People seemed interested and many arrived at my home wanting to learn meditation and hear more about a Buddhist way of life.

I was now the teacher, the representative of Dhamma on the island. I felt it to be a huge and important responsibility and as I was encouraging the members of the group to meditate for one hour a day, I myself began to meditate for two and a half hours a day.

I would wake up at five o'clock in the morning, go downstairs and meditate. I would then go to work and in the one hour lunch break take half an hour to sit again in a small isolated spot I had found. The sound of the machines never stopped and I think in the end this too was a good practice. Most people in the factory knew what I was doing, thought I was mad, but left me alone. In fact people seemed to like me a lot and were always playful and amused by my dedication to something they themselves knew nothing about. They developed new names for me and would often shout across the factory floor, «Hey Gandhi, come here,» or worse, «Oy Buddha.» Very funny! When I would arrive home and the children were in bed I would sit again for another hour. It was a lot, and it was certainly demanding, but I maintained this practice without a break for the next ten years. Poor Fiona.

I studied Buddhist teachings also under the guidance of my teacher and shared my understanding with the group, however, I never took the position of the one who knows everything. If I was asked a question to which I did not know the answer I would always give one of two responses. The first would be that I don't know but I will contact my teacher and ask him and give you his answer the following week. The second response was that I would give an answer according to Buddhist teaching.

Not my answer, but an answer according to Buddhist tradition. People could then decide for themselves if it was useful or not.

Jack was always a great help and support to me and we became very close. We began to meet outside the group to meditate together and take my sons to the beach. They would run and play and we would walk and talk about the next thing we could do to develop the group, and what more the group could offer.

The answer came in a moment.

A five part meditation course open to the public to look at the different aspects of Anapanasati, Vipassana Bhavana and Metta Bhavana in more detail. For the first time there was to be an idea of money. So far we had financed everything ourselves from publicity, church hall rental and cups of tea. Now although the course itself would be free, we would ask for donations to help support the enterprise.

The Quaker's meeting hall was offered to us and we accepted. We then placed an advert in the local paper and waited for the response. Once again the amount was surprising. We took names and gave details.

The hall was full, with perhaps thirty people attending. This was a huge number for the Isle of Man and would be considered a very successful event even today.

At the end of the first session which lasted for about two hours and examined, explained and tested the first part of the meditation practice called Anapanasati, everybody left offering their thanks. However, it seems that they had forgotten the Dana (donation) box completely.

The next week the numbers were lower, perhaps twenty three, but almost all of them also missed the Dana box, and so it went on. Each week the numbers were lower than the week before, and the Dana box remained almost empty. The final week was the culmination of the practice that took Siddhartha Gotama, the man who became the Buddha, to complete Awakening. Now the few people who had actually attended the five week course had something for their life, all they had to do from this point was to use it. We said thank you to them, they said thank you to us and we parted company. All we found in the Dana box that night were two buttons.

Dana is something beautiful, not only in Buddhist teaching, but in the world. Usually it is translated as donation, but that is as with most translations, overly simplistic.

Dana means generosity and is first on the list of the Ten Perfections (Dasa Paramitas). Perfect generosity can only exist when there is no fear, and so no holding something in reserve. It doesn't mean giving everything away, but sharing what we have. When the heart is open through love, we share. When the heart is closed through fear, we keep everything for ourselves. One brings benefit to ourselves and the world whilst the other divides and separates into have and have nots.

However, coming from that first course were a tiny group of

people who wanted to go further and so became part of the Isle of Man Buddhist group.

The group continued to gain momentum and I enjoyed my place as guide and teacher, with Sayadaw Rewata Dhamma as the spiritual director.

Because I took my responsibility very seriously I studied more and more. I wanted always to represent the Buddha, my teacher and the Dhamma in an honorable and respectful way, and so I always took care with my words and actions.

I would take time to prepare what I wanted to say, basing my talks on traditional Buddhist teaching such as the Dhammapada, and the Suttanta Pitaka. On one occasion I even went to the extent of preparing a long and very special discourse especially for a group member who was struggling with life's difficulties. Of course they would not know it was especially for them, but the words would hit their heart and they would know they were not alone. Unfortunately, they didn't come that week and as I had nothing other to say, I gave the talk to a roomful of people it wasn't meant for. It was well received of course but it was the last time I ever tried to give teachings to specific people in a group.

Fiona went to her rifle club, and I taught Buddhism and meditation in our living room on the same evening, and life went on.

Occasionally guest speakers would arrive to give teachings. I don't remember how we contacted each other, but I welcomed the opportunity to hear other people talk about the subject I loved so much.

One memorable guest was an elderly English lady who claimed to be a Buddhist. She arrived at my house, took her place on a chair in front of everyone and began to speak. I'm sure her talk was fine and in keeping with conventional teaching, because I don't remember anything about it. However, at the end, as is the tradition she asked if there were any questions. I'm sure she was disappointed when I gestured that I would like to ask something as tea and biscuits were about to be offered.

«You have spoken a lot about Buddhism,» I said, «but you have not mentioned meditation. What do you think about that?»

«Oh, you don't need to bother with that,» she said dismissing the question with a gesture of her arm, «just hold a nice thought in your head and that's enough.»

Of course, it isn't enough. Meditation in Dhamma training is not about feeling good or even at peace with life, it is about understanding the mind and its influence in what we call our life.

Insights arose spontaneously and unexpectedly with the result that my life often became more difficult. Insight is a clearing of part of the delusion that holds us in our unhappiness and endless frustration of life. Once we can see we can no longer pretend that we can't see. Life continues, but not as before.

In our bedroom at home I had installed an aquarium. It wasn't exotic but it supported a relaxing atmosphere in the room where I spent a great deal of time meditating. Of course it needed maintenance and one time when I was cleaning it I had a powerful insight about Kamma.

Kamma is a huge and important teaching in Dhamma and according to my wonderful teacher, a lifetime's study. With that in mind, I feel blessed to have experienced such an important and significant understanding apparently by chance.

There had been a difficult time in my wife's family regarding the behavior of Fiona's brother and I was asked what I thought about it.

«It's not my place to say,» I replied, really only wanting to avoid the inevitable taking of sides.

Later that day I was standing on a chair in the bedroom carefully cleaning the aquarium when I began to reflect upon my simple comments, and suddenly I knew, without doubt the reality of

Kamma in the universe.

Insights are almost impossible to describe as language does not even come close to the experience and then the understanding of the moment.

Of course 'It's not my place to say,' the universe does not need me to take any position at any time for or against anything. We meet without fail the consequence of the mind states that we empower and we cannot avoid or sidestep them. The seed of the consequence is planted in the moment of the action. This is the reality of Kamma. It is not reward or punishment, simply consequence. My personal views and opinions do not change the Vipaka (consequence) of anything, and in fact only become another burden to carry. The idea that the world and everything in it should always be the way I want it to be is, in the end, only more suffering.

A quietness came into my life and I recognized that even with the best and most noble intentions I couldn't teach anything, I could only share my love and enthusiasm for what was in those days for me, Buddhism. This was a great relief for me and meant that there was no pressure to be someone that I most certainly was not.

Later this understanding would deepen again when I realized that there was actually nothing that could be taught and that freedom is not something to get, it is something to realize.

Liberation then, is not a three, five or ten step programme, it is an unlearning process, and letting go, letting go, letting go of the true cause of our unhappiness.

By this time Jack, for his own reasons, had decided to make retreats with Bhante Kemmadhammo, the teacher of the German monk who some years in the future would be asked to leave my teacher's monastery. Of course, Dhamma is Dhamma but unity in presentation can be strengthening and supportive. However, this particular Buddhist monk became well known to me as a colleague of my own teacher, and later as the founder and my superior when he asked if I would join the Buddhist prison chaplaincy called Angulimala, and so take Buddhist teachings into the prison on the Isle of Man.

By now Angulimala was well established in the rest of Great Britain but as there was no automatic religious rights on the island I, with support from Venerable Khemadhammo, had to approach the prison service and ask if my presence as a Buddhist teacher would be allowed.

One of the most dedicated members of our Buddhist group at this time was a young man called Peter Kelly. Over time we became friends and once again the universe smiled on me. Peter's father was the reverend Kelly, the vicar of Castletown and chief of religious affairs in the prison. He was enthusiastic about me coming to give teachings and arranged everything. A Monday evening was agreed and set aside for me to give a talk to any prisoners who wanted to attend. I didn't think many people would be interested but the whole prison, which amounted to about eighty men, arrived to hear me speak. I later realised that these men searched endlessly for things to help pass the time, and I of course was just another distraction. The talk finished and two or three prisoners were interested to go further, and so it began. I visited the prison every Monday evening for the next eight years, and with a small group of perhaps seven alternating inmates sat in meditation and looked at life from a Buddhist perspective.

One Monday evening I arrived to be met by a large shaven headed, tattooed man who asked in a friendly and quite polite way if I was the Dhamma Lama? I said I was and one more member was added to the group.

Although I was always told of their crimes in advance, they were never mentioned at any meeting and even with violent offenders, I never felt afraid.

Occasionally I would be asked to visit the female side of the prison which was slightly more uncomfortable for me as I would be left alone with two or more inmates, but integrity was preserved from both sides and nothing untoward ever happened.

Later when my teacher would come to the island to make retreats we would visit the prison on a Sunday afternoon for a special group meeting. The officers and staff were always helpful, friendly and courteous to both my teacher and me whether we were together or not, and the authorities were happy to provide tea and biscuits for these special occasions.

On one of these special Sundays when the group was quite large we were joined by two young women prisoners whom I had already met and given meditation instruction to. They arrived with a female officer, a large friendly lady, who sat close to her two charges. With me sitting next to my teacher I gave the instruction for everyone to close their eyes and begin the meditation of Vipassana to be followed by the Loving Kindness practice. Partway through I opened my eyes and gently looked around as is my habit, to ensure that everyone is comfortable and not struggling too much. Everyone had their eyes closed except the female officer who was keeping guard on not only her own responsibilities, but on everyone else as well.

I had to stop myself from laughing as the thought arose that perhaps if she had joined the meditation and sat for thirty minutes with her eyes closed, when she opened them again, the room would be empty. How could that be explained?

I was still attending as many retreats as I could and on one occasion a group of four friends who were all part of our weekly meetings said they would like to come with me to my teacher's monastery in Birmingham to experience a weekend retreat. They asked many questions about retreat conditions and I answered as honestly and enthusiastically as I could. They were easily accepting of everything from getting up at four o'clock in the morning to retiring at ten o'clock in the evening, and then spending the day in silent sitting and walking meditation. The part they could not be comfortable with was the idea that all meals had to be finished at lunch time and for the rest of the day until the next breakfast, there would be no food. I accept that because of our culture and comfortable life style this seems an unnecessary difficulty, but it is part of the monks Vinaya rules and in those days when on retreat, we followed that.

The origination of this rule is quite simple. The monks who were training with the Buddha would spend most of the day wandering around the town trying to find food from the lay people. The townspeople eventually became irritated by continually finding a monk at their door waiting for food, and so they complained to the Buddha. He understood of course and immediately made the rule that all food must be obtained and consumed by lunch time. No food should be saved for later.

Actually to follow this rule is not so difficult when we have the intention to submit to the training. We simply don't eat in the afternoon or evening. We can take a hot drink as we like, but no food.

It is always the mind that creates the difficulties for us and not the reality of the situation, but as long as we blindly follow it we will never transcend its limitations.

Traveling over on the boat together I noticed they each had bags of Mars bars, sweets and other confectionary to secretly eat in their rooms when they felt hungry in the evening.

The greatest obstacle to the teacher is the mind of the student, and the greatest obstacle to the student is also the mind of the student. The Isle of Man Buddhist group became bigger, stronger and more enthusiastic and so the idea was proposed that perhaps my teacher, Sayadaw Rewata Dhamma would visit us to make a retreat. This was the moment to make my declaration and I stood in front of everyone and said clearly and forcefully, «Things seem to be moving quite quickly now and so I want to make a simple statement so everyone is certain about my feelings. My only interest is in Dhamma and its practice. The moment any kind of politics arrives in the group, I will leave. I won't hesitate, I will leave.»

Nobody spoke although I don't think anyone was particularly surprised. It was a simple statement of fact, which I have lived by ever since.

Dhamma is too precious to become a part of the world, to be bought and sold as a commodity and so must always be protected. It may not always be apparent, but integrity is everything.

Organising such an event would be difficult but I was interested in the possibility and felt confident that Jack and I could put something together. We made enquiries for a venue and eventually found an outward bound centre in a remote part of the island. There was enough space for a Dhamma hall, two private rooms for sleeping and male and female dormitories, with simple iron bunk beds. There was also a kitchen of course, but we would have to prepare food in advance and reheat it for lunch. Breakfast would be cereal or toast with tea.

By modern standards this is almost barbaric as people now want single rooms with private shower and toilet and of course wifi. But these were the days of simplicity of practice and the only thing that had value was contact with the teacher. The rest existed only to enable that.

At the end of my next retreat in Birmingham I broached the question of Bhante coming to the island. Naturally he said he would be delighted and he would come with his junior monk, Bodhidhamma, the man who had first opened the door to me some years before as Peter Ridley. He had ordained a year earlier with the intention to stay in the robes for only two years. This plan did not work as devised, and Bodhidhamma is still in robes and now a senior monk with his own small monastery in England. We arranged dates as were available on the Isle of Man, and everything was set.

«Oh, just one thing Bhante, we don't have a Buddha statue for a shrine, will it be alright?» I asked.

«Don't worry about that,» he said, «I will bring one with me.»

I arrived home and the retreat organization began in earnest. Soon the appointed day came to welcome the first two Buddhist monks to arrive on the island. It was the spring of 1985. Bodhidhamma was carrying a large tartan shopping bag with something covered protruding out of the top. I welcomed them both and drove immediately to the venue. Once there he handed the bag to me and said, «This is for you from Bhante.»

I removed the cover to find the head of a beautiful Buddha. I was already familiar with this particular statue as it usually resided in the small private Dhamma room at the top of the monastery in Birmingham. I had been there on many occasions with my teacher when I was alone on retreat. On the final occasion he spoke personally and intimately about the death of his father. As the light in this small room faded the candle burned brighter and I heard the voice of not only my teacher, but of a man.

It was a touching moment and because of difficulties with the then ruling junta in Burma, he had not been allowed to enter the country, or if he had, he would not be permitted to leave.

I lifted the Buddha out of the bag and placed it on our makeshift shrine. I was touched by the kindness of my teacher, to offer this beautiful gift to the group.

Later that evening, when Jack and I sat together making sure that everything was in place and that we were all ready to begin our first retreat on the island, Jack leaned in and looking at the shrine said in a loud whisper, «You know why he brought that Buddha statue, don't you?»

Well, I certainly didn't know and from the question I assumed that Bodhidhamma had revealed something privately to Jack, but this was not the case.

«It's for you,» he continued.
«No, I don't think so,» I countered, «it's for the group.»
«No,» he insisted, «it's for you. Think about it, he only knows you, he has never met anyone else here.»
It was true, Jack had only ever sat with Venerable Khemadhammo and the behaviour of the four students who had made the retreat with me in Birmingham was not seen to have been inspiring by the Master.
I could not accept this conclusion and for seventeen years insisted that the Buddha statue brought to the island on the first visit of Sayadaw Rewata Dhamma was a gift to the Isle of Man Buddhist group.
The truth was finally revealed to me on my last ever meeting with Bhante as we sat in his room in his new monastery.
I had just had the honor and privilege to lead the first retreat in the Dhamma Talaka monastery and had come to say goodbye as I was going now to live in France.
We spoke in a friendly way and towards the end I mentioned the gift of the Buddha statue all those years before.
«Bhante, I'm going to live in France now and I want to return the Buddha Rupa that you brought for the group (long disbanded by this time) on the Isle of Man.»
He looked at me for a moment with his beautiful loving eyes and said, «I didn't bring it for the group, it was my gift for you. Now you must take it to France and show the Dhamma there.»
It is difficult to share the feelings that arose within me after hearing such a thing, but loving gratitude may come close, not for the Buddha statue, but for the honour to be thought of in such a way by this person that I respected so much. This was not the first time he had spoken such precious words to me, but those other times were still in the future from our first Isle of Man retreat.

The retreat was considered to be a great success, not only with the numbers of people attending, but with the organization itself and so became the first of many that we presented on the Isle of Man. For myself, I can only remember the peace and joy of presenting my teacher to the group and sitting with him in meditation. On this retreat I also had the repeated experience of accidentally dropping into another Jhanic state. This time of course I felt no need to mention it to anyone and allowed it to arise and pass away according to its nature. When there is no more fascination with meditation, the work can really begin.

Now I had the opportunity to bring my teacher to the island as often as possible to make two and five day retreats and to visit the prison, but also travel to Birmingham to be with him in his monastery to assist him and sit longer retreats. But the universe had not finished with me yet.

One evening I was at home when I received a telephone call from one of the group members. She was an older, almost aristocratic lady, and she and her husband, a former tea planter in Darjeeling, had become firm members of the group. They were both well travelled and familiar with Tibetan Buddhism. She too was a disciple and a disciplined teacher of Iyengar yoga, so she was well connected on the island and in the world.

«Michael,» she began, «a friend of mine from Sweden (a duke or a lord as it turned out) has a house on the Isle of Man in Onchan and as it's empty, would like to offer it freely for our group meetings and retreats, what do you think?»

Of course it was a beautiful surprise and my only feeling was, 'let's do it!'

Our conversation continued and everything was arranged. No contracts to be signed, only a virtual handshake over the telephone. I immediately called my teacher and gave him the news. Now we can have our own Buddhist Centre on the island. He too was delighted and immediately gave it the Pali name of the 'Manusa Dipa Vihara.' This was certainly very clever as the word Manusa means human realm, Dipa means island and Vihara means something like a Buddhist pilgrim's resting place. So all together it came to the Isle of Man Buddhist Centre. Brilliant.

We spent some time cleaning and preparing the house in Wybourn Drive for our grand opening. We would send out printed invitations and notify the media including Border television, our local broadcaster. My teacher would come and there would be an afternoon celebration and house blessing for the invited guests before beginning the first five day retreat in our new centre.

I really wanted to share this special event in my life with my father, but he was more than suspicious of 'those Buddhists' and so refused. This was painful for me, but I could not persuade him. He was a product of his own generation and honestly thought that I was being brainwashed and corrupted by outside forces.

Happily three small events changed his mind and the time came when we could be together in peace again.

The first happened whilst driving home from work together on a Friday afternoon when he asked me what I would do if he died and left all his money to me.

«Oh, I would try to get a bigger house, maybe a new car, and things like that,» I said.

«You wouldn't give it to the Buddhists?» he asked.

«What, no, why would you even think that? I would take care of my family of course,» I replied somewhat taken aback by his strange thought processes.

He relaxed a little happy to know I wasn't being brainwashed by 'those Buddhists.'

The second event came when I had resolved never to speak of Buddhism again to him unless he asked.

During this first retreat at the Manusa Dipa Vihara, I had spoken to Bhante about the difficulty I was experiencing with my father and actually how upsetting it was for me. As I kneeled in front of him he listened carefully and then spoke. His words, so simple, so healing arrived immediately in my heart. The pain disappeared and clarity manifested once more into my life.

«Ah yes,» he said, «the Buddha had trouble with his father too.» The truth is obvious, we all have difficulties with other people and often the closer the relationship the more intense the difficulty. This is how it is to be alive and living in the world.

Before liberation it is the same for everyone, even the Buddha.

But now came the teaching, and this is how Dhamma really works, first the identification of the problem, then the remedy.

«Your father is an ordinary man living his ordinary life,» said my teacher, «he is not on the Dhamma path, so the responsibility for the quality of the relationship lies with you. You must be kind and considerate to him whilst at the same time, not being the victim in the situation. If he asks you about Buddhism answer his question and explain directly and clearly what you feel, but never give a lesson!

Don't allow him to feel foolish or small in front of you. Share the beauty of Dhamma but never permit a situation to arise where he feels humiliated or condemned for how he has lived his life.»

The responsibility for the quality of the situation was with me, that means in reality, I am in control, now what to do?

I resolved mentally never to speak of Buddhism again to my father unless he asked first and then to follow my teacher's beautiful advice.

This plan worked quickly and perfectly and I began to see that every time I had spoken about Buddhism to my father he felt it as a personal attack on the way he had lived so far and consequently retaliated.

So the second event happened some months after the visit of my teacher when my father asked me a simple question about Buddhist life and I answered with a brief and friendly illustration of the five precepts, the lay Buddhist moral code of conduct.

Not to harm, not to steal, not to abuse or exploit others, not to use our speech in cruel or harmful ways and not to take drugs that cloud the mind.

When I had finished he looked relieved and said, «But that's what I taught you when you were a little boy.» He was absolutely right!

The third event happened when I had been invited to teach a Saturday morning course of simple Buddhism at the college on the island. I did this of course, to great success and in fact would teach perhaps hundreds of courses there during the next twenty five years. From simple Buddhist teachings to the practice of meditation the Isle of Man college became a wonderful venue to meet and receive new interested people into the ever evolving Buddhist group.

On the following Monday morning at work my father, with his arm around my shoulder proudly paraded me through the factory telling everyone about 'my boy, who teaches at the college.' It was a nice moment for me to see him so happy at what he considered a success in my life.

One week before the grand opening, house blessing and first retreat at the newly established Manusa Dipa Vihara, was about to begin, I received a telephone call from my teacher. This was highly unusual as it was me who usually called him, mostly to simply maintain a contact with the man I respected so much.

«Michael,» he said, «I will arrive soon with Bodhidhamma, but I would like to know if it is acceptable for me to also bring someone else?»

«Yes Bhante, of course. Who is it?»

«Ah, it is my closest friend, the Venerable Hamalawa Saddhatissa. Do you know him?»

I almost cried with surprise and joy. Through the writings of this man I had been able to train alone and stay on the Dhamma path for seven years. Through the writings of this man my Dhamma understanding had developed in the correct way, and through the writings of this man I had met my teacher and been accepted as his disciple.

So I answered, «Yes Bhante, I know him. He has been a great inspiration in my life. It will be an honor to welcome you all to our little island next week.»

The day arrived and once again I found myself at the quay in Douglas watching the ferry dock and the passengers alight.

Eventually the three Buddhist monks appeared. Venerable Saddhatissa was a tall Sri Lankan monk, wearing a large cloak over his robes. He looked so elegant and refined, not like my teacher who was always less concerned about his appearance. There were so many idiosyncrasies about Sayadaw Rewata Dhamma that I loved, his appearance being one of them. Often he would enter the Dhamma hall with his upper robe carelessly thrown around his left shoulder as is the tradition, but with a long part dragging on the floor behind him. At one time he had a hole in his sock with a toe poking through at a special occasion, sitting on his high seat offering the most beautiful Dhamma, but as always, he didn't mind.

I presented Anjali, welcomed these three special guests and excitedly took them to our new centre in Onchan. We naturally had prepared their rooms with care and once they were established and rested we invited them to give a formal Dhamma talk in our new Dhamma hall. Such an honor for us simple lay people.

The next day was Sunday and the official opening of the Manusa Dipa Vihara.

We fed the monks at lunch time and once we had eaten and the invited guests arrived the ceremony could commence.

Reporters from our local newspaper had arrived and were welcomed as was the local T.V. channel. This was a surprise and I think Jack and I could hardly believe we had hit the 'big time,' with our organizational skills.

The first thing to do was to bless the house and so the three monks walked around the building three times in single file chanting a blessing for all beings.
After customary Dhamma talks for everyone, the television people asked if we could bring the monks outside to film them. Jack and I gathered them together and led them into the garden. Here we stood in a straight line in the beautiful afternoon sunshine, with Jack on one end and me on the other.
We stood there immobile as the camera panned past us one at a time. Having reached the other end of the line the producer said to me, «Can you get them to do something?»
Truly, I thought, what? They don't dance or sing and I'm sure they can't juggle. This is what they do. They radiate peace and calm and share their love with the world, not great television, but a blessing for all beings.
So I answered, «No, I don't think so. They are monks, not entertainers.»
Needless to say when we watched the news report that evening, we were not on it.

As the retreat went on I naturally took every opportunity to be with my teacher. On one of these occasions he was sitting with Venerable Saddhatissa and turned to him and said, «Michael will take temporary ordination with me next year.»

A few months earlier I had just finished another retreat in Birmingham and was drinking a cup of tea in the kitchen with Mar Mar Lwin when she opened a door in my life that I had not even considered could be possible.
«You know,» she said, «you could take temporary ordination. It is sure Bhante would accept you.»
She had barely finished the sentence before I found myself rather excitedly and inelegantly bounding up the stairs to his room.

I composed myself and knocked on the jamb - still no door.
I entered and asked if it would be possible to take temporary ordination. He made his usual jokes about it not being impossible, but we discussed it as something with potential.
«How old are you now?» he asked.
«I'm thirty four,» I replied.
«Then we will ordain you next year in May when you are thirty five. This was the age of the Buddha when he became enlightened. It is an auspicious time.»
So it was settled.

What I didn't know then or discover until well after the event was that Mar Mar Lwin would become my chief sponsor when I was in robes and made an enormous donation to the monastery to support my time there.
It may not be a truth that we understand very well, but in the end everything has to be paid for. My robes and bowl did not just arrive by magic, and each mouthful of food I took had been grown, bought and paid for by someone, as well as the heating and water I used to shower etc, when I was a monk. This is why the monk's life is so precious. It is dependent entirely upon the support of the lay community, and in response to this selfless generosity a monk must guard and keep the highest moral principles.
«If my life is not pure,» my teacher said, «why should people support me?»
Of course Dana, the purity of giving, is not part of western culture anymore and during all my years connected to my teacher's monastery, it was the Western community who used it for teachings and meditation, and the Burmese community who supported it financially and made sure the roof didn't leak and the bills were paid.

Venerable Saddhatissa looked at me and said, «When you are in

robes, I will come to visit you.»
I thought that this was a beautiful thing to say, but didn't really believe it. It was simply a nice comment from a lovely old man.

The next day something uncomfortable happened in the Dhamma hall.
We had finished a meditation session and as both Bhante and Venerable Saddhatissa kept their places, it was a spontaneous opportunity for questions.
I don't remember any of the simple questions until Jack, sitting next to me asked about himself being seen as a Dhamma teacher. For myself I have never had ambition to be someone in front of others, only to serve with integrity my teacher, the Buddha himself and the purity of Dhamma. Although I live from Dhamma now, it was never a career path for me, and was always in the service of fellow beings.
But Jack had some ambition in that direction, to be someone, to be known as different from the other people, to be seen. In my enthusiasm for Dhamma I had not been aware of this until perhaps a few months before the moment of the question.
Dhamma training is not a learning process, but an unlearning process. It is not a series of new ideas and things to remember, but a gentle and consistent releasing of self identity until all that is left is the smile of liberation. If this is not understood properly 'self' will always seek its place.
So Jack asked his question from a perspective of ignorance and ambition revealing in a moment his complete lack of Dhammic understanding.
My teacher listened to the question, inclined forward slightly and said ten of the most powerful words I have ever heard.
«Jack,» he said, «before you can teach Dhamma you must know Dhamma.»
He was telling him that he didn't know anything, and worse than

that, he and I were not equals. I was my teacher's disciple serving Dhamma. Jack was only my assistant, helping me to do that.

It seems that in life we always show our true intentions sooner or later. My teacher's comments were received perhaps even harder than they were meant as Jack had spoken with me a few months earlier telling me that even after such a short time of training, he now knew as much as me.

I didn't say anything or tell anyone, but I felt a sadness in my heart to receive such words.

The Manusa Dipa Vihara was a great success and our meetings and short retreats were held there for many years until the condition of the house deteriorated to the point where we could no longer maintain it, and so the owner took it back, restored it and sold it. However, I have a store of happy memories of this place and perhaps the most cherished were the times that my eldest son Michael, still a very little boy would accompany me when we needed to cut the grass, paint a wall, prepare for a visit from my teacher, or for just Bodhidhamma who came many times by himself to offer retreats. We would work and Michael would play in the garden until suddenly he would stop and run into the house and up the stairs. I don't know if he was aware that we were watching him, but he would arrive at the Dhamma hall, kick off his little shoes and enter with a great deal of respect. Once in front of the Buddha he would bow three times and take his posture for meditation. There he would sit completely immobile until his meditation session was finished, usually after two or three minutes, then back into the garden to shout and roll in the grass. So lovely.

Life continued and the focus now for me was to organize my time so that I could take temporary ordination the following year. This was not so easy, but surprisingly I received huge support from

Fiona. Perhaps she had given up any idea of trying to hold me by this time and simply accepted the inevitable, but she agreed to stay alone with our sons for my time in robes. On the day that I disrobed she would visit the monastery in Birmingham so we could spend some time in the city and then travel home together. This was the night when the ceiling of the room she was sleeping in collapsed onto her bed, missing her by seconds. But that was yet to come.

Harder to arrange was time away from work. The customary time in Asia for temporary ordination is the three months of the rainy season, but in the west different conditions apply. After much wrangling and negotiations I was able to take all my holidays plus some unpaid leave adding up to one full month, to ordain. The arrangement was that later I would write something for the factory magazine. I agreed and as my work was in no way important or even close to being essential as later events would testify, it was securely organized.

The Buddhist group was excited about this situation and the prestige it may bring to us to have their leader spend time as a monk, and both Jack and Peter Kelly quickly decided to come with me as support.

The rest of the year passed without incident and as May of my thirty fifth year approached, my wish to be a monk was coming true.

Jack, Peter and I arrived at the monastery on Saturday 9th May 1987. I was excited by the prospect of reaching the furthest peak of being a Buddhist, to take the robe.

The ceremony would take place the next morning, and many monks from other countries had been invited. May 10, the day of the ordination was also the Vesaka Puja, usually called in English the Buddha Day. This is the triple celebration of the Birth of Siddhartha at Lumbini in modern day Nepal, the enlightenment of Gotama the ascetic under the Bodhi tree in what is now Budh Gaya, and the final passing of the Buddha, the Parinibanna in Kusinagar. These three moments in the life of Siddhartha Gotoma, the Buddha were all said to take place of the full moon day of Vesak which corresponds to the western month of May.

I met with my teacher and bowed at his feet. We spoke and he gave me some simple instructions. There was really nothing complicated to remember. Simply say yes when asked if I wanted to be a monk, and answer any other questions honestly. The whole event was one of joy and celebration and so nothing to be nervous about.

Leaving his room I met a friend of mine who had taken temporary ordination some time earlier and so we sat and talked a little.

There was a special meditation and Dhamma talk that evening and because we had spoken so long I was a few minutes late arriving in the Dhamma Hall. It was not disrespectful as nothing had begun and my teacher and the guest of honor had not yet arrived, but it did mean that the only place left to sit was right at the front. As any experienced meditator will tell you, being at the back is better!

However, I took my place and sat quietly. Soon we heard the rustling of movement outside and the door opened quietly and two people walked in. The first was my teacher who took his usual place and the second was the guest of honor. At this time I did not know him at all but as he was dressed in the simple Burmese style of lunghi, shirt and bandana around his head I made the assumption that he and Bhante were friends from Burma.

Later I discovered exactly who this man was, and during the next two weeks we became very close.

His name was U.Nu, (U, being the socially honorific title of 'uncle') and he had been the first prime minister of the new Burma once it had gained full independence from Great Britain. More than that, he was a Buddhist scholar and authority on Theravada Buddhism, and so when he spoke it was always with the voice based in the certainty of direct experience. He once told me that his favourite teaching was the Kalama Sutta, where the Buddha encourages a community of people (the Kalamas) not to accept anything that they have simply heard or cannot test for themselves and so reach a conclusion based only upon their own experience. This is an early but very important teaching, and to the Buddha's enormous credit, for there are not many spiritual teachers, then or now, who tell their followers not to believe them, but to test their words.

The evening Dhamma talk was divided into two parts, the first from my teacher and the second from U.Nu. His talk was quite long and as I remember, quite technical based upon another well known Sutta, with lots of, 'what did the Buddha mean when he said this? Or 'what did the Buddha show by this example?' and so on. Nevertheless it was a privilege to sit in this Dhamma hall with these great men, and be inspired by their words. At the end of the second talk, U.Nu, looked at the assembled group of mostly western Buddhists and asked if there were any questions. Everyone immediately looked down at the carpet and began to brush imaginary fluff off their trousers, but his eyes rested on me, «You,» he said, pointing directly at me, «you have a question for me.»

Actually I didn't, but in a moment I was able to come up with something inconsequential, inviting him to speak about the situation of Buddhsim in Burma in those days. The evening passed and finally we all went to our beds. I shared a room with Peter and a Burmese man who was the loudest snorer we had ever heard, but I think I slept well enough, and woke ready for the big day.

We began as always with chanting and meditation in the Dhamma hall, and then breakfast for the monks. Then, the rest. Toast and tea was the offering which we all gratefully accepted. This was followed by the hair cutting and head shaving, in itself a special ceremonial moment that took place in the Dhamma hall. I sat in a chair whilst Mar Mar Lwin and an older Burmese lady held a towel in front of me to catch the falling locks. My teacher was with me also reminding me to reflect upon the five unwholesome aspects of the body and to mentally repeat, 'hair on the head, hair on the body, skin, teeth and nails.'

Without reflection these things may not seem to be unwholesome but if we find one from somebody else, even someone we love, on our plate the reaction may be quite severe. This is known as assimilated beauty, that when everything is held together and presented as a complete unit, we can feel very attracted to another person, but when we meet various parts of the body and its contents outside its usual environment there is a natural repulsion. Actually all I could really think about was how thick and shiny my falling hair was as I looked at it in the towel.

Next was the head shaving. This was performed in the bathroom by Bodhidhamma whose hand was not the steadiest and so many cuts appeared on my new and shiny bald head. Then the ceremony. What I remember most was the joyful feeling and the pleasant teasing and gentle mocking of me by my teacher.

At the point where he gave me my Buddhist monk's name he said, «I give you the name Paññadipa, which means Island of Wisdom - not because you are wise, but because you come from an island.» How blessed to know this man.

In the time of the Buddha the ceremony was very short and someone would approach Gotama and ask to be accepted as a disciple. If the Buddha was happy with this person he would say, «Ehipassiko,» which means, 'come and see,' test this Dhamma for yourself so you will know the truth beyond belief or faith and personal opinions.

Over the two thousand six hundred year since the time of the Buddha the ceremony has evolved and now lasts about an hour and a half.

It begins by asking for acceptance into the Bhikkhu sangha and then receiving the ten precepts.

These begin with the five important training rules of the lay Buddhist and then are expanded to become the training rules of the Samanara, by adding the next five as follows; not to take food at inappropriate times (after midday), not to be involved in singing, dancing, playing music or attending entertainment shows, not to wear perfume, make up or ornamentation, not use high social positions, not to accept money.

There were four of us taking ordination that day and kneeling next to me was a retired psychiatrist and next to him two young Burmese men. We faced my teacher and the gathered monks with our new and unworn robes resting in the crook of our arms as we presented Anjali and waited for permission to leave the Dhamma hall to be instructed on how to wear our robes.

We filed out to the small anteroom, each with a senior monk, and undressed. It was all very modest of course, and as I stood with my bottom robe in place the very senior monk from Thailand was kneeling at my feet arranging it so it was even all around. He then looked at me and said, «Pants off,» referring to my underwear.

Happily Bodhidhamma was next to me and he answered on my behalf, «No, Bhante, in this country we leave our underwear on.» The monk obviously did not understand and repeated his instruction, «Pants off.»

Once again Bodhidhamma came to my aid, and repeated that in England monks kept their underwear.

There was a moment of stillness until the monk from Thailand repeated for the third time his simple instruction to me, «Pants off.»

For the third and final time my friend Bodhidhamma answered on my behalf.

Another moment of stillness until a hand arrived inside my robe, grabbed my underwear and pulled it down, then as it lay at my ankles he gave a great smile of relief and said happily, «Pants off!»

This was an important event for me as my whole intention was always to be true and authentic to my practice and as monks in the east do not wear underwear, I was more than happy to be a part of this noble sangha. As we four new Samanaras arrived back in the Dhamma hall, I can honestly say that I was the only one naked under my robes.

We took our places once again in the Dhamma Hall for the Upasampada, or full ordination. Now the ten training rules of the Samanara are lost to the two hundred and twenty seven rules of the fully ordained monk.

The atmosphere was joyful, but demanded our full attention as we had to request in the Pali language our place in the Bhikkhu Sangha, and then answer simple questions directly.

Do you suffer from leprosy?
Have you got boils?
Have you got eczema?
Have you got tuberculosis?
Do you get epilepsy?
Are you a human being?
Are you a man?
Are you a free man?
Are you free from government service?
Have you got your parents' permission to be ordained?
Have you got a set of three robes and an alms bowl?
What is your name?
What is your preceptor's name?

These questions may seem strange to the modern western psychology, but it was accepted that in the later days of the Buddha's dispensation not all men wishing to take ordination did so for the right reasons and so they had to be tested.

These are the questions asked and each must be answered correctly for acceptance into the Bhikkhu sangha. The first five deal with physical health, for one must be quite strong and in good health to follow the Dhamma life as a mendicant monk.

It was also understood that beings from other realms could take on human form, and so the next two questions are asked.

When my teacher asked me, «Are you a man?» my answer was obviously, «Yes Bhante.» He turned away and then suddenly turned back to face me with a huge smile on his face and asked, «Are you sure?»

And so it went on. I was given my monk's name of Paññadipa, and was invited to sit with the other monks. I don't know if it was deliberate or not, but I was the first of our small group to receive full ordination and that made me the senior of the new monks.

I became a fully ordained monk at exactly 10.32 am, on 10th May 1987. It was a special day in my life. I was thirty five years old.

At the end of the ceremony, gifts were offered by the lay community to the monks. From Jack and Peter I received a woollen hat for my newly shaved head, and thick socks. Then a Dhamma talk from Santa Citto, a visiting guest monk from Amaravati Monastery, about the four requisites. This is an important talk as it distinguishes the difference between needing something and simply wanting something.

It is so easy to get lost in the fantasy of need, but the Buddha reminded us that in reality we only need four things to sustain us. Beginning with simple nourishment for the body, followed by simple clothes to protect us from the elements, shelter from the elements and medicine if we are sick. As human beings we need only these four things, everything else is simply desire. Of course desire is only desire, but liberation comes from not confusing it with need.

Next was lunch and we were served our meal in our bowls. Sitting in a long line, eating rice and dhal with our fingers while Burmese lay supporters continued to offer more and more food. I was not very hungry, still feeling overwhelmed by the events of the morning and so I took very little. After the meal it was time to rest before the afternoon's activities began.

I went to my room to be away from the noise of the lay community below and to meet properly the retired psychiatrist who had ordained with me. He was a very pleasant, quiet man called Barry in his worldly life, but now he was Dhammasami. This is a very powerful name, and means, 'Lord of the Dhamma.'

We spoke for a short time and were then joined by Bodhidhamma who gave us the itinerary for the afternoon. We would all walk in procession to the local church hall where we would sit on the stage and be presented to the local lay people for their approval and to listen to Dhamma talks from my teacher and U.Nu.

That all sounded fine, and that is what we did.

We arrived at the church hall and were escorted onto the stage for full viewing. I sat as still and as monk like as I could in respect for the situation and waited for the proceedings to begin.

It seems to me that anything connected with Dhamma, Vipassana and Buddhism is not subject to the same rules of time as anything else, and so patience becomes an important quality to develop and it is in fact one of the ten Perfections (Khanti Paramita) necessary for Buddhahood. We say that we apply, 'Indian time,' and so when asked, «When do we begin?» the flowing answer is, «When enough people get here.» This can be a huge frustration for the western mentality but in the end will serve us well.

When we understand in this way, everything presents itself as practice, and so everything becomes our teacher.

Finally enough people arrived and the proceedings began. I learned many things that day, and one of them was that Asian people have a big and loving relationship with microphones and loud speakers.

My teacher began by coughing and clearing his throat into the microphone and then tapping his fingers on it, just to make sure it was working. It was!

More coughing, electronic feedback and then the chanting. Of course we new monks were not familiar with all of it so we chanted what we knew and mimed the rest. Then a few words of welcome which seemed to last an eternity, and then the microphone was passed to the guest of honor, U.Nu.

Another thing I learned that day was that often, at any one moment, only one quarter of an Asian audience are listening to what is being said. The rest are sleeping or eating or reading the newspaper, etc, and so the speaker plans his talk to accommodate that dynamic. U.Nu was an accomplished speaker, having been a prominent politician and prime minister (twice) in his time and so he knew his audience well. He made his speech and then arrived at the phrase that I learned to hate that afternoon. «But this is not my most important point,» he would say, and off he would go again addressing another quarter of the crowd. And so it went on. In the end it was the longest talk I have ever sat through and although it was uncomfortable it was manageable without moving. This was not the case for Dhammasami however. Barry, the retired psychiatrist, had a problem with his legs and hadn't told anyone about it. He could sit on a meditation stool, but cross legged on the floor was difficult and this became apparent very quickly. I noticed him shuffling and squirming next to me and had the feeling that something was wrong. It was uncomfortable, it's true, but we were monks now and should make an effort and be an example to those watching us from the auditorium.

However, such was his pain and difficulty that he just couldn't be still and in one moment, because of the constant movement, his upper robe fell off.

Now I was sitting next to a half naked, skinny middle aged man, jerking and twitching because of his pain. Immediately two monks jumped up to rescue and take care of him. This they would do off the stage so it was not in the public eye. They quickly took an arm each to help him stand and lifted. However, so bad was the situation that his legs no longer worked and the two helpful monks simply dragged him off the stage. As they descended the few stairs at the side all I could hear was the bump, bump, bump as his dead legs hit them. He was rested and re-dressed in his upper robe and when he felt strong enough was sent back to the monastery to wait until we returned. Poor Barry, even now when I remember this moment, my heart goes out to him.

However, U.Nu continued his talk, oblivious to the scene behind him, «But this is not my most important point,» he would say, and send his theme around the audience one more time.

Finally it was over. A little more chanting and then finished. It felt as though I was sitting on a fire, a strange combination of pain, and no feeling at all, but there was a bright light, a beacon of hope in the distance. At the back of the church hall two Asian ladies arrived from the kitchen with a huge tea urn.

«Ah, tea,» I thought, «now everything will be well.»

When I could move elegantly I descended the stage and casually began to make my way towards the awaiting tea. However, because I was now the only other western monk along with Bodhidhamma in the hall, many people including other monks, wanted their photograph taken with me. Of course I obliged but my attention really was on the tea. I almost made it too, except just at the last moment somebody grabbed my arm and led me to where the Coca Cola was being distributed.

«Here Bhante,» he said, «this is for you.»

That was the third thing I learned that afternoon, that monks love Coca Cola, and it is considered a special treat for them. For myself, monk or not, I still prefer tea.

My time as a monk passed without major incident. The programme was intense, but that is exactly what I wanted. We rose at 4.00am to chant and meditate in the cold Dhamma hall. Then a pause and breakfast, prepared by one of the lay people, or Mar Mar Lwin. It was not always possible for this food to be served formally, so we understood that everything on the table was for us monks, and so took what we wanted accordingly. More resting and then one of my favourite parts of the day; an informal session with Rewata Dhamma in the small room opposite the Dhamma hall. We would arrive with cups of tea and our questions.

«Bhante, what do you think about...?»

«What is the Buddhist perspective on...?» and so on.

Bodhidhamma and I had a mutual friend who was a gay man, so this was a question and answer we were both interested in.

«Bhante, what is the Buddhist view of homosexuality?» The answer was disappointingly Dhammic.

«Oh we don't mind. In the end desire is desire and only the object changes from person to person and moment to moment. For complete liberation, all desire must be transcended, otherwise no matter how much we can explain and justify it, we are still trapped in the mind.»

This was a wonderful teaching for me and one I took to heart and reflected upon for a long time until I understood completely.

Desire is desire, fear is fear, anger is anger. Only the object changes in different moments, but the desire for a cup of tea is the same as the desire for sexual activity, or a million pounds or a new partner, or a new car, or anything that the mind can create.

In the afternoon and evening when there were no visitors there would be a formal session in the Dhamma hall where particular Suttas and details of teachings would be examined.

On one occasion Bhante asked me what I would like him to speak about that evening. Without hesitation I asked for the Sammanapala Sutta. This had been a favourite of mine for a long time as its contents matched my personal experience of the life of a Buddhist practitioner.

The Sutta simply asks the question, 'What are the benefits of practicing a true Dhamma life?' The Buddha answers in a graduated way, showing the benefits from simple happiness, peace and respect in the world, to the complete liberation from suffering.

I meditated a lot, conducted myself with integrity and spent every afternoon for the first two weeks with U.Nu immediately after the formal discourse from my teacher.

It was always he who would come and seek me out. He was a close friend of my teacher and was staying at the monastery with his daughter and her husband before continuing his travels. We would sit at the table in the library and talk in a polite and friendly way with a cup of tea each, mine without milk as is the monks rule. Here we would discuss every conceivable aspect of Buddhism and perhaps more importantly, Dhamma practice. It seems we liked each other a lot, but why he was so attracted to me I did I not discover for several years.

On the morning at the end of his visit he found me in the Dhamma Hall and approached me very respectfully.

«Paññadipa, I have come to say goodbye. We are leaving in a few minutes and I didn't want to miss this opportunity to see you for one last time.»

We spoke about how enjoyable it had been for both of us to meet in these circumstances and wished each other well.

We were both standing in this moment and he immediately dropped to his knees and prostrated before me three times, touching my feet. I was not surprised and he was certainly not the first Burmese lay disciple to do such a thing, after all this is a Buddhist monastery and I am a Buddhist monk, so I accepted his prostration gracefully and said, «Sukkha, Sukkha, Sukkha» happiness, happiness, happiness.

I and my teacher accompanied the small family to the door and watched them drive away. It was the last time I saw him, though not his daughter and husband who were kind enough to give me lunch in New Delhi when I first arrived there five years later.

Later my teacher told me how special U.Nu really was in Buddhist terms.
According to Theravada Buddhism there are two roads to enlightenment. The first is the path of the Arahat. This is the more conventional path for as disciples of the Buddha we take him as the teacher and investigate and then apply for ourselves the validity and instructions of his teachings.
The second path is the Bodhisattva Path. Here one lets go of the Arahat ideal and vows to become a future Buddha. This path can take thousands of lifetimes as it involves perfecting ten aspects of the Dhamma heart, each one bringing the Bodhisattva closer to Buddhahood.
The ten qualities are; Generosity (dana), Moral conduct (sila), Renunciation (nekkhamma), Wisdom (Paññā), Energy (viriya), Patience (khanti), Honesty (sacca), Determination (adhitthana), Loving-Kindness (metta), Equanimity (upekkha).
U.Nu had taken the vow to walk the Bodhisattva path and so become a future Buddha.
Again, to the western mind this may sound illogical, but the kammic consequence of such a noble endeavor cannot be ignored.

One morning, some days after my ordination, I was in my room meditating when my teacher arrived, «Paññadipa,» he said, «Venerable Saddhatissa is downstairs waiting to see you.»
I could hardly believe it. This great man whom I had met for the first time the year before, was as good as his word, and had travelled all this way to see me. I arranged my robes and went downstairs to meet him.

Venerable Saddhatissa was sitting in an armchair in the anteroom of the monastery and so I immediately knelt in front of him, bowed three times and presented Anjali.

«Bhante,» I began, «thank you so much for coming. It is a pleasure and a privilege to see you here.»

«Yes, yes, yes,» he said gently touching my arm, «now tell me, are you getting enough to eat?»

My teacher arrived later to join us and we spoke and shared a loving relationship until it was time for him to leave. This man had a direct influence in my Dhamma life, and I am happy I had the opportunity to tell, and show him how grateful I was for his wisdom.

Dhamma training is the way to be free, to live with love and be aware. To find happiness for ourselves so that we can share that happiness with all beings. The greatest teachers manifest this happiness and love in their relationship with their students.

The fundamental things are the ones we have to address. Are you comfortable, are you warm, do you have enough to eat?

The Buddha himself discovered that we have to be strong and healthy to make the practice and so the basic requirements for life are the primary concern.

The real Masters are like loving parents, hard when they need to be, but always loving. Their advice is pure Dhamma. Take care of you, so that you can take care of others. When you have energy you will share that. When you are tired you will share that. Be something of value in the world.

There are no secrets in Dhamma. Truth is truth, love is love, wisdom is wisdom and these qualities always manifest in the simple and spontaneous acts of caring and kindness.

On another day Venerable Bodhidhamma announced that we would be going to the Shrewsbury Buddhist Group to give a talk that evening. This sounded like good fun and so together we took a coach for the hour long journey. It was an interesting ride as we got to know each other much better and I began to realise the reality of being a monk. We do it to learn, and so until we awaken, monks are always men in training. This means that we must deal with our own story until it's finished. The robes and the monks discipline help us with this, but in the end it is always ourselves who must do the necessary work of letting go of self identity, because only in this place is peace. We arrived at the Shrewsbury Buddhist Group and were welcomed graciously. The evening proceeded with meditation and Dhamma talks from both Bodhidhamma and me, the Venerable Paññadipa Bhikkhu.

At the end of the evening we were told that we would spend the night at the home of one of the members of the group. This was fine with us because as Buddhist monks our needs are few and our requirements minimal.

We arrived at the house to meet an incredible and undisguised hostility from the wife of the man. She was ironing and not happy at all that these two strange men in their orange robes and shaven heads should be staying in her house, obviously against her wishes. We were given a cup of tea each and a room with a bed and a mattress on the floor.

I, as the junior monk took the mattress and fell immediately into sleep, only to be awoken some time later with the face of Bodhidhamma only inches from mine whispering at me.

«Paññadipa», he said, «you're snoring!»

I turned over and that was that.

The next morning we found ourselves in a cold and empty house. Breakfast of toast and jam was left on the table for us and a pot of tea.

We ate what had been offered, chanted the Metta Sutta, wishing all beings a comfortable and fear free life, and left.

The journey home was uneventful, and we arrived at the monastery ready for what the rest of the day had to offer.

By this time now Dhammasami had disrobed and gone home, as had the two young Burmese men. We had enjoyed a nice relationship together for two weeks, but I had spent most of my time either alone in meditation, with my teacher or Bodhidhamma.

Also staying at the monastery for a short time was a Burmese Buddhist nun called sister Paññaramsi. Her name means 'the golden rays of wisdom,' but actually she gave herself the place of washing the dishes and making cups of tea for the monks. This was slightly awkward for me as a westerner and having grown up in a familial culture of gender equality, but we could not dissuade her from this path.
One day she told my teacher that she wanted to be a man.
«Perhaps in your next lifetime it can happen,» he said kindly.
«I don't want to be a man in my next lifetime,» she said, «I want to be a man now!»
Even with patience and strong social conditioning it is still possible to see the injustice of simply not being born male.

I had been told that my teacher had the ability to read minds, a claim I had not really taken seriously until it happened to me.
One day I was alone in the Dhamma hall meditating completely consumed by sexual desire, the most explicit images arising into my mind.
Having your head shaved and wearing simple robes does not suddenly free you from yourself, it only helps create the environment where you can meet yourself, including the mind of desire.
I was sitting immobile trying as much as possible to not be overwhelmed by these images when Bhante walked in. He came straight to me, waited until I opened my eyes and said quite simply and compassionately, «Tonight Paññadipa, I will speak about sexual desire.» He then turned and left.

I was devastated. My only thought was, 'my god, he knows!'
I don't remember the talk that evening, but I'm sure it was helpful.

It was always my intention to be the best monk that I could be, out of respect for the Buddha, my own teacher, Sayadaw Rewata Dhamma, my wife and my friends, and so I undertook the 'samana' training.

Samana, means, 'one whose senses are under control', and so I spent many hours each day in silence and in meditation, and always conducted myself with mindfulness and dignity. The result of this training was the very deep feeling of peace and calm. All desires and aversions seemed to have fallen away.

One day I was invited to attend a house blessing celebration with my teacher and Bodhidhamma. This was a very special occasion for the Burmese lay people who were doctors and had just moved into a new house. They had invited many friends and relatives and everyone was dressed in their finest clothes. The ladies, in traditional Burmese costume, looked especially elegant.

Arriving late, the first thing to do was to eat. In the Theravada tradition it is a monk's rule that no food should be taken after midday, and so in accordance with this, we were directed straight to the dining room.

The families must have been awake for many hours preparing the delicious food for our benefit. Huge amounts of salad, rice, noodles and vegetables were waiting for us on the fully laden dining-room table, and more elegantly dressed Burmese women waiting to serve us.

However, as we walked in, me deeply engrossed in my practice of mindfulness, something caught my eye.

There on a plate in the middle of the table was a chocolate éclair. It was the biggest éclair I have ever seen, filled with fresh cream and covered by a thick layer of chocolate. It was a type of food that I had not eaten for some time and so the moment my eye caught sight of this beautiful object, my mind screamed, 'I want that!'

We sat down and ate, having the most delicious food almost forced upon us, but I kept one eye on the éclair. I wanted it, and in some way felt certain that by looking at it I could make sure no one else took it.

The generosity of the Burmese people is well-known and finally, I could eat no more. The Burmese lay people had managed to fill at least one Buddhist monk to capacity and I was not able to take another mouthful.

The éclair was left on a plate, until, I suppose, someone else took it. With so much food inside me, I was definitely past caring about its destiny.

Naturally I was shocked by the intensity of the desire that had arisen within me, but happily Bhante explained the reality of the situation which is first, that in the environment of such deep calm everything that disrupts that calm is exaggerated and secondly, to remember that it too will pass. The impermanence of all phenomena is a crucial part of Dhamma training and although easy to speak about, resting in the ever flowing and changing conditions of life takes great dedication to the practice that ultimately dissolves self identity.

As a Buddhist monk living in a monastery I was almost invisible to the world, outside the protection of the monastic walls however it was a different story. On the long journey back from the house blessing in Ipswich, we agreed to take a short rest and a cup of tea at a famous service station in England known as the Watford Gap. Historically this is the oldest service station in Englad opening as it did on the same day as the motorway it serves, and is a very popular stop for travellers.

The moment that we arrived and left our small car two busses of noisy football fans arrived. They alighted from their busses singing and chanting football songs and looked over at us three Buddhist monks in our flowing orange robes. I was pleased and relieved that they completely ignored us, but happy also that, just by chance, we fell in line behind three Roman catholic nuns who had also stopped for a cup of tea.

There is an English expression which says that there is 'safety in numbers,' and that certainly felt true on that day.

On another occasion Bodhidhamma and I took a stroll around the local park close to our monastery.

We were quietly walking in our conspicuous orange robes, myself once again feeling very exposed as a new monk, when we were met by two local skinheads who immediately began to chant, Hari Krishna, Hari Krishna at us.

My only idea was to walk on quietly and not engage these two young men, but my colleague however had other ideas and stopped and spoke to them telling them that we were monks of the Theravadin Buddhist tradition and that we do not dance or sing!

He then described our simple life in a few words and in a way that was not only non-confrontational, but allowed them their dignity even in their misunderstanding. They were actually interested enough to ask simple questions in return as to our reasons for following this particular life-style, and this meeting and my friend's response became a great teaching of non-judgement for me.

One day, Bhante asked me to clean the small pool in the garden and as the sun was shining it seemed like a good opportunity to be outside for a time.

I began by gently catching the many small fish that lived there and re-housing them temporarily in a bucket of water. Next was the situation with the frogs - wonderful creatures for me, and having put them to one side I began to clean the pool. Not difficult and so it didn't take too long. The sun was shining, the birds were singing and I was happily focused in my small work.

Soon I had replaced the water and gently again put the fishes back one by one. But now something happened.

As I sat there with my shaven head and monk's robes watching these small creatures finding once more their freedom I had a tremendous insight - the insight of 'Oneness,' the interconnectedness of all life.

This intuitive understanding brought with it an immense sense of peace and completeness and I sat gazing into the water watching these small creatures, now no longer beings outside and separate from me.

My teacher arrived and saw me sitting quite still just looking into the water.

«Paññadipa what are you doing? You don't have to sit there all afternoon,» he said in his usual playful way.

«Yes Bhante, I know, but I have just understood the reality of oneness. There is no separation between me, these fish and everything else that exists.» I replied.

He looked at me for a moment, smiled and went back inside.

Such an obvious truth needs no comment for when the heart is truly open everything is seen to be the way it is, and spontaneously has equal value.

Hatred, violence, discrimination and murder now have no place in our life, for to bring pain to one being is to bring pain to ourselves.

During my time as a monk, and in all my many years with my teacher I had been encouraged to investigate, understand and practice Loving Kindness for all beings, beginning with myself.

Very often, the teaching of love is seen as something that has value when things are going well and then ignored in more difficult times. This of course is not the Dhamma way of training where the opposite is true. The difficulties in life are recognised as the perfect opportunity to practice Loving Kindness.

As Bhante's lay disciple, whenever I would go to his room to complain about my life, how unfair it seemed, how wrong things were for me or for others, he would always say the same thing, «Michael, now you need Loving Kindness,» and he was always right!
Because he was my teacher and because I wanted to awaken to truth more than anything else in life, I would always listen with an open heart and then practice what I had heard. It never failed. It is the truth of Vipassana and Metta Bhavana, the way to peace, happiness and Awakening. All we need to do is apply it to our life. Of course it wasn't always easy, but I persevered. I lived a life around the beautiful teachings of the Buddha, the Zen Masters and Gandhi, people who had cultivated what I wanted most, an open, loving and kind heart.
I began to realise through my own experience that love is not weak, it is real strength. The perfect balance of love and wisdom does not cultivate the mentality of a victim, blaming others for our experience of unhappiness, but rather it develops confidence and personal power. With wisdom, we know how to live for ourselves. With love we do not insist that others follow our way.
Love and awareness are the most important requirements of spiritual development, for without them we cannot ever proceed beyond the limitations we place upon ourselves. To open our heart and allow love and wisdom to flow freely, spontaneously and without limit is truly a blessing for ourselves and ultimately all beings.
Before I had ordained I was given the gift of a mala, a Buddhist rosary of 108 beads and this is what I used now twice a day to compliment my Loving Kindness practice. The mala was made of human bone and I felt pleased to have such a gift to remind me of death and so encourage me not to miss a moment of love in life.
In the morning I would make one round of the 108 beads and on each one mentally recite, 'May I be well and happy'.

In the afternoon I would repeat the process, this time reciting 'May all beings be well and happy.' It was a good and wonderful practice and has always served me well.

Eventually, my short time in temporary ordination was finished, and I had to renounce the robe. This small ceremony was only a formality, but I didn't like it. I knelt in front of my teacher in the Dhamma hall and renounced the Buddha, Dhamma, Sangha and then left to change from my robes into my ordinary western clothes.

Returning, I took refuge again, (see next page) expressing my confidence and commitment to the Buddha, Dhamma, Sangha.

Taking refuge is the small ceremony that means to actively become a Buddhist. In the Theravada tradition it is chanted in Pali usually with the teacher. The principle part being when we repeat three times the refuges.

And so, from this moment we take as our foundation for life, Wisdom (the Buddha) Truth (the Dhamma) and the community of wise beings (the Sangha).

The ceremony completed, I was a Buddhist again and I could once more breathe easily.

BUDDHAM SARANAM GACCHAMI
I take the Buddha as my refuge.
DHAMMAM SARANAM GACCHAMI
I take the Dhamma as my refuge.
SANGHAM SARANAM GACCHAMI
I take the Sangha as my refuge.

DUTIYAM PI BUDHAM SARANAM GACCHAMI
(for the second time I take ...)
DUTIYAM PI DHAMMAM SARANAM GACCHAMI
(for the second time I take...)
DUTIYAM PI DHAMMAM SARANAM GACCHAMI
(for the second time I take...)

TATIYAM PI BUDHAM SARANAM GACCHAMI
(for the third time I take...)
TATIYAM PI DHAMMAM SARANAM GACCHAMI
(for the third time I take...)
TATIYAM PI SANGHAM SARANAM GACCHAMI
(for the third time I take...)

I offered the robes and bowl to my teacher, but he would not accept them.
«I want you to take these robes and this alms bowl back to the Isle of Man to show the presence of Dhamma,» he said.
I humbly did this and still have them in my small Dhamma hall in France today.
My time as a monk was over, it was brief, but I will never forget it. The natural restrictions of wearing robes and following the Vinaya become a wonderful opportunity to observe the mind and everything it presents. Its quest for perfection never ends. I enjoyed so much the shared meals with my teacher as he would suddenly find the desire to talk about Dhamma or his early life in

Burma and so many other things in a friendly and informal way. To see him looking for his woolly hat when it was folded in half and resting on his head, or to offer him his favourite breakfast of banana on toast with a big mug of tea sweetened with condensed milk.

These are fond memories for me, but there are others.

During my time as a monk I met the same mental conditions as I had when I was a layman: desire, aversion, interest, boredom and all the rest. During the periods of boredom I would wish to be back in my other life, to talk with friends, play my guitar, listen to music, etc. For a short time that life seemed very attractive. Of course, I had done the same thing in reverse when I was a layman, thinking about how wonderful it would be to be in robes.

Without wisdom the mind is never in peace and it looks outward comparing what it has with what it perceives others have, and how it can be happy by giving up what it has for something more attractive.

But the truth we need to understand is that however your life is right now, these are the perfect conditions for enlightenment. There is nothing to get and nothing to do. Surrender into the reality of each moment and let the comparing mind fall away. Everything is fine, just as it is.

Later that afternoon Fiona arrived to spend the weekend together in Birmingham. Mar Mar Lwin had given me two tickets for the Ideal Home Exhibition in the town centre, and so we visited that as a married couple. It felt strange to be together again, and my worldly life began to reappear.

That evening in the monastery we went to our beds. Mar Mar Lwin had offered Fiona her room to use for this weekend and I of course kept my monk's room on another floor.

In the morning I came to Fiona's room to greet her and offer a cup of tea. I entered not only to find the room empty, but half the ceiling lying on the bed!

When I eventually found her she told me what had happened. As she was lying in bed preparing to sleep, she had become aware of a creaking sound. This is not uncommon in buildings during the night, and I had certainly heard this old house straining and groaning under its own weight on the occasions I had practiced all night meditation alone in the Dhamma hall. This however, was different and the sounds got louder and louder until in one instance she leapt out of the bed, just as the ceiling collapsed onto it. She was safe, but frightened, and had run to the ever reliable Mar Mar Lwin's room where they had organized another bed for her.

After the shock came the amusement and the lingering thought that perhaps the universe wanted me to remain a monk, and so had tried to kill my wife?

The next day we travelled home together and after some time to adjust and allow my hair to grow again, I found myself back in my ordinary life.

I was a disciple with my teacher for twenty two years. I lived with him as a layman and then for a short time, as a monk. Being the disciple was always the important part, and never the amount of time I spent as a Bhikkhu. It was a wonderful experience and in those early days after I had disrobed I would fantasize about the time when I could take the robe again. It never happened, and I eventually found my true life beyond a monastic tradition.

As agreed I wrote an account of my time as a monk for the work's magazine, a quarterly assortment of articles and photographs for six hundred people who worked at the factory and of which almost none were interested in my or any other story contained within its glossy pages.

It was called, 'Taking the Robe,' and the subtitle read, 'The ideal of spending one month of your annual holiday with a shaven head and wearing little more than an orange tablecloth and bed sheet

may not appeal to everyone, but for me it was the opportunity of a lifetime.'
This approach did not please Jack when he read it as he thought my flippancy was disrespectful, but my intuitive feeling then and now, is to speak to people in a way they can understand and relate to. It is not possible for me to disrespect the Buddha, the Dhamma or my own teachers no matter what I say or how I say it. I consider these things as the greatest gifts and blessings in my life.

So, there was a return to normalcy, working a lot, two and a half hours of meditation every day, retreat and family commitments.
There were moments when I really struggled with my life as a non-monk, even to the point of occasionally wearing my robes again when I was alone in the house, but happily the frustration I met by not being in the monastery finally faded away, and I could begin to enjoy my ordinary life.
Letting go is the path to happiness. The more we carry resentment and disapponintment in life, the more we struggle. I had been a monk, it was over, move on!
This is when we began our family holidays in Majorca. They were wonderful experiences, either alone or with our closest friends and their children from the Isle of Man, and some of the happiest memories of my married life. Sunshine, speaking a little Spanish and a restaurant in the evening after a day relaxing at the pool. Of course I would still sit every day before everyone else awoke, and then walk into the town and drink a café cortado in the early morning before the family day began. Ten or fourteen days in the sunshine, seemingly without responsibilities, money in our pockets and time on our hands. Wonderful.
Then the flight home and back to work, and always the questioning of my life. Why am I doing this? What's the point of it and how can I escape this drudge?
Here once again I had the beauty of my relationship with a living

and caring Master.

On one occasion during this period of doubt I knelt in front of my teacher and complained. I felt my life to be very difficult and unrelenting. Here I was married with two small children, a huge mortgage, three jobs to pay for everything and no end in sight. I felt exhausted and wanted to be free from this situation. I asked him if I could run away from all this, ordain again as a monk and live a simple life with him?
«Of course we can ordain you easily anytime you want,' he said, 'but this is not your Kamma now. Right now your Kamma is to be with your family, to take care of them, to serve them and find the Dhamma there. When you do this you will understand properly.»
Bhante had a way to speak that would always touch my heart. Listening to his words it became obvious, the Dhamma life, the true Dhamma life, is not about running away until everything is easy, it is about facing our difficulties and using them for our own liberation.
It may be a much more romantic idea to sit in a cave in the Himalayas contemplating the navel, but it is much more realistic to meet the consequences of our actions and use them as they present themselves moment by moment.
Without our suffering, how could we end our suffering?
Our life is the mirror of our mind and it will always bring good results if we use it wisely. Knowing what to do and what to leave undone. When to speak and when to be silent. What to empower and what to let go of.
There is a time to be a monk or a nun, and a time to meet our worldly Kamma. Being married brings responsibilities. Being a parent brings responsibilities. Being a student of Dhamma brings responsibilities. Once we recognise this everything is practice and we use our ordinary daily life as our path.
As a disciple of Dhamma and of my teacher I heard these beautiful

words and saw the problem. It wasn't the situation, it was my relationship to the situation! Once I changed, everything changed. In that moment I resolved to be the best husband that I could be, the best father that I could be, the best disciple that I could be.

Complaining has no value at all. Running away from life's difficulties is endless, for wherever we go we will always meet ourselves, the originator of these difficulties. Now, with Dhamma understanding we can see the truth and use this very moment for our own liberation.

So I surrendered into the situation and as much as I could used it as my vehicle for freedom. Not always easy, but always valuable.

Rumors began to grow at work that the factory was experiencing difficult times as it was the era of 'glasnost,' and peace had broken out. This meant that orders for component parts that go to make up the world famous Martin Baker ejector seats were diminishing and so something would have to be done.

I had now been working at the factory for eleven years, and even if I didn't like it, I had used it as a place to train myself in Dhamma and was now quite popular and well established. However, in the early days I had experienced many doubts about working in such a place. Ejector seats are fitted only to fighter aircraft and they are used for war and the destruction of property and fellow beings, how could I as a Buddhist support such activity? But, on the other hand, this was a safety device used to save someone's life, and so my very small and extremely limited place in this situation had some value. I went with that second argument and felt at peace.

Now things were changing and perhaps it was the time to move on?

I was still working at my Saturday job as the storeman at Newsons on the quay in Douglas, and one day the boss casually told me that they would be looking for a full time storeman, and would I be interested. We discussed hours and rates of pay and everything was an improvement on my factory life. I could walk to work. I could almost choose my own hours and so I could begin and finish early to be at home for Michael and Adam when they finished school, and I would work alone. Perfect.

I agreed and went immediately to tell my father. He was delighted. Of course, because this meant that I would also be working with Eileen, who was the senior assistant in the shop.

Back at the factory I obtained a 'termination of employment' form, took it home and filled it in. I would have to give a weeks notice, but that was fine of course and usual. My new job was waiting for me.

The next morning I arrived at the factory with my end of employment form filled in and ready to hand over to the office. However, there was an ominous feeling throughout all the departments and before I could do anything we were all summoned to the canteen where Mr Richard Holt, the boss, would address us all.

Six hundred men and women stood together waiting for who knows what?

I don't remember the speech he gave except to say that two hundred people were to be made redundant immediately and for all of us to return to our work space and wait.

This was shocking news. This was a family owned business and the only reason I was employed there was because my father, now retired, had also worked there. This was a job for life! The idea of redundancy could not have been further from anybody's mind. We returned to our workspace in a state of stunned silence and waited. One of the office staff arrived sad-faced and handed me an envelope. Inside was my redundancy paper and a cheque for five thousand pounds. I was in shock. I didn't want to stay but I didn't want to be pushed out either. I looked around to see big, grown men crying. Not only the third made redundant but those who had kept their jobs also. Now their life and everything in it

was uncertain and there could be no going back from this point.
I took my coat, said goodbye to my former colleagues and began to leave. It was not a sudden departure as so many of us met, spoke, embraced each other. Then it happened.
One person came to me to say goodbye and wish me well.
«Did you hear about the guy who was about to put his notice in, but then received his redundancy cheque?» he said.
A moment of clarity followed by a smile, «Yes,» I said, «it was me.» I took out the paper and held it for a moment. Once again the universe had taken care of me. If I had handed in this paper I would have received nothing, but it is said that in life timing is everything and to be in harmony with life's impersonal presentations brings good results.

I began my new job a week later and found it to be more pleasurable full time than only on Saturdays. I worked alone on three floors of an old-fashioned warehouse, hoisting boxes up to the different floors via an old pulley system and then leaning out into the air to pull them in. As I worked alone, I was left alone and any contact was made through a walkie talkie hanging from my belt. Newsons was divided into two establishments and the quite modern shop where Eileen worked sold jeans, tee shirts, belts and the like, whereas the shop immediately underneath the warehouse where I worked sold working men's attire and camping equipment.
I sought out my discreet places where I would not be easily discovered. Not to avoid work but rather so that I could chant every day, six or seven times.
I would walk to work early in the morning chanting the 'Metta Sutta,' the Buddha's teaching of Loving Kindness and used my time alone during my official breaks to reflect and chant even more.
This worked well for some months until the day my father died.

On Saturday 7th July, 1990 I was awakened at about 7.00 am by the telephone next to the bed ringing. It was Eileen, my stepmother and my father's wife for twenty five years suddenly talking in my ear. She was speaking so quickly, telling me a strange story about my father, how he had been unable to sleep that night because of a pain in his lower back and had dressed in the middle of the night and gone downstairs to watch television. She had slept again of course and when she had got up and arrived downstairs about fifteen minutes earlier she went into the living room to see how my father was feeling now. By this time I had realized where these almost nonsensical words were leading and I waited for the reality of such an early telephone call, «and your father is dead,» came the five words I had accurately anticipated.

A strange calm washed over me and I spoke in a gentle authoritative voice, «O.K. Eileen,» I said «I'm on my way. I'll be there in twenty minutes.»

Fiona looked at me and asked in a sleepy voice, «What is it?»

«My dad's dead.» I replied, «I have to go to the house.»

Fiona wept and I dressed. Everything was happening in a calm slow-motion and a sense of disbelief filled the bedroom. Perhaps I was still asleep? I arrived at the house twenty minutes later, embraced my stepmother and went alone into the room where my dead father sat in his favorite armchair.

Eileen had called the doctor who was writing the death certificate. He was friendly and compassionate, but stayed only a moment. «It was an embolism,» he said, «It was painless and he died peacefully.» He looked almost as I had seen him on so many Sunday afternoons, dozing after a big lunch, peaceful with one piece of hair hanging down on his forehead. Of course the complexion was different and there was a sense of stillness I had not met before. Without any reflection or intention (I was completely alone) my hands went together in Anjali and I said to the man I admired and loved, «May you be well and happy, and thank you for being a part of my life.»

For almost twenty years now I had been involved in a serious and committed Dhamma practice. Once I had found Vipassana and my teacher, I never deviated from the path and used my life and what it presented as the tools to work with for my own liberation. Little by little, often without realising it, the reality of freedom had put its arms around me, and I felt more and more secure and at peace with the uncertainties of life.

I had trained in Loving Kindness, reciting many times each day the whole of the Metta meditation verses,

> May I be free from anger and ill will.
> May I be free from fear and anxiety.
> May I be free from suffering and pain.
> May I be free from ignorance and desire.
> May I be happy and peaceful.
> May I be harmonious.
> May I be liberated from greed, hatred and delusion.
> May I realise the deeper peace within.

> May all beings be free from anger and ill will.
> May all beings be free from fear and anxiety.
> May all beings be free from suffering and pain.
> May all beings be free from ignorance and desire.
> May all beings be happy and peaceful.
> May all beings be harmonious.
> May all beings be liberated from greed, hatred and delusion.
> May all beings realise the deeper peace within.

And more particularly the central part of the Metta Sutta, in both English and Pali,

> May all beings be happy and secure,
> may their hearts be wholesome.
> Whatever living beings there may be,
> feeble or strong, tall, stout or medium,
> long, short or small, seen or unseen,
> those living far or near,
> those who are born and those who are to be born,
> may all beings, without exception, be happy minded.

I had also practised every day for some years the Maranusati, the reflection of death, again from its simple form of reminding myself of the reality of life:

One day, in no particular order, and for no particular reason, I and all the beings that I know will die. This is the truth that I live with. May all beings be happy.

To the more profound sitting meditation reflection that death in any moment is only one heartbeat away.

Naturally these reflections are not meant to frighten the disciple, but to bring them into the reality of life.
The Buddha said; 'The one who holds death in front of them lives in this moment now.'
With all this genuine and sincere training, I felt secure in the unpredictability of life and so had not missed the moment to tell my father that I loved and admired him, and so even when he died so suddenly there was no sense of regret. Nothing was left unsaid. He knew exactly how I felt about him, and I think he was happy with that.

He was sixty five years old, apparently in good health and so had taken early retirement two years before.

Because he had always worked so hard in his life my sister and I were sure he would be very quickly bored, but not a bit. He spent his days in his workshop working with the carpentry he loved so much, grooming and attending the two ponies he bought for the sheer pleasure of their company and who became such great friends to him in their little field next to the house, and cooking for Eileen when she was at work.

He was delighted to tell me that one day he was taking the oats to the ponies when he slipped on the grass and sat down hard. He wasn't injured, but it took a moment to recover his composure. However, in that moment one of the ponies arrived and nuzzled him, as if to say, «Come on, get up, you'll be fine.»

When I would go to visit he would offer me something to eat. This was, and I think still is a family trait, beginning in my lifetime with my grandmother who could never just offer a cup of tea. By the time the kettle had boiled the table was filled with the most delightful things and then forced upon the unsuspecting guest.

My father would be in the kitchen and shout, «Michael, I'm making a pan of chips, do you want some?»

«No, not for me, I'm leaving soon.» I would reply.

«Are you sure?»

«Yes,» I would reply now slightly irritated because he wouldn't accept my first answer, «I'm sure. I'm not hungry at all.»

Some time later a big plate of chips would arrive, steaming and golden and too hot to touch. They would be offered to me and I would reluctantly accept them. I would eat the whole plateful without waiting for them to reach the correct temperature for the human palate, puffing and breathing trying to cool them before they burned my tongue too much. He just stood and watched me. When the last chip was devoured he would reach for the plate and say in his lovely humourous way, «Not bad for someone who wasn't hungry.»

I was going to miss this man.

Without realizing it he was my first Dhamma teacher and showed without intention a way of joy, love and compassion. By the time he died he was already vegetarian. Eileen would say later that it was my influence, but I don't think so. His beautiful Kamma was evident on so many occasions it was only a question of time.

On one of these occasions my father and Eileen were celebrating another year of marriage and invited a small group of family and friends to share this happy event with.
We sat at a large round table in a smart restaurant, my father and his wife, my sister and her husband, Fiona and I and a cousin of my father and his wife.
The conversation was of the usual quality in family situations like this with lots of jokes and good humour, until the subject turned to corporal punishment.
The Isle of Man, where we were all born and lived, had kept the whipping of certain offenders on its statute books and occasionally meted it out as punishment. It was known as the birch, but was in fact a bunch of willow branches tied together and used to lash the bare buttocks of the usually young male offender. The logic being that this would teach them a lesson they would not forget.
However, the court of Human Rights had just made this type of punishment illegal throughout Europe, and although it was still on the Manx statute books it was illegal now to use this barbaric form of punishment.
This enforced change in the law had angered many people on the Isle of Man, and even today, so many years later, it is sure that there are still residents, Manx and others, who would like to see its return. Such is the nature of fear.
At the table of this dinner party my fathers cousin expressed his favour of continuing this brutal and unforgiving form of punishment and ended his disposition with the familiar Manx expression exclaiming that we should, 'birch the buggars!'

He then turned to my father who had been silently continuing his meal and asked, «What do you think Noel?»
My father gently returned his fork to his place and said in the calmest, quietest and most profoundly beautiful voice I had ever heard, «No-one should be beaten,» picked up his fork again and continued his meal gracefully.
It was the first time I had seen such beautiful Dhamma in action, and not only does the power of that simple comment stay with me all these years later, it was the first time that I realized that truth never has to be argued for. It can always be expressed in a few words and left for the other to contemplate. Truth is always like a joke, we either get it or we don't, but it can't be explained.

This was the moment when I realised that my father was in fact, my first Dhamma teacher.

There were things to do now and I was the elder male in the family. I had to take care of my stepmother, my sister, my wife. I had to organize everything. However, such is the way of things, that many people knew what needed to be done and so offered all kinds of welcome assistance.
The first thing however was the funeral director. His business was at the top of the road and so he arrived quickly in an unmarked transit van. He and his colleague entered the house with what I now know from watching American movies was a black body bag.
He told Eileen and I to have a cup of tea in the kitchen and they would do everything necessary. Sometime later there was a gentle tap on the door and he stood there with his professional compassionate smile. Everything was done and the body would be taken to the funeral home, and please do not hesitate even for a moment if there is something he could do for us or help us with. I showed them to the door and watched them drive away in the

plain unmarked van. I went back inside to the room where my father had died.
I looked at the place where his body had been. All that was left was a dent in the cushions from his posture and his clothes folded next to it.
Although this was the last time I ever saw the physical form of my father, I can honestly say that he, in one way or another, is with me every day.

The funeral was a simple affair with the very Reverend Canon Bagley as the man in charge. This was the man who some years earlier had married Fiona and I in St Peter's Church in Onchan, and who had befriended my father in the intervening years. He gave the sermon standing next to the coffin rather than in the pulpit and had a lot to say, most of it funny, loving and touched with a tinge of sadness.
After the ceremony, as is the tradition, came the wake. Drinks and sandwiches in a local bar, and many, many stories about the presence of my father in the life of others. His cousin and best friend, Willie, now a retired police sergeant, had us all laughing at his stories like the time when my father fell off the wall whilst leaning back to see the bikes go past during the famous T.T. Races and nobody knew where he has disappeared to until he spoke.
«Where did Noel go?» somebody asked
«I'm here,» said a voice in the grass, «help me up.»
Or the time when he went to the cash dispenser outside the bank. This was still a very new thing on the Isle of Man so he was a little bit excited to see how it worked. He put in his card and the machine immediately spat it out onto the ground. He picked it up, wiped it clean and tried again only to meet with the same result. For the third time now he inserted his card only to meet the same situation except this time it was accompanied by a voice from behind the screen saying, «Can you wait a minute mate, the

machine's not working and we're trying to repair it!»
The wake was a huge success, and ironically my father would have enjoyed it most. Perhaps he did?

Our life was different now. Every Sunday morning I would visit Eileen, drink a coffee with her and eat a piece of home made cake. We had always got along well and my father used to say that she thought the world of me.
I don't know if that is true but she was often complimentary about my demeanor and felt I had certain qualities similar to my father. One Sunday morning she asked me to teach her meditation. I knew what she was really asking, but I wanted her to understand for herself, so I asked her why.
«Because I want to go past the death of your father, and put it out of my life.» she said.
I took her hand and answered gently, «Eileen, that's not how it works. To let go of the pain we must meet it again and again until we understand its origins and then gently, lovingly and beautifully, let it go. There is no quick fix into liberation, but if you ask me again in another year, we will do it for sure.»
So we met, drank coffee, ate cake and talked about my father, his romantic side and his last and possibly greatest gift to me.
On the night he died he and Eileen went out to a local bar for a drink. Neither of them was very interested in alcohol, but it is a way to get dressed up a little, leave the house and be together.
On their return my father asked Eileen for the key to the house.
«I haven't got it.» she said.
«Yes,» said my father, «I asked you to pick it up.»
«Well I don't have it,» she continued.
Now my father was in a bad mood. He would have to break the small piece of glass next to the door, reach in and turn the lock so they could enter. Then he would have to repair the glass so no burglar could do the same. He didn't want to do any of these

things, but there was no option, and so he did what was necessary all the while mumbling under his breath.

My father was always proud to say that in twenty five years of marriage they had never argued, and this was developing into the first.

Finally everything was done and it was time for bed. After lying together in silence for several minutes, my father spoke, «Eileen, I want to apologize for my behavior this evening. I was upset by what needed to be done but even so, there was no reason to be unkind to you. I am truly sorry and I hope you will accept my apology.»

Of course she accepted immediately. They kissed and embraced and went to sleep.

Six hours later he was dead.

There is an old English superstition that insists things happen in sets of three, and superstition or not, that is exactly what happened that year.

First was my redundancy from the factory, then the sudden and unexpected death of my father, and now the third thing was about to come.

One Sunday morning just a few weeks after the funeral of my father, Fiona and I woke up together and almost immediately she announced that she wanted a divorce.

I was shocked and hurt.

How could she possibly want a divorce from me? I was a loving caring Buddhist husband. It's true that I had ignored her for most of our married life and that she always took second place to my so called Dhamma and Buddhist practice, and arising with that was the view that her worldly needs were as nothing compared to my much more spiritual ones.

This had become evident many years before, after returning from the very first retreat with my teacher. Buddhism is also about family unity and harmony and so there is a simple rule which says that a person must receive their partners permission to attend retreats and the like, and so, filled with enthusiasm for what I had met, I asked Fiona for her permission to make more retreats.

She answered without hesitation a great and incontrovertible, no! I couldn't believe it, so I replied simply, clearly and completely unsympathetically, «Well, I'm going!» and that was that. The dye was cast.

She had struggled with my emotional distance, my prison visits, my traveling to and from Birmingham and our house filled with people wanting to learn about meditation and Buddhism. Actually all she had wanted was a husband to be with her and to live a so called normal life. It could not be me.

Although now I see clearly my behavior was not always as kind, caring and considerate as I had thought it was, I believed at the time that I had done nothing wrong, that the fault was completely with her and so was angry at the idea that we would separate. Perhaps I felt something similar to my father who told me that he had felt ashamed when his marriage failed. But these were different days and divorce was already commonplace, but there was something more than that; she had preempted me.

All those hours walking silently in Summer Hill Glen with my sons playing in the trees and the stream, all those days riding to the factory on my little motor bike, and then having to stay there just to pay the mortgage, all those empty conversations with work colleagues, family and friends about things of no significance, all those moments when I felt my life slipping away.

In all those times the only thing that had sustained me was the dream that when Adam, my youngest son was sixteen years old, I would renounce the family life and become a monk. But that would still be some years in the future and now it was too soon. I wasn't ready, and although we had spoken of divorce in the past, this time she was completely serious. She packed a few things and left for her parent's house. This was new and suddenly my wife and I had separated. I was stunned. What would I do? I made plans. I rejected them. I made other plans and so it went on.

She came back after two days and told me that she had been to see a lawyer and that it was time to talk. By this time the shock, the anger and the frustration had subsided, and a conversation could take place. It was clear that we didn't fit together as a couple and it would be better to part, but in a good way so as to not hurt our children.

«After all,» she said, «I'm still young enough to find my Mister Right, and you want to go to India.»

It was over. We arranged everything as comfortably as we could, even trying to use one lawyer to dissolve the marriage, but that proved impossible as he told us that he couldn't act for both of us, so I had to find my own legal representation. My lawyer was quite bewildered by the situation, where we would not fight or argue about possessions, money and most importantly, access to our children until finally he was so concerned with what I wanted to do he insisted that I sign a waver, freeing him from any responsibility.

So we began the procedure of dissolving our legal relationship.

My teacher was teaching in Scotland and had already asked me to manage the retreat for him. Both Fiona and I thought I should go as this would be a good opportunity to explain the situation to him and receive some wise words.

I took some time away from work and travelled to Scotland.

When I could be alone with him I explained the unfolding situation. He was resting on his bed and listened lovingly, until finally he spoke.

«In Burma, when a couple divorce often the man moves to the other side of the country and never sees his children again.»

I didn't say anything, but the strong all pervasive thought came, 'that will never happen to me.'

Perhaps that is why he spoke like that, for me to resolve that even without a marriage I could always be a father, after all, this is not Burma.

Then came the next part of our conversation. «Bhante, do you think it is possible I could come to live with you?»

Without hesitation he said «Yes, you are always welcome, but you cannot come straight away. As Buddhist people we cannot be seen to encourage the break up of families, but come in some weeks and you will be welcome.»

Simply put, that is what happened. Fiona and I sorted out our affairs, I took my few items of clothing, the little bit of money that was due to me, cut off my hair and left everything else.

I married Isis on the fifth day of May,
But I could not hold on to her very long
so I cut off my hair and I rode straight away,
for the wild unknown country where I could not go wrong.
Isis, by Bob Dylan 1975

Once I settled in at the monastery I began to adjust to a new life. Except for the time I spent with Bhante, I didn't like it so much. The monastery was cold and I was still not sure about the next phase of my life. Is this what I really wanted?

Once again Bhante came to the rescue. Perhaps he realised that I needed something more dramatic than simply changing my address.

«Michael, do you have money?» he asked one morning.

«Yes, a little,» I replied.

«Enough to go to India?» he continued.

«I think so,» I replied cautiously.

«Good,» he said, «I want you to go to the four holy places and make a pilgrimage.»

Although there are many places in India special to Buddhist

tradition, the four principle places are Lumbini, the place of the Buddha's birth, about twenty eight kilometers inside the Nepalese border, Budh Gaya, the place of his enlightenment thirty five years later, the deer sanctuary at Sarnarth close to Varanasi, where he gave his first teaching, and Kusinagar where he died at the age of eighty.

I was excited because now I had a quest. Suddenly everything became clear, I would go to India, make my pilgrimage and come back to ordain again with my teacher, and live the rest of my life as a Buddhist monk.

Wonderful, that's what I would do.

I bought a Hindi language course, but never got past the first cassette. In the end I gave it away to another resident at the monastery, who I think did the same thing as me.

I also visited a small shop close to the monastery which was owned by a married couple from India. In my excitement I mentioned that I would be going to make a pilgrimage there in a few weeks. «Ah,» they said, «you will need many things to take with you.» and immediately sold me everything they could think of, convincing me that I would need it.

I arrived back at the monastery with lotion for sunburn, soap, toothpaste and toilet rolls. Everything in fact, as I found out immediately upon my arrival, you can buy anywhere in any town in India.

I applied for my six month tourist visa from the Indian consulate, bought a return ticket with British Airways, and on the eighth of December in my thirty ninth year took my place on the plane and left for India. Who knew what it could offer?

- PART 2 -

THE INDIA YEARS

A journey to Awakening

The flight to India was uneventful. Three movies, poor but exciting airplane food and no sleep.

My first taste of India had actually come at the check-in desk at Heathrow airport when I found myself in a mass of Indian families armed with so much luggage you could hardly believe it, plus black bin liners also filled with all the things believed necessary for the journey. As we all checked in it became evident that not everyone was traveling and whole families of three or more generations had come to say goodbye to one of their members.

I had been given a small bag by my teacher who told me it was filled with clothes that U.Nu had left behind and would I please take it to his daughter's house in New Delhi. I agreed of course, and when I was asked if I had packed the bag myself I lied convincingly and said «Yes.» I trusted my teacher and so I felt confident with my response.

We boarded our flight, took our seats, stood up, sat down, moved and finally settled and waited for take off.

Nine hours later we arrived at Indira Ghandi airport in New Delhi. As we began to disembark I suddenly felt nervous and my old friend fear arrived to taunt me again. In the same way as Mara had spoken to the Buddha just before his enlightenment, the voice was calm and reasonable, but worse, persistent.

'What are you doing here?' it said, 'coming half way around the world, and for what? What difference will it make if you see these four holy places, how will that change your life?'

And so it went on. I looked around to see if I could attach myself to anyone for company, but everyone else seemed secure in their choice to be here.

I followed the crowd, passed through the Indian security measures, collected my backpack and the small bag for U.Nu, changed my money into Indian Rupees, and looked for a prepaid taxi.

First stop was the apartment of Than Than Nu, the daughter of U.Nu, where I was graciously welcomed by her and her husband as an old friend, having met at the monastery during my time as a monk some years before. They offered me lunch and advised me to go to Budh Gaya, and most importantly instructed me on how to buy a train ticket.

I took another taxi to the railway station and joined a long, snake like queue of Westerners all waiting to buy their tickets out of New Delhi in the special office for non Indian travelers. Finally it was my turn.

«I would like a train to Budh Gaya,» I said.

«That is Gaya junction,» said the official without lifting his head. «Next train, three days.» Disappointed I accepted, showed my passport, paid my money and received my ticket.

Our business concluded I left, needing to find a place to stay for the next three days.

Although traveling in India is second nature to me now, this was my first time and I was nervous, tired and lost.

A married couple on the Isle of Man had given me the address of a retired army colonel and his wife who now had an upmarket guest house and so I went there.

I took a room, had dinner and went to bed only to be attacked so ferociously by hungry mosquitoes that eventually I had to drape clean underwear across my face to sleep.

The next day I took a pleasant breakfast, joined by a young married American couple and went to the famous Connaught Place. I bought a copy of the Lonely Planet guide book, and a few gifts to take home with me.

I didn't know how to find food that I could eat safely and began to struggle with my time in India. I felt that if things didn't improve quickly I would be home again for Christmas. I found myself wandering aimlessly until I had a strange and interesting experience. I was approached by a large and imposing Sikh man in a modern western three piece suit, a black turban and long beard.

«Come with me sir and I will tell you three things.»

What? What three things? What does he want from me? Lost in the moment I followed him.

We took a turning into a small alleyway and he told me he was a gifted psychic and could tell me my future, of course I would have to pay, but it would be in my best interest. However, to prove he could do these things he would write down on a piece of paper the three things he had mentioned. The first would be the name of my mother. The second would be my date of birth and the third would be the name of the woman who had hurt me.

O.K. I thought, let's do it, and handed over some rupees.

He took a piece of paper and a pencil from his pocket, wrote something and put the paper into my hand. A few more rupees and then the command to open the paper.

The first word was Violet, the correct name of my mother. The second was the digits of my birth, 13/12/1951, also correct and the third was the name of the woman who had hurt me, Fiona. I'm not sure that I agreed with his definition of her, but nevertheless, he was correct again.

Naturally I was completely impressed and handed over more money.

Then he told the things about my future he had promised. I don't remember any of them now except the one thing that was proven to be true less than one month later.

He said, «There is someone where you come from who is working behind your back. It is a man, and his name begins with the letter J.»

When I had left the Isle of Man to stay with my teacher before coming to India, I had left my treasured Buddhist group and prison visits in the capable hands of Jack. These were the things I loved and as Jack and I had worked so closely together for all those years, making retreats, bringing Sayadaw Rewata Dhamma, the spiritual director of the group, to the island, taking Dhamma into the prison, I felt sure that it would be safe and well protected in his hands.

One month after the meeting with this Sikh man in New Delhi I received two letters from people in the group saying that the group had disbanded because of Jack's behavior. He had attempted to be supremely authoritative and given orders to people as to what their new duties would be and tried to oust Sayadaw Rewata Dhamma as the spiritual director of the group and replace him with his own teacher, Ven Kemmadhammo. Of course, Ven Kemmadhammo immediately refused, himself being a disciple of Sayadaw Rewata Dhamma, and rebuked Jack for what could really be called a schism.

Later, when I returned from India I asked Jack about the situation with the prison and he informed me that he had contacted the authorities there and told them if they get any Buddhist prisoner's to let him know and he would come to see them.

There are no prisoners religious rights on the Isle of Man, and I had always felt that my responsibility was to make myself available and not wait to be called.

Perhaps this is why now I am so against what can be called popular spirituality where there can be a presentation of something honorable and noble, but no integrity or depth of understanding.

I shook hands with my fortune teller and said goodbye.

I took a motor rickshaw back to my lodgings, had a meal and went to my room. The next day, the door to my love for India opened.

I returned to Connaught Place in the morning, passing the time and shopping for more souvenirs when I found myself in a large store around lunch time. In my mind I was still working on a plan to go home as early as possible and meet my teacher without losing face, when one of the shop assistants approached me, «Excuse me sir,» he said, «it is time for lunch and we will close our shop now.»

«Oh,» I replied, «I'm sorry, I will leave.»

«No sir,» he continued, «that is not necessary. We would like to invite you to eat with us.»

This was a life changing moment. An opportunity to put down at least some of my fears and anxieties and surrender into the present. I took a breath and jumped at this gift in front of me.

«Thank you,» I said, «I will be very happy to join you.»

We sat together, perhaps ten men, in a large circle on the floor and ate using our hands, sharing not only a delicious meal, but a friendship based in a simple acceptance of the other.

The next day I took my train. I arrived at the station in good time only to be overwhelmed by the sheer number of people on the platform. I saw one young Western man sitting quite high on some boxes and made my way towards him.

We nodded at each other and I spoke.

«Wow, the platform is really full,» I said in the most casual voice I could muster, the anxiety having presented itself again.

«Yes,» he said quite dreamily, «a sea of people.»

I hated him for that. For not supporting my fear. For thinking this is quite acceptable, so many people wandering around obviously knowing exactly what they were supposed to do. I wanted to leave this terrible person, but I stayed close, for my own sense of protection.

Eventually the train arrived and everybody boarded. According to Indian train regulations, everyone must have a ticket and a seat, hence the delay of three days. I found my place in the third class compartment and sat on the hard wooden bench, surrounded by some of the poorest people I had ever met. It felt like a scene from the film 'Gandhi' and I was suddenly the romantic hero on my epic journey.

«Sir, sir,» came a friendly and helpful voice, «this is not your place, your seat is at the other end of the train, in 2A.C.»

I said thank you, took my backpack and left the carriage.

I moved to the other end of this long train and found my name on a list on the door of a compartment. Second Class with Air

Conditioning. This is where westerners and educated Indians travel. I found my seat, breathed a sigh of relief, greeted the middle class Indian men, all with excellent English, and for the second time in two days began to feel slightly more comfortable in this strange country. This, although different from Europe, felt much more familiar than the chaos outside and at the other end of the train, and very much more organized, with guards, ticket collectors in their uniforms and specific duties.

Vegetarian food was brought and an endless supply of chai and coffee, plus clean sheets and a blanket for the overnight part of the journey.

Now I really relaxed and actually began to enjoy the long train journey. There is something special for me about the Indian trains. People speak, share food, engage with each other. The journeys are long with many stops, and there is an endless supply of food and drink. Of course, by the end of such long journeys the toilets leave something to be desired, but nevertheless, I love Indian trains.

I slept when it was time to sleep and was awakened with a breakfast of a 'bread omelette', with chili and ketchup, delicious. The train was only four hours late arriving at Gaya junction, which in those days was almost early, and I said goodbye to the welcoming company I had enjoyed and disembarked.

Gaya town is a place to pass through as quickly as possible and that is exactly what I did. The dirt, noise and enormous crowds of people was once again overwhelming but a young rickshaw driver grabbed my arm and said, «Come, come, Budh Gaya sir.»

I went with him to his cycle rickshaw, we negotiated a price and we set off. Actually I gave him what he asked for and ever since have encouraged Europeans and all other travelers to give generously and more than is asked, to these hard working people. After half an hour we were outside the town into what I describe now as Buddha country. This is where the Buddha had lived for the six years before his enlightenment and now I was seeing it, not from a bus or auto rickshaw, but sitting in the morning sun, listening to nature and the heavy breathing of the rickshaw boy as he brought me nearer to the first part of my pilgrimage.

We stopped for chai along the way, and I felt the excitement rising to soon see the famous Bodhi tree, the place of the Buddha's enlightenment. I imagined a field with cows wandering freely and a large tree, something like an English oak standing in the middle. 'I'll take a look,' I thought 'and then see what I will do after that. Maybe I can still be home for Christmas?'

Eventually we arrived on the outskirts of Budh Gaya at the famous Burmese Vihar, a small monastery combined with simple guest accomodation. I paid Koulu the rickshaw boy, took a small room, rather like a monk's cell equipped with only a hard wooden bed and a slim mattress for five rupees a night and went to see the tree in the field.

In those days Budh Gaya consisted of one long narrow street with the Gandhi statue at the end. The road then forked to the Indian market on the left or right to the field.

Except of course it wasn't a field.

The place of the Bodhi tree is something like a small spiritual park, identifying seven events in the life of the Buddha beginning with his enlightenment. Four are considered to be accurate representations that happened in this place and three are symbolic, the actual events having happened slightly further afield.

It is a well kept holy place and visitors are invited and made welcome. The huge tower stands at the foot of the steps and pathway of the entrance and then three paths in concentric circles following the circumference of the whole park, each path slightly shorter than the preceeding one as it was closer to the Bodhi tree itself. In those early days there were no railings around the tree and we could touch it easily and meditate underneath its branches as Siddhartha had done. This however, is not the original tree, but a third generation descendant.

It took my breath away and with it all my doubts. Now I knew why I was here. I wandered around this beautiful place drinking in the atmosphere, tears in my eyes.

I had arrived. It was December thirteenth, my fortieth birthday, and my new life had begun.

I went into the small restaurant and shop area of the town and ate. No problem with food here. I saw other Westerners and we spoke a little in a friendly way. They were all here to make some kind of spiritual practice, and were happy to talk about it.

I wandered back to the Burmese Vihar all the while trying to decide how long I would stay in Budh Gaya for, then I had it! According to the Buddhist story the Buddha stayed here for seven weeks after his enlightenment, and so that is what I would do. I devised a daily spiritual practice for myself, bought Indian clothes, and surrendered into Budh Gaya. This was the best birthday gift I had ever received.

Now I had my plan and a reason to be here. Budh Gaya then was a small, hospitable social place and so it was easy to meet people and interact with them. First the tailor. I needed Indian clothes for the warm weather and I wanted to be part of the town as someone who lived here rather than just a tourist or traveller. I dressed in the simple Indian style of kurta and pajama (long shirt and wide trousers) and presented myself all in white as this is the colour of the clothes of pilgrims and Buddhist devotees, called Anagarikas. I created my own programme which I adhered to every day without fail.

I would rise early, meditate alone for an hour in the Dhamma hall at the Vihara, then go to the temple complex and perform Kora. This means to circumambulate the whole area of the stupa three times in silent contemplation. This was always such a beautiful experience for me as the sun was rising and as often as possible I would walk barefoot.

The Kora would take about one hour. Then back to the Burmese Vihar and to Gautam's café opposite for a breakfast of cinnamon roll and coffee, plus a meeting with a small group of people who were staying long term for their own reasons. Next a shower in cold water (this was not by choice, there was simply no hot water available) which although was uncomfortable suited my then still quite strong ascetic tendencies.

My self-imposed discipline would continue and I would visit every temple in the town and bow three times in front of its Buddha statue. This would be followed by lunch, more conversation and resting until it would be time to hear the Theravada monks chanting at the stupa in the evening, followed by another set of three Kora, this time in the light of oil lamps placed by the Tibetan community on the low walls approximately every meter.

This routine represented a perfect day for me and I felt a new clarity in the direction of my life. It was clear now that I would visit the four holy places, go home and ordain with my teacher and now, as a development of that idea, live in a kuti, a small wooden hut, in the garden of the monastery. This plan became known in the town, and it seemed that I gained some small degree of fame until I was even invited to ordain immediately under the Bodhi tree by the monks at the Mahabodhi Temple, the governing body of the main temple complex. I was flattered of course but declined for two principle reasons. The first was that I really wanted to stay close to my teacher in England, and the second was that I enjoyed 'good' ground coffee in the morning, and that was impossible to find here. The best that was offered was a well-known instant blend.

So, my destiny was fixed, at least in my mind, what could possibly go wrong?

As my routine became more familiar to the local residents of Budh Gaya I soon became known as a dedicated disciple and was called Yatra, simply meaning pilgrim.

As always, even if my commitment was complete, I was as invisible as I could be and did not make an obvious show of any kind of special behavior.

This has always been my way of training, never to make a deliberate show of what I was doing.

One day a young western man approached me in the street and asked if I was the Vipassana man. I wasn't sure if I was but I said a hesitant yes.

«Will you teach the meditation to a few of us in Budh Gaya please, it seems that there is only Tibetan Buddhism here?» he continued. I was reluctant. I hadn't come for this and actually I was enjoying my simple daily routine, but in honor of my teacher and the place I was in, the true home of Vipassana meditation, I agreed and set about organising something.

I had spoken many times with Sayadaw U Nyaneindagane, also conveniently known as Bhante, the abbot of the Burmese Vihar and he had met my teacher some years before so when I asked if I could use his Dhamma hall to present Vipassana meditation and teachings he readily agreed. I announced my intention to offer short teachings in the Burmese Vihar and was surprised by the response. We began at three o'clock that afternoon with perhaps fifteen people sitting and receiving instruction.

So here I was, teaching Vipassana practice in the holy town of Budh Gaya, what more could the universe offer?

One day, after the one hour Dhamma session with the newly formed meditation group, I arrived at café Om to drink a cup of green tea and take a slice of cake for which café Om was famous. It was empty at that time of day except for a young man I had met before sitting with an attractive young woman. I joined them and we spoke a little until the young man stood up, threw his backpack over his shoulder and announced that he was leaving for New Delhi. I was a little taken aback, but wished him a safe journey and he left, leaving me alone with this attractive young woman.

Her name was Maria and she was a German woman of twenty seven. Her personality was to be bright, funny and intelligent and she impressively spoke five languages. I don't know what she saw in me but we immediately liked each other.

After some time I said that I had to leave to hear the monks chanting at the stupa.

«Oh, I would love to hear the monks chant,» she said, and that was that. She became another great blessing in my life and for those few weeks we knew each other in Budh Gaya we became close and affectionate friends. I taught her meditation to calm her mind, and she threw my life into incredible confusion. What a gift she was.

From that moment of meeting, outside my own pilgrim practice and meditation teaching, I spent most of my time with Maria. I took her around the stupa and explained the significance of the seven areas located inside the perimeter walls and shared the story of the break up of my marriage.

On one occasion whilst walking together around the stupa in the warm December sunshine I asked her what on earth she saw in me, a forty year old married man, father of two sons, who had been working as a storeman in a warehouse on a small island in the Irish Sea?

She stopped and looked at me with amazement in her eyes, «But that's not how we know you,» she said.

It was a powerful teaching for me. That list of things was not who I was, it was only a once convenient identity I carried with me, now no longer useful.

However, this eye opening teaching was not her most important point, as U.Nu had said repeatedly as I sat on a fire of pain as a new monk, all those years ago.

One afternoon we were sitting together in the famous café Om, discussing many things when, as part of the conversation, I said the four words that changed the direction of my life.

«I just like people,» said in reference to a comment from her.
She suddenly became serious, grabbed my arm and said, «Michael, you must come with me,» and marched me to what was then the smartest place in Budh Gaya, the Ashok Hotel and ordered tea and cucumber sandwiches for both of us.
This was all very nice, but I felt a sense of foreboding. I waited, and then she spoke.
«Michael, we are friends and so I speak in an honest way to you. You must not become a monk again.»
These words were like a knife in my heart. My plans were made, my new life was clear. Why did she say that?
«Because,» she began, «you are able to share this teaching in a way that is accessible for others, Buddhist or not. If you become a monk, only people interested in Buddhism will come to hear you, and so your voice will be lost to the others. None of your students here are Buddhist, and yet we all hold onto your words. I tell you now as your friend, you must not become a monk again. And also,» she finished, «perhaps you are really only looking for another family to replace the one you think you have lost?»
She was right of course, and ultimately I saw the wisdom of her argument, but it was not easy for me to let go of my plan.
Buddhism in the Theravada style, had been such a great gift in my life. A support for my practice and a structure for my day to day life and my way to be. But now it was time to put it down and be 'no-one' and 'no-thing'.
The Buddha was not Buddhist and he was my hero, and so I committed myself to sharing Dhamma so that all beings could benefit from hearing and then applying the teachings of liberation, which ultimately of course, are not Buddhist.
I sat there in shock, not only at her words but at the impact I felt in my heart.
Perhaps she was right? Perhaps I should not be a monk? Perhaps I should stay in the world? But what would I do? How and where

would I live? My head spun like this and sleep did not come easy. Monk or not my Dhamma practice in my life was well established and I would not abandon that, and so I arose at my usual time and sat in my room, went to the stupa and performed my Kora. Arriving at Gautams café my head was clear. Thank you Maria, I knew now that I would not be a monk again. I would stay in the world, serve my teacher, play my guitar and live my life.
I told my group of breakfast friends and they supported my decision.
This clarity however, did not last and a few hours later my doubts reappeared and my decision changed. Of course I would be a monk. What else was there for me? I have dreamed of this life for so many years, and anyway, my teacher is waiting.
I played this intellectual game of tennis, going backwards and forwards in my mind for five weeks until one evening in Varanasi, sitting with another young woman drinking coffee, everything became clear. No decision had to be made, the universe showed me the way. Finally there was a peace around this situation that has never left me.
The young woman was a Swedish traveler called Titti, who had come to learn meditation with me at the Burmese Vihar. We also became friends and when it was time for her to leave India to return to her boyfriend in Sweden she asked if I would accompany her to Varanasi where she would take a flight for the first part of her journey home.
I said yes, and we travelled together on the short journey by train. It is not uncommon for single women to ask fellow male travelers to accompany them on train journeys as often the staring eyes of Indian men can make them feel uncomfortable.
That evening we sat outside at the Mir Ghat, the main access to the holy river Ganges, and drank a coffee.
«Please tell me again about Loving Kindness practice,» she asked. I spoke for some time about the thing I loved so much and I

noticed her gently gazing at me.
«What?» I asked.
«You know, you speak so beautifully, so clearly and so wisely about Loving Kindness, there is no doubt for me that you were born to do this,» she answered.
«You should make your life teaching this and helping others.»
And that was it. In that moment all the doubts and confusion lifted from me and never returned.
We left for the airport and embraced and said goodbye. She said that I had changed her life. Little did she know of the impact she had on mine.
I watched her enter the departure lounge, one final smile and wave, and she was gone. I never saw her again.
I took the train back to Budh Gaya, went to my simple cell at the Burmese Vihar, and slept a deep and peaceful sleep.
The next morning I continued my practice, but this time with a smile in my heart.

Christmas arrived and as the sun shone down on a bright December day I and a group of friends held a picnic on the flat roof of the Burmese Vihar. It didn't feel like Christmas but we shared a few gifts and sang the words to the carols we could remember and enjoyed the experience. Very spicy curry for lunch was not a tradition I was used to, but an Indian chef made an offer of food for us and so we accepted.
«Is it spicy?» somebody asked.
«No sir, not spicy,» came the reply we knew to be a lie.
It almost burned the tongues out of our mouths. Wonderful!
Then new year.
I was now forty and was living a life I never could have imagined. I was finding a part of me that had long been asleep, encouraged first by Maria and Titti, and everyone else. India gives the idea that anything is possible and I was in the process of laying an old

me down to sleep, never to awaken.

To celebrate this change I wanted to do something significant, and so on the thirty first of December, whilst sitting in the Burmese Vihar, I publicly had my beard shaved off.

Apart from the time when I was a monk, I had worn my beard consistently for fourteen years, principally because I didn't like to shave, but also it was a fashion in those days. I had forgotten how my face looked without it and was surprised when a still young open face appeared from behind the shaving cream, to the laughter and applause of those watching.

We sat around together drinking chai until eleven o'clock when we went to the Japanese temple for the new year ceremony. There was meditation, chanting, incense and monks banging on blocks of wood shaped like fish. All very enjoyable.

At midnight we went outside to bang the big temple bell.

This was done by slowly swinging a huge piece of wood suspended on ropes backward and forward until it's momentum brought it crashing into the bell. The sound was deep and powerful and everybody took a turn. It was always starting at the beginning as each time the bell was struck the momentum stopped. The ceremony lasted a long time, well into the night.

Then a small group of us walked back to our beds at the Burmese Vihar, quietly, gently and with great emotion, singing in unison, 'You've Got a Friend,' by James Taylor.

I think I have never felt as close to anyone as I did walking through the empty streets of Budh Gaya that night.

Now it was a new year, a new life and a new me. What was next?

Budh Gaya is considered to be not only a holy place, but a deeply spiritual place and this spirituality can reveal itself often in mysterious ways. Two instances during my first visit there come to mind, the first arriving at the beginning of my second week.

An apparently well-known Japanese Zen Master arrived in the

town with his disciples. There was a lot of excitement when it was advertised that he would give a public Dhamma Talk at the Japanese temple. I think that all the western travelers and at least one famous western teacher were there and we sat together and waited.

The Master arrived in his black robes, took his place and looked out at the audience. He began with a koan, speaking in his thick Japanese accent. Although I had never heard this particular koan before I understood it immediately, the insight cutting through any delusion about life and death like a knife. I realized in that moment that the universe had brought me to the right place at exactly the right time.

'The Buddha always resides at Vulture Peak' was the koan and it was the understanding of this that changed my relationship with life and death.

Vulture Peak (Gridhkut in Hindi) is an outcrop of rock, just outside the town of Rag Ghir, about two hours by car from Budh Gaya. This is the place where some two thousand six hundred years ago, the Buddha would spend the rains retreats with his attendant Ananda. This he did for many, many seasons and of course it is now possible to visit this place, to walk up Bimbisara's road to the outcrop of rock. Here many devoted Buddhists place garlands to honour the Buddha himself. During my first days in Budh Gaya I met a young guide who happily took me everywhere he said that the Buddha had been and on one occasion I went to Vulture Peak to place my garland and to pay my respects. The place is in the hills, and the view across the plain is quite magnificent. However, as much as I looked around Vulture Peak I did not see the Buddha there. He was not hiding behind any rocks, he was not trying to avoid being seen. He was simply not there. And yet, there was a certain feeling. A certain sense of awe, of peacefulness, of calm. A certain connectedness with the Buddha himself. Physically we can say that he definitely was not there, but emotionally and spiritually, the Buddha was everywhere, all in the same moment. It was only five months before this event that my father had died. It had been sudden with no warning whatsoever. My father and I were close, and although I peacefully accepted his death, I missed him no longer being in my life. There was an unfilled space that was still new to me. However, like the Buddha at Vulture Peak, he didn't go anywhere. He always lives in my memory and my heart, and in any moment, I need only turn my attention to him to see us together, laughing and sharing our time. Sitting in this crowded Dhamma Hall, listening to the Master, I understood this koan, fully and completely.

The Buddha is not here, but he is always here.

My father is not here, but he is always here.

The dead do not leave us, they do not go away never to return, they live with us forever in our hearts and in our memories. Physically, they could be living in another country and not able to visit us, but in our own personal reality, they don't go anywhere.

This is the understanding of the koan.

Some time after this experience I attended a Tibetan Buddhist Dhamma Talk. I have never been attracted to Tibetan Buddhism as I always found it too religious and 'high church' for my simple tastes, but it was an opportunity not to be missed.

The lama was an American Rimpoche and the theme was 'the wish fulfilling gem.'

Simply put, the highly symbolic teaching is that even if you could have a magic precious stone that could grant any wish, it's power is nothing compared to the supreme wisdom of Awakening.

The group attending was quite small, and I was definitely the outsider, missing the meaning of many of the subtle terms used by the devotees. Nevertheless the talk was quite interesting, and as my mind was still spinning from my recent conversation in the Ashok hotel with Maria only a few days earlier, this served as a good distraction from my still prominent confusion about my life. However, it became much more than that as I lay in my sleeping bag on my hard bed in my monks cell in the Burmese Vihar later that evening. At the end of my usual long practice filled day I fell into sleep and had two incredibly powerful dreams.

In the first dream I was holding in my hands the wish fulfilling gem. Suddenly its power consumed me and I was filled with brilliant light and physically began to tremble. It was then that it revealed its truth to me, that no matter what path I took in my life, I would always make Dhamma and the integrity of Dhamma my priority. The trembling in the dream shook me awake and I lay still and felt the clarity of what I had understood. The surface may be confused, but the depths were calm and clear. I was excited by what I had felt, but it was a complete revelation with no further questions to be answered. The road ahead may not always be clear, but it is always straight and so I relaxed and surrendered once more into sleep.

In the second dream a kindly but disembodied voice spoke to me and simply said, «take the red one, take the red one.»

Of course I didn't grasp what it could mean, but as it was only a dream, I didn't think too much about it until some months later, standing next to the Dalai Lama in McCloud Ganj, I understood its meaning.

My allotted time of seven weeks was moving smoothly along with my daily routine, now well established. Early morning meditation, Kora and meeting with friends and the students of our small Vipassana group, including Maria for breakfast and catching up of the news around the town.

One day we heard that an American Theravada Buddhist monk was coming to Budh Gaya and he would give a talk at the Burmese Vihar that evening. What was so interesting for me was that he lived in a cave in Thailand and he would give a film show to accompany his talk. My Dhamma life still had the quality of the ascetic, hence the bizzare pleasure of the hard bed in my simple monks cell and only cold water to shower with, and so I was excited at the prospect of hearing and seeing this man.

That evening we gathered in the large room above the monk's quarters in the Burmese Vihar and waited. The American monk arrived and as expected he was a lovely man and was able to tell a good story and so keep his audience interested.

Next came the film show and he talked us through his life of living in a cave.

Although I could not say that this monk was arrogant, he did belong to a tradition that are very proud of their practice, and that showed through as the film show began.

I think that I was not alone when we finally got to see the cave he lived in and many of us later agreed that it was better than the homes we had left in Europe and further afield. We could not say it was luxurious, but it was certainly well equipped and comfortable, not at all the way it sounded through the simple sentence, 'I live in a cave.'

The days passed and soon Maria was ready to leave. Budh Gaya is a small town and you really need a good reason to stay. I had one, she didn't, so it was time for her to move on.

She asked me to go with her, to be her traveling companion, but I declined. I had a purpose to be in India now and I felt comfortable in this place. It is only another reflection of my life that I would not be deterred from my objective.

Her train from Gaya junction to her next destination was in the middle of the night so we agreed to share a hotel room in Gaya and rest until it was time to go to the station. It was a pleasant, funny and sad evening as we had both touched and lightened the heart of the other, but impermanence is a truth of our life, and whatever begins must end.

We arrived on the platform with hundreds of Indian men, women and children and eventually the train pulled in. There is never an

urgency to board so we had time to say 'thank you,' and goodbye. We embraced each other as close friends do and held on to this moment of parting. I became aware of someone tapping me on the shoulder and so I broke our embrace to see what was happening. I turned to find an Indian man smiling at me, «Excuse me sir,» he said, «what is your country?»
This is a common question asked a hundred times a day. My usual response was always England. If I had mentioned the Isle of Man who knows where the conversation would have taken us, so I said with impatience, «England.»
«I have a friend in England, maybe you know him?» he continued. Maria boarded the train at the appropriate carriage and found her place. Eventually the train slowly began the long journey to its next destination and this woman who had so radically changed my life was moving away into the distance and into a memory. I went back to the hotel to sleep and think about the gift she had given me. Thank you Maria. We never met again.
Living in Budh Gaya at that time was a large Italian man named Roberto who had opened a restaurant serving very good Indian style Italian food.
I would go there often and Roberto and I became friends. Later he helped me to find a place to teach in Budh Gaya, but that was a year in the future.
The same group of travelers would assemble for lunch most days and one of this particular group was a young English woman called Sarah. We became friends, as was so easy to do in Budh Gaya and shared our ideas of traveling through India. I told her of my plans to visit the remaining three Buddhist holy places and she said that she would like to accompany me, if I would go with her later to Daramsala, to meet the Dalai Lama. By this time I was quite comfortable in India and with the idea of traveling by train or bus, both an adventure compared to similar journeys in Europe, so I readily agreed, but also stipulating that I would not stay in

Daramsala but just accompany her there.

I was still thinking about home and my sons and was feeling ready to finish my pilgrimage. So we were both happy with the arrangement and made our plans to move. My seven weeks were finished and so it was time.

I said goodbye to everyone I knew, which amounted to a lot of people, both local and travelers by this time, and took a train to Varanasi with Sarah.

The next place on my pilgrim's list was Sarnarth, the place of the Buddha's first teaching of Dhamma after his enlightenment under the Bodhi tree, known as the Dhammacakkapattavana Sutta, 'the turning of the wheel of the law.'

Sarnarth is a small village just thirteen kilometers from Varanasi and so a self-made opportunity to visit India's holiest city and river in advance of the great stupa where the Dhamma teachings of Siddhartha Gotoma were first heard easily presented itself.

We found a small guest house in Varanasi close to the river and shared a room, once again, not unusual for men and women simply traveling together.

The following morning I went alone to the Ganges and took a boat. We negotiated a price and I sat in the back in the pre-dawn light. The boatman rowed down the river past the hundreds of Indian men and women taking their early morning bath, the men almost naked and the women fully clothed in their saris. It was a wonderful and inspiring sight. Many people say that India is a deeply spiritual country, for myself I will say that it is a deeply religious country, and this religion is found on every corner, every home, every café and en masse at the beautiful river Ganges.

I sat looking at the river, the rising sun and the buildings that lined the banks in turn, lost in a fascination of the power of the place. Before you arrive on the Ganges, it is just a river, after you have traveled on it your life will never be the same!

The boat turned and my boatman began to row upstream. This is hard work and is why I always ensure that I pay the right price to all the hardworking people in India. Not too much, I'm not a day old traveller any more, but I will not argue and negotiate like some westerners over five rupees.

I let my hand trail in the holy water reminding myself not to put it near my mouth until I had washed it well. The morning had been cold but now as the sun pulled itself above the horizon its gentle warming heat met me. I took as many photographs as I could, but this was the pre digital age and so I had to take care to leave some unused film in the camera. Finally we reached the furthermost part of our journey and the boatman pulled into the side to rest and smoke a bidi, a cheap Indian cigarette.

«Burning Ghats sir,» he said pointing at a neatly arranged stack of wood, «no pictures.»

My life has been blessed with significant spiritual moments and this was another.

A funeral was in process and a small wrapped body was placed on the stack of wood, which was of course the funeral pyre, and the family, led by the oldest surviving male carrying a flaming torch, walked around chanting. At the prescribed moment the torch touched the oil-soaked wood and the flames rose up.

It was such a powerful moment for me. There was death, not hidden or discreet, but in full view, and there was the family actively participating in the final moments of the body. My own father had died and everything was so clean and clinical. My stepmother and I were told to wait in the other room whilst the funeral director took care of the unpleasant aspect of dealing with a dead body. He was placed in a black bag and I never saw him again. But here it was not like that. Death was not seen as the enemy, but only a natural consequence of life. I reflected that if anything ever happened to my sons that caused their demise, I would like to walk around the pyre and light it to say a final goodbye.

I sat in the boat mesmerized by this beautiful scene and realized my hand was gently moving in the water. In the moment of that recognition a strange image came into my head of all the fear that I carried in my life running down my arm and into the river Ganges to be gently washed away by the current, never to return. That image stayed with me until twenty years later, once more in Varanasi, that slightly prophetic vision would come to pass.
We began downstream again and arrived quickly at the place we had started from. I stiffly climbed out of the boat, looked around, saw a chai stall and took my first drink of the day. It was now ten o'clock in the morning, time for breakfast and then Sarnarth.

We took an auto rickshaw for the thirteen kilometers to the village of Sarnarth and the enormous stupa that marks the place of the Buddha's first teaching. According to the legend, the Buddha left the forest of Uruvela and the Bodhi tree when a great compassion arose in his heart and he realized that it was his responsibility to share his understanding with the world, even if it would make difficulties for him sometimes. He headed for the holiest city in India which was then, as now, Varanasi. This would be equivalent to Jesus traveling to Jerusalem in the Christian tradition.
He reflected who he could first share this new revelation in the world with and he remembered his five former colleagues. They had all been training together with Gotama as the leader and inspiration to the others but they had become disillusioned with him when they saw him one day accept food rather than starving himself. This becomes an important part of the Buddhist story and the Dhamma path, that we need our strength to continue with the work that needs to be done. It was Venerable Saddhatissa's first question to me when I was a monk in robes and he had come to visit my teacher's monastery, 'are you getting enough to eat?'
For many years Gotama the ascetic ate almost nothing until he became a walking skeleton, (known as Kankal Buddha in the

Theravada tradition) and so fragile that one day he collapsed in the dirt and lay there weak from hunger, unable to move. He was found by a shepherd and nursed back to health and this is when he was seen accepting food. His five colleagues abandoned him and went to continue their ascetic training alone. They arrived at a small deer park on the outskirts of Varanasi, and lived quietly and without leadership continuing their hard-line ascetic practices.

The Buddha heard they were there and out of universal compassion and friendship went to them to share what he had understood. They were hostile at first, but in the face of love and wisdom their resistance faded and their hearts opened to receive Dhamma.

Naturally for me to be there was incredibly special, but the place itself is not particularly inspiring. There was a temple, the huge park that housed the stupa, a small area with deer and some excavations of an ancient monastery. I was pleased to be there, but was happier when we found a place to rest and take a cup of tea.

We returned to Varanasi and stayed for some days whilst we arranged our travel to the third place on my pilgrim list, Lumbini, just inside the border of Nepal.

Varanasi is a fantastic city, filled with millions of people of course, but alive and vibrant. To walk in the crowd and hear a particular drum beat getting closer and louder and watch a dead body on a stretcher being passed over your head on the way to the burning Ghats, is something special. To visit so many restaurants or eat in the street with everything happening around you, or just to sit at the river and reflect on the significance or lack of it in life. I fell in love with this place and in all my years of traveling in India never missed an opportunity to visit and receive its special energy.

The simplest way to reach Lumbini from Varanasi was by overnight bus. As with so many things, it was simple but not easy, but we were young and nothing seemed impossible, also it was part of the overall experience of India. We booked our tickets, arrived at the bus station in good time and eventually found our bus. This was not so comfortable for me as I was not feeling strong and thought that I might be a little ill. However, we took our turn for boarding, as our bags were thrown on the roof of the bus, and settled down. Unfortunately for me it was a video bus, which meant that films were shown all night and the volume was horrendous. By this time I had a fever, and slipped in and out of wakefulness and delirium as we continued our long and bumpy journey. The next day I felt better but nevertheless was happy to arrive at the border town of Sunauli where we would cross the border the next day. We found a small hotel and took a meal. The hotel was simple and clean and the one thing I really remember was a huge poster on the wall in the dining room showing Chinese mountains and rivers with a caption that added, 'if you find a place that makes you happy, go there.' Wonderful.

We crossed the border, having bought our visas for Nepal, and hired a taxi to take us to the birth place of the baby Siddhartha, the being destined to become the Buddha.

We arrived, had photographs taken at the historic sights, met a traveling Burmese monk who knew my teacher and had our photograph taken all together at the pillar that marks the birth place of the Buddha, played with the local children and shared biscuits with them. We found a guest house and stayed the night. As with so many things, the expectation was greater than the reality, and although I could not feel excited to be in these places, I do feel privileged to have seen them and walked where tradition said the greatest hero in my life had been.

Many years later in the house of Shakespeare in Stratford upon Avon, I had a similar feeling.

So, that was three down and one to go, what next.

We decided that we should visit Kathmandu, another simple but long bus ride. This is what we did and arrived in the early evening. The air was much cooler here, hotels more expensive and food many times better. In short it was wonderful. We did the expected tourist things and went to the district of Boudhnath and respectfully barefooted climbed the stupa there with its famous Buddha eyes, and the equally famous Kopan temple close by. This is a large Tibetan monastery, mostly closed to tourists, but where people can stay to have introductory courses in Tibetan Buddhism.

We also visited the tourist shopping area of Thamel, where I bought more gifts to eventually take home to my estranged wife and our children.

I had always been close to my father, and then in turn to my sons so it was not really surprising that I missed them a lot and so on impulse I decided to telephone them.

I called the house but was met by an answering machine telling me that there was no one there to take my call at the moment, but if I left a message someone would get back to me.

Surprisingly this shocked me.

We did not have an answering machine when I lived there, so that was new, but more than that, there was the uncomfortable revelation that life had not collapsed for my family because I was no longer there. This became a great teaching for me in later days when I was able to digest and reflect upon the significance, but in that moment it was like a knife in my stomach.

I carried this pain for two days until the teaching became clear. Life goes on and our place in any relationship, even if desired, is not really essential for happiness. No matter how highly we place ourselves in the life of others, the reality is that everyone will survive without us. As with all Dhamma truths, its realization brings peace and balance.

I wrote and sent more postcards to them and left it at that.

Eventually our time in Kathmandu was finished and we left for the fourth and last place on my pilgrim's list. This is where the Buddha died at the age of eighty having spent forty five years sharing his wisdom of love, compassion and equality to everyone who was interested. He met many difficulties as his very message of equality shook the foundations of Indian life, and now, as an old man, he sought a quiet forest place to surrender into death. He travelled with Ananda, his cousin and attendant and arrived at Kusinagar. This then was our next and last stop.

We took yet another bus ride and arrived at our destination. The journey itself took almost twelve hours and as with all these journeys contained dangers of landslides, rockfalls and small accidents that are always better not to think about.

However, we arrived and visited the temples and found another guest house.

Kusinagar is no longer a quiet forest but a bustling little town so finding somewhere to stay was not so difficult, however, finding food was.

There was some confusion about a meal and we waited and waited for the food we had ordered to arrive in our room. It never came but a crisis did.

On certain occasions I suffered and still sometimes suffer from hypoglycemia, where the blood sugar level drops rapidly. Mostly this means that my hands tremble a little bit and that I should eat something. However, it can be far more serious than that with the situation having the power to affect the mental processes creating a special form of amnesia and disorientation. In other words, feeling lost, confused and physically unstable. This is what was happening to me and Sarah and I left our room to find something to eat. This proved not to be as easy as we had hoped and I was failing fast. Happily, help arrived in the shape of a Burmese Buddhist monk who in some uncanny way saw my predicament, sat me down near a fire, shouted to someone to bring food. A plate of cabbage, rice and chapatti appeared as if by magic and I felt the gratitude well up inside me. I always feel blessed in my life, and although like everyone else, I meet difficulties, it seems that the universe sends someone to help me sooner or later.

As the food arrived in my stomach I immediately began to feel better and the three of us sat and talked until I was able to go back to our hotel room.

During certain Dhamma talks now, based upon this incident, I will often jokingly say that the Buddha died in Kusinagar, but I'm not surprised, I've been there and I almost died myself.

So, my pilgrimage was over. I had visited the four holy places and now, according to Buddhist tradition I was guaranteed a good rebirth. If that's really all it took, I could relax. Sarah had been a good companion and we served each other well, but now it was time to fulfill my part of the bargain, to accompany her to Dharamsala. She wanted to meet the Dalai Lama who would be there as it would soon be Tibetan New Year, and also attend some Tibetan Buddhist courses at the famous Tushita monastery.

I reiterated that I would travel with her but not stay. I had no interest in Tibetan Buddhism and was aching to go home.

Another two days of rough bus travel took us to Pathankot and then a short ride to Dharamsala and the old British army hill station of McLeod Ganj, where the residence in India of His Holiness the fourteenth Dalai Lama could be found. The bus wound its way up the hill, displaying the magnificent scenery of snow covered mountains and deep valleys of the outer chain of the Himalayas.

Finally we stopped at our destination and everyone got off. It was time to say goodbye, but something had happened to me. Suddenly and without warning I was in love with this place. I needed to be here, and I didn't know why, but I felt comfortable and almost at home. More and more I was in love with India, but this place had a similar emotional effect on me as Budh Gaya.

I told Sarah that I would stay for some days and she seemed happy with that. We looked for a room and found one at a guest house owned by the Tibetan lady who came to Budh Gaya each season and ran the café Om. She recognized me and offered a double

room at a good rate, and so we stayed.
Sarah began her daytime courses at the Tushita monastery, and I walked alone and meditated in the mountains. I found a small bar in Bhagsu Nag, a few kilometers along the quiet road, that served surprisingly good coffee, and spent time there in peace.
I loved this place and for whatever reason, it was nourishing the deepest part of me.
Sarah and I would meet every evening in a restaurant to share a meal together.
On one occasion I sat at a table and waited for my friend. She arrived like a demon, so angry and frustrated that it was impossible for her to be discreet about her feelings. She reached our table, noisily pulled out the chair and dramatically threw herself into it. Sighing out loud she looked at me, paused and sighed again. «What happened?» I asked, and so she recounted her experience at Tushita that afternoon. A course had been presented by a western Tibetan nun in which she had made the proclamation that birth is suffering, aging is suffering, sickness is suffering, death in suffering etc, etc. In short, life is suffering! This teaching had shocked her so much that she had been overwhelmed by fear and desperation, hence her bad mood. I listened patiently until she had finished talking and spoke simply and calmly, «But the Buddha never said that life was suffering.» I said. She glared at me and asked, «How do you know that?»
«Because he didn't speak English,» was my reply.
The First Noble Truth (Dukkha Ariya Sacca) often translated as 'life is suffering,' is truly one of the greatest teachings ever given to the world at any time in human history. However, the overly simplistic translation of the word Dukkha, reducing the First Noble Truth to 'life is suffering' is to misunderstand the gift of the Buddha completely. Life is not suffering, although it certainly can contain the qualities that we may call suffering, but even these moments, no matter how unpleasant they appear, are not absolute

truths, they are unique and personal to the being experiencing them.
What one person calls suffering, another simply may not.
We know from our own direct understanding that not everything in life is unpleasant, but until Awakening, whatever we meet will always have the quality of being unsatisfactory in one way or another. This means that every situation, gross or subtle, can be bettered in some way according to our own mind and preconceptions of how things should be. Happiness then, is always perceived as a goal in the future, something that will be achieved when everything is the way we need it to be so that we feel secure. Once we begin to grasp the notion that life does not change, but is only a continuing process of change, our understanding of the First Noble Truth spontaneously opens and can no longer be a simple repetition of what we have read or heard others say due to their own lack of understanding. Life is only what it is. The internal conditions and reactions that we each individually meet in life come from us and cannot be taken from us or given away. The world that we experience is the one that we create for ourselves, moment after moment. If the foundation for that world is that everything is suffering, how will we ever meet the joy that lives in our heart? We are responsible for the world we experience in every moment and so the purest Dhamma teaching, beyond gender inequality, beyond politics, beyond religion, beyond social or group manipulation, beyond self righteous segregation and cruelty, beyond the limitations of the fear based mind is simple: live with love and be aware. In this way you will be happy and share that happiness with all beings.

The days passed quietly and I reflected on my life. I was now forty years old, half way across the world from my little island, and had never felt happier. Everything seemed to be complete, the ambiance, friends from Budh Gaya arriving and afternoon cake and tea at the 'Chocolate Log,' a small tea house on a hill. We would meet there, eat cake and just 'be'.

Soon it was Tibetan New Year and everybody had the opportunity to meet briefly the Dalai Lama. Honestly, I didn't feel very interested, but as it only consisted of joining a very long queue and waiting for my turn, I did it. The line snaked closer to the compound, then through the gate, and finally, there he was.

He was standing in the same position for many hours greeting westerners as they were almost pushed past him by his attendant monks. I realized as my turn approached that I didn't know if I should say something or not, and then I was pushed directly in front of him. I lowered my head, put my hands together in Anjali and said, «Namaste Bhante.» Then I became aware of something and looked up. He had covered my hands with his and his big smiling face was only inches from mine. Our noses touched and he said, «Tasha Delek,» and that was that.

The moment seemed endless, and both space and time opened up before me.

I was gently maneuvered out of way so the next person could meet this beautiful man. Standing now in front of me were two more Tibetan monks handing out the traditional scarves called kata. One monk had white, the other had red.

«Take a red one,» the voice in the dream had said, so I took a red one.

I wandered away somewhat emotionally confused and saw a friend of mine from Budh Gaya standing in the distance. She was an older lady called Mira, who, the moment she saw me, opened her arms and welcomed me into them. I burst into tears and took shelter there.

Later I met Sarah and everyone else at the Chocolate Log, and we shared our moment of meeting the Dalai Lama. It was a nice day and we were all happy for it.

The next day Sarah and I had a big dispute.

I had travelled with this young woman who believed herself to be a Tibetan Buddhist and had come to receive teachings at the Tushita monastery. We were walking down the steep hill to the old Tibetan library when she asked me a question. «Do you believe that the Dalai Lama is enlightened?» As we had both individually met him the day before, the question did not seem to be strange. However, according to Buddhist teaching, it is not possible for someone who is not enlightened to recognize enlightenment in another, and so I answered in accordance with this. «I don't know,» I replied. There was a pause and suddenly she stopped in the middle of the road with her hands on her hips and fury in her eyes and exclaimed, «I don't believe you don't believe the Dalai Lama is enlightened!» Wanting something to be true does not make it true, and cultivating a belief around an idea only becomes divisive and ultimately destructive as all belief systems by their very nature end up by being in competition with each other. Whose god is the greatest, the most powerful, the most loving? Which spiritual system is quickest, the most efficient, the best?

The answer is always the same – mine! We build a life around belief, simply accepting what we have been told or what has been socially or culturally conditioned into us without ever investigating the possibility that it is mistaken. To simply accept as reality stories, fables and our pre-determined place in the universe helps us feel a part of a greater whole, and answers the need to feel secure in life at all times. Whenever we don't understand something, feel confused or disagree with another philosophy, we fall back on our belief system to feel secure again. We are right, you are wrong.

The view that the 'Dalai Lama is enlightened' makes me feel secure in my pursuit of Buddhist teaching. If you don't agree with me, suddenly I'm afraid and alone again. So I need that you not only agree with me, but that my belief is never challenged.

Life is always uncertain, but that uncertainty is not threatening once the fear based controlling aspect of mind (ego) has fallen away. Then we will be at peace with the reality of the moment. It is not possible to know everything about everything and so sometimes it is simply honest to say, 'I don't know,' and to be at peace with that.

To be empty of belief means to be free. It is the mind that holds us prisoner, and our views, opinions and beliefs that make that prison comfortable. True Dhamma training is a very mature approach to life and living and tells you always not to accept things at face value and never believe anything. Not books, not stories, not even the words of the teacher. Belief is not the truth, belief is what we cultivate when we don't know the truth! So as disciples of Dhamma we turn away from belief and blind faith and take our attention to the constant ebb and flow, to the apparent reality of this being we call 'self' and surrender into truth. There is nothing that you really are and no way that you have to be, and however you can point to books, teachings and traditions, you are responsible for you and your speech and actions in every moment, so take care with your life, because every delusion or misunderstood truth you empower has a consequence. Live with love for yourself and all beings, in this place you will not feel the need of any kind of belief.

So, in the end there is no need to believe something, just be open to all possibilities. Don't reject, but don't grasp either.

Of course it was not more than a difference of opinion, but everything in India was teaching me something, and one of the things it showed me was that even here, in the land of the Buddha and Buddhism, I am still destined to be the 'odd one,' the one who takes Dhamma above belief systems in every moment.

The days passed and life went on. It is easy to stay somewhere comfortable in India for westerners where our money goes a long way. We can be poor in our own country but live like millionaires there.

Sarah continued her courses at Tushita and I continued my practice of meditating in the mountains and drinking coffee in Bhagsu Nag. The weather began to change and it was time to leave.

We travelled together, eventually arriving in Varanasi, where we finally said goodbye. She continued on to Puna, close to Bombay, where she abandoned her interest in Tibetan Buddhism and became a follower of Osho, the new identity of Bhagwan Shree Rajneesh.

For whatever reason I kept delaying my return to the United Kingdom, whilst being curious how life would be after India. That I was different was evident, but that I also looked different was clear. My hair was long again, my skin tanned and healthy and I wore two earrings now, the first I put in my earlobe on the Isle of Man using the almost closed hole from my youth, before Fiona and I separated, and the second, a small yin and yang stud, I had inserted via a piercing gun in a shop in the tourist area of Kathmandu. I'm happy tattoos and the now fashionable style of body piercing was not popular in those days, if so who knows what I would have come home with?

In the end I changed my flight date once more and arrived in New Delhi ready to go home. I had decided to go via Birmingham and see my teacher, and from there I would fly to the Isle of Man when I was ready. In all I had stayed in India for six months. Everything in my life felt different, but it was over and I knew I would never go back. I put my hands together in Anjali and said thank you to this wonderful country, but I must have been distracted for a moment because I didn't hear her say, «Not so fast my son, we've only just begun our relationship. I have gifts for you, so I will wait for you next time.»

I arrived at the monastery in Birmingham and rang the bell.

Someone that I didn't know answered but standing in the hallway smiling broadly at me was Sayadaw Rewata Dhamma, my teacher and greatest inspiration in my life.

News of me teaching in Budh Gaya had apparently arrived at the monastery before me and as I entered to pay my respects he said in his loving laughing voice, «So Michael, now you are a guru?»

«No, no Bhante,» I answered, «I just share with others what you have shared with me.»

He lowered his voice and said as my father would have said, «This is good and you can do it, but make sure you receive enough money. If you are not a monk you must live in the world, for this you need an income.»

Burmese monk or not, he knew how the world worked and his blessing naturally meant everything to me.

I stayed some days and spoke about my experiences during the past six months. I was often gently mocked (such an important part of training - don't take yourself so seriously) but incredibly supported by Bhante and Mar Mar Lwin. However, I wanted to see my boys so I booked a flight home and arrived at Ronaldsway airport.

Now, the next part of my life.

The family reunion was everything I wished it could be. For my sons and even Fiona, I arrived as a traveling hero, somehow exotic and interesting with a backpack full of Indian gifts.

An older lady friend of mine called Pam, a long time member of the now defunct Isle of Man Buddhist group offered me a place to stay indefinitely and I took it. I was now back on the Isle of Man, living in the town of Ramsey, visiting the house I used to own and wondering how I could make my way in the world as a Vipassana teacher.

Pam was like my favourite auntie and enthusiastic meditation student rolled into one. We would sit up until the early hours of the morning talking about Vipassana and Dhamma training and she was one of the kindest people I ever met.

A few years before my life changing venture to India I had given Pam a ride home in my car after a meditation meeting. With me were Fiona and Michael and Adam, and so Pam sat in the back between the boys who would be around six and eight years old respectively. She was an attractive older lady with a slightly hooked nose and now wearing a large fur coat.

Michael and Adam were fascinated by her presence in the car and couldn't help looking at her.

There was a pause until she looked at the two children sitting next to her and with a twinkle in her eye and a whispered voice announced, «I'm a witch.»

In that moment you could not imagine two more delighted boys. A witch, a real witch in our car. How could life be better than this? Pam became a firm favourite of all of us from that moment.

I wanted to see Jack again and so contacted him and called at his house. He looked the same as when we had last been together, but his behavior towards me was different.

«Since you left,» he said, «I have found another Path and have discovered many things.»

He then told me that he had been a disciple of the Buddha in a previous life. He had apparently discovered this with the use of a pendulum and by asking questions and spelling out words with the letters it pointed to, he was able to discover things about his past lives.

In this life, he was an ordinary working man, holding down a job in a factory and living with his family. So I pointed this out.

«You used to be a disciple of the Buddha, living the homeless life and seeking enlightenment, but now you are a married man and work in a factory. Are you sure you're going in the right direction?»

This comment was not well received, and it emphasized the

ending of a relationship that had been a wonderful gift in my life for many, many reasons, and for ever, I put my hands together and say thank you to this particular being and everything he brought to me. But, Dhamma is precious and it requires integrity. If we don't stay on the path how will we ever arrive in the place of freedom? Picking up new identities and ideas are in the end, only more things to carry.

I have always felt blessed with my training and especially that I had a teacher who out of love and compassion for me would never let the idea of being someone special in front of others take a place in my mind. My raison d'etre was to serve and honour Dhamma, as he had done.

Many years before whilst on one of my hundreds of intensive ten day Vipassana and Loving Kindness retreat with my teacher, myself and the small group I was part of were meditating in the Dhamma hall. Sayadaw Rewata Dhamma was in front of us and when the meditation ended, he did not move. This could only mean one thing, he was going to present a Dhamma talk. This was always a source of joy to me, to listen to his words, to take them inside and reflect upon what he had said. The Buddha himself (according to Theravada tradition) has said that to hear the Dhamma is one of the thirty eight blessings in life (The Mangala Sutta), and certainly this was always my experience.

I could and did, meditate at home three times a day, but to hear the words of Dhamma from him was always something exceptional and to be with a true Master, having already been accepted as a disciple, can only ever be experienced as an honour and a privilege.

However, the only role of the Master is to present Dhamma and not allow the disciple to be fooled by anything – especially by themselves.

As we were sitting quietly my teacher looked at me and spoke.

«Michael, what do you understand by the word, ardent?» Ardent is a word found many times in the suttas to describe the necessary attitude of the true disciple. I felt pleased and honoured that in front of the others he would choose me to define this important word and so I gave the standard definition.

«Bhante, ardent means to be determined, to be focused on practice, to be disciplined and to make liberation our goal.»

«Yes,» he replied, «So why are you sitting with your watch in front of you?»

He got me!

I wasn't sitting for enlightenment, liberation or Nibbana, I was sitting for an hour.

It's not the same thing!

Every time I would enter the Dhamma hall I would take off my wristwatch and gently place it in front of me. Then I would time the meditation. One hour (in those days) and not a second more. If someone didn't ring the bell at the right moment a lot of coughing and throat clearing would follow!

It may be obvious that from that moment I never brought my watch into the Dhamma hall again, and always surrendered completely to the meditation.

The gift of the Master is the training given to their disciples. There was no intention in my teacher's mind to embarrass or humiliate me, such a thought would not occur to him, only to show directly that beyond the physicality of my sitting posture, something was missing.

Dividing our life into time slots is common and can be useful in daily life, but Dhamma demands much more than that. Dhamma demands total immersion whether we are sitting, standing, walking or lying down.

Dhamma demands that we are determined, focused on our practice, disciplined and that we make liberation our goal.

Dhamma demands that we are ardent.

I had been encouraged to be a professional meditation teacher, by friends in India where everything seems possible, to my teacher who reminded me to ensure I received enough money to live. But how, how could I do it?

I would lie in my bed at night reflecting on how I could possibly make this work but never found a solution. In fact, the fear of the empty space in my life opening in front of me like a deep black abyss manifested on at least two separate occasions when I woke up in the morning so full of fear I wanted to vomit.

Happily help arrived in the shape of my Buddhist monk friend Bodhidhamma. He had come to stay with me at Pam's to make a small weekend retreat in her house. We spoke at length and he too supported my idea to be a professional meditation teacher.

I was still struggling with the notion of how to put this into practice and felt that time was running out.

«You need to give yourself seven years to see if it is a viable proposition,» he said.

Seven years, that seems like a life time. Thank you Bodhidhamma for lifting the self-imposed stress from my shoulders. Seven years, that's better, now I can relax a little bit. But still, I didn't know how to do it!

Then, many weeks later I finally experienced relief, I had the solution and I knew what I had to do.

All of this had begun in India, and it was India who had the answer. I would return and see what she had to say about my predicament. I collected the remaining money I had from my separation from Fiona and booked a flight to India. In the pre internet days the best way to find cheap flights was through a 'bucket shop,' and so I called a number and made my enquiries. A very pleasant young man found an excellent price for me with an airline called 'Ariane'.

«I haven't heard of them,» I said, «are they good?»

«Oh yes,» he lied, «we have very good reports about them.»

«And I fly from Heathrow?» I continued sounding like a seasoned

traveler.
«No, the India leg begins at Prague, but this is all part of your ticket price.»
«O.K. I'll take it,» I finished, and that was that.
The day came and I said goodbye to everyone once again. The Buddhist group had reformed under my guidance newly returned from India and the four holy places, but now would rest again until I came back.
I said goodbye to my family and set off to find some direction and clarity in my life.
I arrived at Prague airport and was put with a small group of westerners all waiting for the flight to India. It was here that we found that Ariane Airlines was in fact the national airline of Afghanistan, and as a consequence this would not be an easy journey.
A young drunken Scotsman took issue with me about meditation but I remained calm and did not react in any way, all the while being discreetly observed by a young man traveling with his girlfriend.
Finally the flight was called and we took to the skies, first stop, Kabul. We circled the airfield at Kabul many times before landing able to see the burnt out areoplanes pushed off the runway to enable other planes to take off and land. Soon it was our turn. We landed and taxied without difficulty but I think all of us were nervous about the sights we were looking at and what lay ahead. There were militiamen with automatic weapons everywhere and we were escorted into a building to await a connecting flight. Actually there was no problem at all but we were all happy to board the next flight to New Delhi.
Finally we arrived and I felt as though I was in home ground again.
I took a small room in the Paharganj district and went to the station, at the end of the long street of a thousand shops and stalls,

and a million people. I was able to get a ticket to Gaya Junction for the next afternoon so now I could change from my jeans and tee shirt into more comfortable Indian style dress.

This time the journey was easy. I was a traveler now, I knew how to do things and not be exploited too much by the street people in New Delhi. In truth, I never really minded paying more than the real price. These people are poor and we are like millionaires by comparison. It was only that I didn't ever want to be taken for a fool.

Two rules of being in the beautiful country of India, never be in a hurry, and never tell anyone it's your first time even if it's apparent to them that it really is. In this way all will go well.

I slept and rested in the morning and eventually went for lunch. I was sitting in the window eating something simple with my bag at my side in preparation for my train journey later that day when a young couple walking past noticed me and tapped on the window. It was two of my fellow passengers from the flight the day before. They came in and sat with me. The young man was called Henry and the young woman, Clara. Henry bombarded me with questions about meditation telling me that he had been impressed by my peaceful refusal to be drawn into an argument in Prague airport when I was confronted by the young Scotsman.

We spoke a lot and I answered his questions as best I could, until finally it was time to take my train. I said goodbye and maybe we will meet again.

When I was out of earshot Henry told Clara that I was the happiest person he had ever met, and he definitely wanted to meet me again.

We did, some months later. This was Henry Bowen, the man who became my retreat manager, assistant teacher, best friend and first true disciple. Our journey had just begun.

I arrived back in Budh Gaya in November that year where I checked into the Burmese Vihar and immediately felt at home.

On the first morning I took my breakfast of coffee and cinnamon roll at Gautam's across the road and found myself in conversation with new friends. One of them was a young Italian woman named Francesca who quickly took her own place in shaping my life again. We spoke, made our Dhamma connection and I revealed my reason for returning to India.

«I only do this because my teacher told me to,» I said, «and my life is in turmoil. I teach on his direct instruction, and I certainly don't want to fail him.»

Francesca was impressed by that and offered to help me.

We wandered down to Roberto's restaurant where I received a bear hug from this giant man and a beautiful welcome back to India and Budh Gaya.

Once again I explained the situation and it was Roberto who gave the solution.

«You must teach here in Budh Gaya, something simple like on your island. An introduction to Vipassana and Metta Bhavana. No one else is doing that, and last year you began in the Burmese Vihar.» His mind was moving quickly now like something from a Hollywood movie about a bank heist.

«I have the very place, and it's available, come with me.»

I felt myself carried along by the enthusiasm of these two Italian people, perhaps it's cultural, but I was surprised and a little nervous that things were happening so quickly.

We arrived at the main stupa and then to the Lotus Tank. This is a huge pool of water covered by lotus flowers and a giant statue of the Buddha in the middle with a great snake (Naga) protecting him from a storm while he continues his meditation.

In the far corner was a stone bench and space for people to sit on the ground.

«Here,» he said, «you can do it here.»

This needed some thought but for Roberto and Francesca it was already arranged. First we would need some posters and at the same time tell everyone we could that free Vipassana teachings would be given at the Lotus Tank every morning at nine o'clock, and we'll begin next Monday.

I stood silently by, almost in shock, at the speed of what was happening, but realized, that this is exactly why I had returned!

Francesca and I sat in the Burmese Vihar preparing posters and meeting people. My name it seems was still favorably remembered from the year before when I gave teachings in the Dhamma hall of the Burmese Vihar, and it was helpful when some of those old students appeared in Budh Gaya and spread the word by speaking kindly about me to fellow travelers.

The rest of the week passed quietly and the great day of Monday arrived. Waiting for me at what was to become known for the next few years as 'the Vipassana corner' at the Lotus Tank was a good number of people, perhaps ten or twelve all sitting on blankets and cushions that they had brought with them. I arrived with Francesca and took the teacher's place, a concrete bench in the corner while she introduced herself and presented me. It was interesting for me that people were so impressed when she announced that I was actually in India sharing these most important teachings expressly on my own teachers instruction. Even now I do not know any other western teachers who were instructed to do this by their own Masters.

The course began and we met twice a day. Once in the morning for instruction and practice and once in the afternoon for a Dhamma talk. This introductory course to Vipassana and Dhamma practice was very successful and lasted five days. Then a pause for the weekend and recommencing the following Monday. At the end of each course Francesca would ask people to leave a donation to support the life of the teacher. That doesn't take very much in India, and people were aware of that. Nevertheless, money arrived and certainly helped me in my simple monk style life in Budh Gaya.

One morning as I was crossing the street to take my usual breakfast of cinnamon roll and coffee I saw something that appeared in front of me almost like a vision. A young slim man with a head of unkempt black hair, dressed in simple clothes and wearing Ghandi style glasses and simple worn-out Kung fu slippers was walking so elegantly towards me as a silhouette against the early morning light.
I shook my head as if to awaken from a dream and entered Gautam's to meet Francesca and others and prepare for the day.
An hour later at the lotus tank he was there sitting quietly and completely still with an aura of peace about him.
I gave the lesson and everybody left at the end except him, and so we spoke.
His name was Oved, an Israeli who had finished his time in the army and like so many Israelis found himself traveling. He had just arrived in India from China where he had studied Tai Chi Chuan at the Wu Dang mountain monastery. He had been the first non Chinese person ever to have been accepted there and I think that the real connection between us was that his absolute dedication to his training in Tai Chi and mine to Vipassana had been the same.
We became friends immediately, a friendship that lasts to this day, even to sharing a house together in Israel some years later.
On the few occasions I managed to persuade him to demonstrate his Tai Chi for my students, I felt privileged to know him. This was no western style learned in a church hall one evening a week, this was 'the real thing.' Slow, elegant movements, each one measured and exact and then suddenly an explosion of movement, almost shocking to the observer with its power, and then the tranquility again. As he would take his posture to begin there would be a moment when my friend Oved was in front of me laughing and joking, and then his eyes would empty, in exactly the same way as aikido Alan's eyes would just before he would propel me without

any obvious force across the dojo. Now there was the emptiness of self. Tai Chi was presenting itself with no interference from outside. There was nothing to win, nothing to lose, no points to score. Only the beingness in the moment. Then it was over and Oved was back, ready to laugh and drink a coffee. Beautiful.

We shared our time in Budh Gaya and then he moved on. We said goodbye and thank you, never expecting to see each other again. We didn't realize that our friendship had just begun and cannot be ended because we are no longer in the same country.

During my previous visit to India, Sarah had been the great gift as a companion and teacher, now it was the turn of Francesca. We shared many things together and over time we became close and loving friends. Christmas was coming and I asked her what she would like as a present from me. This is Budh Gaya so the choice is minimal, but she saw a three sided photograph stand that she said she would like, and it was my pleasure to make a gift of it.

Christmas lunch once more was on the roof at the Vihar and I offered my gift. She liked it, having actually chosen it herself and we were all happy.

Some weeks later Francesca was experiencing some financial difficulties and had refused my offer of money.

«No, it's fine,» she said, «I have many things that I can sell.»

I arrived at her room one evening to collect her for dinner and saw her proposed sale items stacked on her bed. On the very top was the gift I had given her for Christmas.

«You can't sell that,» I cried, «I gave it to you!»

She looked at me with incredibly strong and wise eyes and answered, «Yes, it was from you, now did you give it to me or not?»

I understood immediately. Whenever we give something we must cut our attachment to it the moment it leaves our hands. It's not ours anymore and we renounce all rights to it. If there are conditions attached it cannot be called a gift, it is a trade or a deal or perhaps even only a loan, but not a gift.

This is why Buddhist monks are not supposed to offer even a glance or gesture of gratitude for what they receive, so that the gift is pure with 'no strings attached.'

At the end of one of the meditation courses a young English man asked if there was a possibility to make a retreat with me. Immediately others in the group were interested and once again Francesca took control and said that we would try to find a place. It seems to me that the whole of my Dhamma life has been organic, and as my fear diminished more space appeared to allow things to happen naturally.

Impatience and setting time limits only increases the fear and creates pressure to make things happen from nothing. I had met that fear in my bedroom on the Isle of Man just a few months earlier and I knew it did not bring a good result. Now, because there was no intention to be seen as someone doing something, I could stand back and let things happen.

Budh Gaya was a small town of temples and guest houses in those days and so we wandered from place to place asking various monks and priests about the possibility of using their temple or guest accommodation to present a Vipassana retreat. Through kindness and smiles they all reluctantly said no.

Finally we arrived at the International Meditation Centre just at the outskirts of the town. We were greeted in a very friendly way by a young Theravada monk who took us to meet the abbot, the Venerable Rastrapal.

He also was friendly, helpful and interested. He asked many questions about me and my training, and after drinking tea together he told us that he would telephone the Burmese Vihar later that evening.

What I didn't discover until later was that Venerable Rastrapal, like me was very protective of the teachings of Vipassana and Dhamma and immediately on my leaving his office had contacted the Bhante at the Burmese Vihar to make further enquiries about me. Having received a good report he then contacted my teacher in England to see what he felt about the situation. Another good report followed and it was decided, I could make a retreat at his small meditation centre without interference from him or his staff. Vegetarian meals would be provided and the price would be fixed. Venerable Rastrapal was not only a well educated, kind and knowledgeable senior monk, he was also an excellent business man. However, because Dhamma and money always seemed strange bedfellows to me, I agreed everything and took my pleasure from sharing the Dhamma rather than becoming a rich meditation teacher.

The first ten day retreat began with perhaps twelve people and like the lotus tank teachings, was considered a great success by all. This led to the second retreat and then a third. My life, at least in India was becoming a dream I could never have imagined, simple, Dhamma based and free. What more could I want? More and more I was finding my own voice, telling stories and jokes and sharing what came to be known as, 'the joy of Dhamma'.

That year there were only three retreats for now it was almost February, the temperature was rising and the town was emptying, it was time to move on.

India is filled with gurus, some authentic and some not, but all of them entertaining in one way or another, and all of them teachers of something.

Francesca asked me to travel with her to Lucknow to attend Satsang with a famous Master of Advaita Vedanta, called affectionately Pappaji by his devotees but more accurately known as Sri H. W. L. Poona.

Advaita Vedanta may be expressed simply as a school of nondualism, however, like many convenient definitions it is overly simplistic, but Pappaji was becoming very well known now in his later years as a speaker and man of wisdom.

He himself had been a disciple of the world renowned Master Ramana Maharsi and now had a large following of many western disciples including well-known teachers such as Andrew Cohen and Merle Antoinette Roberson, better known as Gangaji.

Actually, I had already met and had a private lunch with Gangaji and her husband Eli, in Budh Gaya some weeks earlier and as this kind of thing happened on more than one occasion with different teachers, I had the idea that others were 'checking me out,' as the new boy in town, but actually if the truth be told, I was doing the same thing with them.

In my mind, then as now, integrity is everything, and when one student of mine asked me at the Lotus Tank one time, how can we know a good teacher, my answer was simple: «Watch them when they are not teaching. It is here you will see everything.»

The fame of Pappaji was helped along by the recent death of Osho, Bhagwan Shree Rajneesh in Pune whose followers were now looking for a new guru to devote their spiritual enthusiasm towards. With this in mind the Satsangs were full, with perhaps three hundred people sitting in their best Indian clothing waiting to be awakened.

It was a strange environment for me. Here there seemed to be a complete indulgence in emotion, with people suddenly standing up and shouting, «Pappaji, Pappaji, can I come down?» Can I come and kneel before you so that you can look deep into my eyes and my soul, and set me free?

For a Vipassana man such as myself who had received years of instruction to allow everything to arise and pass away according to its nature, this was all very strange and undisciplined behavior. Even so, it was fascinating for me and if I stayed quiet and invisible I could sit and observe a very different version of spiritual enquiry. Francesca and I shared a house with a group of westerners staying in Lucknow to attend Satsang and if we didn't see each other in the morning over coffee and toast, we would all meet later in the Satsang house. One of the people sharing the house with us was a young Dutch woman called Anna. She had sat a retreat with me at the International Meditation Centre in Budh Gaya for ten days a few weeks earlier, and had been a good student. Now one morning during my first week attending these strange meetings, she was standing behind me her eyes on fire with unbridled emotion, waving her arms in the air to be seen shouting «Pappaji, Pappaji, can I come down,».

Poonjaji saw her and beckoned her to approach.

He was a fat jolly man who laughed a lot, and although I really didn't like the system he was allowing to happen, he nevertheless said one of the wisest and most profound things I had ever heard. People could write notes with questions and they would be passed to him. Many were about boyfriend/girlfriend relationships and he refused to answer them, others had a more spiritual content.

One such question was about the nature of mind. His answer was so simple and so profound that he completely blew mine, to use an idiom from my youth.

«There is no unconscious mind,» he said.

Incredible, the power of pure Dhamma. I looked around to see who else had understood this fantastic teaching, but as much as I looked I saw no recognition in the eyes of anyone.

Another technique here was to allow someone to kneel before him with their question and he would 'push his mind into theirs' and say simply, «Who is asking this question?»

The instruction was to try to find a real and lasting person inside who was struggling with life and who from fear and delusion, could ask such a thing. This is the intimacy that my Dutch friend wanted to experience. However, this time with her, it was slightly different. She was enjoying an incredible emotional experience and so when she arrived at the Master she whispered something to him.

He laughed his jolly laugh and told her to turn around and tell us what she had understood.

She turned to face the crowd, almost unrecognizable from the energy pouring out through her ecstatic face and said, «It's so easy!»

The whole room cheered and I looked around in confusion. This was more like an American T.V. game show than any Dhamma hall I'd ever been in, but it hadn't finished there. He told her that she was now enlightened and gave her a Hindu name to support that, and said she should sit next to him now and help him teach. Although she didn't speak for the rest of the meeting except to agree with him when he presented something, she sat on the teacher's seat at the front facing us smiling insanely.

Later we all met outside wondering if it was time to have lunch yet, it was, it always was after Satsang. The close disciples would speak together imitating the Master and when anyone would ask a question they would quite seriously repeat, «Who is asking this question?»

I now felt tired of this presentation, and although happy to have experienced it did not feel I needed to see more.

The next morning I met the young, now supposedly enlightened Dutch woman in the kitchen of the house we were sharing. She was still radiant with her experience and so I greeted her with, «Good morning Anna, are you still enlightened?» She would smile a patronizing smile and answer simply, «Yes.»

The next morning I would ask the same and the morning after that. On the fourth morning I greeted her and asked her if she was still enlightened. She turned to face me, very different now, and answered sadly, «No, it passed.»

That which passes cannot be enlightenment because enlightenment is not the getting of something it is the letting go of everything. Once you are free, you are free. There is no more to be done and nothing left to hold on to.

Later I heard of many westerners who had similar experiences only to return to their own countries and lose it and so meet a profound depression.

The Vipassana way, to my mind, is much more secure.

The disciple arrived before the Master and said, «Master, I think I'm enlightened.»

«You, enlightened,» said the Master, «how could that be? You're an idiot.»

By this time other students of mine had arrived in Lucknow and like me had become disillusioned with what they had met, and so asked if I would present Vipassana talks and meditation instead of going to Satsang. I immediately agreed and we spent the next two weeks meeting every morning in a Vipassana environment.

In all I stayed in Lucknow for one month and then it was time to move on again.

Francesca asked if I would travel with her to a small almost unknown town to westerners called Banda, to meet and spend time with another so-called enlightened guru. I thought, 'why not?' and so off we went.

We arrived at a small family house to be greeted by the guru.

He was a young man looking exactly as you would expect an Indian guru to look. Long white flowing robes, accompanied by long black hair and beard. We had come to make some kind of retreat in his house although sleeping in a small hotel locally. In all there were three men and three women plus the guru and his wife. I became quite friendly with the wife and helped her make and serve chai when the others were listening to his strange Dhamma talks. Neither of us it seems were very impressed by his wild stories about visiting other planets, meeting the beings that lived there and describing events from history in a new and unusual way, from the first person singular.

We would sit for two hours in meditation and then he would join us for the final half an hour. He did not take a place on a teacher's dais or even the floor, but a large chair covered in fabric to look something like a royal throne. He himself had been a disciple of Osho and so his inspiration for presenting his teachings came from that.

He would ring the bell and then ask each one of us in return the same question.

«Did you feel my energy when I entered the room?» The women, all young and already in love with him, in breathless hushed voices all said yes, and more than that, his energy washed all over them and they felt peaceful, calm and loving. The two men answered in a similar way though more forcefully, preserving their masculinity until finally it was me.

«Michael, did you feel my energy when I entered?»

«Well,» I began, «I heard you come in.» Not the response he wanted, but honest from my part. I did not go to India to find a guru, so I did not make the naïve space for one to appear.

When you are deliberately looking for a Master, it is not surprising that suddenly someone will present themselves as exactly what you want.

They will shine in front of you, and blind you with their words and enlightened behavior, until you fall in love with them and become a true follower.

Slowly then comes the beginning of your mental athletics and endless compromising to ensure this person always fits your fantasies of what a Master should be.

Perhaps they will inadvertently reveal their deep seated hidden desires and aversions, but upon questioning, will always be able to present a satisfactory Dhammic explanation of them, and you in your trust and naivety, will seek a truth in their words and what is presented in front of you, but sooner or later the heart speaks and this will be the first step on your own true path.

No one can save you. No one can free you from your past. No one can purify your heart, only you can do that. And this is the truth of liberation.

We are our own saviors. The Master points the way but asks for nothing in return.

Reflect: if the Master is a fully realized being, what could they possibly want from you?

In the end everything is teaching us, but often it takes time to understand the lesson.

Take care with who you sit in front of.

However, surprisingly perhaps, I liked this man very much. Perhaps it was a compassionate view of someone playing a part, I don't know, but it was on one evening after the chai and spending time in the kitchen with his wife that I had a powerful and freeing experience that released me from a huge influence of my past.

From sitting and teaching the three retreats in Budh Gaya, through my experience in Lucknow to these days here in Banda there was a strange feeling in the pit of my stomach. It was emotional I knew that, and certainly connected to my mother.

'Something's coming,' I thought, 'and I'm going to meet a lot of sadness.'

Francesca stayed at the house to sleep with the others on the roof as it was so hot, but I needed to be alone. I arrived in my isolated room just in time.

Suddenly the past exploded out of me like an emotional projectile vomiting and rather than experiencing the sadness I had expected about my mother leaving, there was violent teenage rage. I cried, I screamed silently and I cursed her for abandoning me.

'Why did you leave me, what did I ever do to you? You were my mother, I trusted you, I loved you and you left me - for him - for George Bellis!'

Then in my mind I called her every unkind name I could think of. Tears, saliva and mucus poured down my face and, like physical vomiting, it didn't end until everything was emptied. The whole experience lasted many hours and rather dramatically I fell asleep in the corner of the room propped against the wall.

Later Francesca concerned that I hadn't arrived for breakfast came to find me. She was shocked but now everything was different.

My poor mother, she wanted only to be happy and thought she would find that happiness in another place with another man. She missed her children growing and the important events in their life. My heart was filled only with acceptance and compassion for a suffering being. These feelings have never left me and from that moment I was in peace. It was as though the spectacles I was wearing had become greasy and dirty but I hadn't noticed. During the previous night I had taken them off for the first time and cleaned them. Now everything was clear and in focus. My life would never be the same again. May all beings be happy.

It was a powerful and significant moment in my life, and like everything else did not exist in isolation and so had its influence in every relationship, Dhammic, neutral or romantic after that.

It seemed that this experience and revelation was the great gift of India this time so perhaps it was time to go home. Only one more thing was waiting for me, and that would be in a few days at the airport.

I arranged my things, explained my feelings to Francesca who smiled and said she understood, changed my flight to a convenient date and said goodbye and thank you to the guru and his wife, and took the first available train back to New Delhi.

I was not looking forward to the flight home with Afghanistan's national airline, and I wasn't disappointed with my apprehension, however, there was a very pleasant surprise waiting for me in the departure lounge.

Just as I entered, running up to me like a big friendly dog was the young man I had first seen in Prague airport on the way to India, and the following day in the Paharganj just before I left for Budh Gaya. We had both coincidentally changed our flights many times and after a five month stay in different parts of India had decided to return home. Clara, his female traveling companion was not with him and I think she had decided to stay longer and generously work with orphaned Indian children in the south.

Actually I was not unhappy to meet him and we talked about our respective times in India, him working in the south for a children's charity and mine mostly in Budh Gaya teaching meditation. Henry could talk a lot, and did and by the time we were sitting together on another half empty airplane I was exhausted by his questions. During my time in Budh Gaya encouraged by my students of Vipassana I had written a simple outline of the teachings which in time became the book 'Vipassana - the way to an awakened life.' However, I dug these notes out of my shoulder bag and gave them to Henry. «Here, read this,» I said, mostly so I could have some peace. Happily it worked.

The plane took off, then landed somewhere. Boxes were brought on board by men in suits and ominous bulges in their jackets under their armpits.Then we took off again, and landed. More boxes, more men with what we assumed were guns hidden under their clothes. Nobody said anything and certainly nobody questioned the flight plan.

Eventually, after many unannounced and unscheduled take offs and landings we arrived in Paris. However, as we were so late we were told we would spend the night in a hotel and our flight back to England would be the next day.

A bus took us to a very nice hotel and we queued at the reception desk waiting to be assigned to our rooms. It had been a long and tiring journey and the possibility of a hot, deep luxurious bath and then sleep in a comfortable bed sounded like paradise. Suddenly Henry spoke again, «This is great,» he said, «now we can share a room!»

«Henry,» I countered, «there is not even the slightest possibility of that happening. I'll see you tomorrow for breakfast. Sleep well.»

I went to my room, took my bath and slept like a baby.
Next stop, England.

The rest of the journey was straightforward with no delays or difficulties and Henry and I said goodby at Heathrow airport. I liked him. He was amusing, honest and naive all at the same time, quite a beautiful combination.
I returned to my western life, spent time with my sons, taught at a few meetings at the 'on and off' Buddhist group and went to spend some time, weeks or months was not yet certain with my teacher. I moved in to the monastery and became his assistant, disciple and companion, never replacing Mar Mar Lwin of course, but mostly being available for more menial tasks.
One day it was announced that Sagharakshita, a well-known former British Buddhist monk, author and now leader of his own Buddhist organization, known as the F.W.B.O. Friends of the Western Buddhist Order, would visit the monastery as part of a book promotion tour and to meet my teacher.
I opened the door to him and his assistant with my teacher standing next to me. I stood to one side to let him enter and present his Anjali to Bhante. That being done my teacher welcomed him to the monastery and introduced me. «This is my disciple, Michael,» he said. My heart swelled. To be presented in this way was a great honor and privilege and if I ever needed another reason to respect my teacher and his teachings of love, compassion and joy, this presentation was it.
My life now was quite fluid, spending time at the monastery and assisting my teacher, or traveling home and living back in the house I once paid the mortgage for with Fiona and our sons. Strange as it must have seemed to many people it worked very well and it was Fiona who invited me to live with them again, though still as a divorced couple. Although I played my part in daily duties such as shopping and cooking, also driving people to

different destinations I still feel it was an act of great kindness on her part to let me, now as almost a homeless mendicant, live quite comfortably under her roof.

On one of the occasions when I was spending time at the monastery a junior monk came to me and told me that there was someone on the phone for me.

These were not the days of constant communication with the whole world and so a telephone call still carried some importance. My first thoughts were as I descended the stairs on my way to the phone in the hallway, that it must be from Fiona informing me of some crisis with my sons, and that I would have to return as quickly as possible to the Isle of Man. However, it was a different voice that answered my 'hello' and one I was pleased to hear.

«Hello Mike, it's Henry,» it said.

There had been no contact between us since we parted at Heathrow airport many weeks previously and he was phoning because he would like to come and visit me, discuss the meditation he had been practicing via the copious notes I had given him on the plane, and possibly meet my teacher. He could come the next day, Saturday, if that was convenient.

I said it was and that I would be pleased to meet him at New Street Station. He gave me the scheduled arrival time and I reached the station the next day just as his train was pulling in.

It was a joyful meeting, and we embraced as friends do and smiled into each other's eyes. It's often difficult to understand spontaneous connections between people but certainly I had it with my teacher and Henry.

We walked back to the monastery, stopping for coffee along the way. As always, Henry's enthusiasm was exhausting but his commitment to a Dhamma practice was clear. He wanted to know - everything!

So we talked about the meditation practice and then how to apply the developing understanding to our regular daily life. He asked me then if I would be his teacher, and more, him my disciple. I had never thought about the idea of anyone calling themselves my disciple, but it was a word my teacher had used about me, so I agreed.

We spent the day together and at the monastery I introduced him to Sayadaw Rewata Dhamma. They exchanged pleasantries, but not really more than that.

At the end of the afternoon we walked back to the station together where Henry would take his train home to a small town on the English border with Wales.

We walked together mostly in silence, everything having been said, until Henry very seriously stopped and turned to me.

Of course I had to stop too, which I did, and waited for what would come.

«Mike,» he began, «I want to tell you that if you ever need my help, for anything, you just simply ask me and I will always do my best for you.»

During all the years we knew each other until his death in 2013, no truer word was ever spoken. However, on this occasion I replied simply and spontaneously, «Alright, come to India with me in November and help me run my retreats.»

This had already been arranged with Venerable Rastrapal who had been delighted with the success of the three retreats at his centre and was enthusiastic to host more for western students with a western teacher. Also, the possibility of a greater financial income sat well with him.

There was a slight pause while he reflected and took in the enormity of what I was asking. He would have to find the money to travel and then give up his job or at least ask for special dispensation for a long leave. After that there is the question of a visa, a flight ticket, not to mention what I was actually asking him to do, and as it was now June, there was not a lot of time to delay.

«O.K.» he said, «I'll do it.»

During the next few months we kept a good contact with each other by telephone, letter and occasional visits so we could coordinate our journey. He said he would like to arrive in Budh Gaya a little bit in advance of me to introduce himself to Venerable Rastrapal, get to know the town and begin publicity for me.
That sounded very good and so it was exactly what happened.

In time I made my arrangements to return to India and as this was becoming second nature to me everything went smoothly. Naturally I wanted to spend some time with my sons before I left and so I decided to spend some weeks on the Isle of Man. I told Bhante of my plan and that I would leave soon. We spent the day before my departure together and as was his custom he asked me what time my train would leave, proposing that he would take me to the station in his car. I protested out of habit, but his generosity to me was always humbling and so I accepted whilst feeling unworthy of his care.
The next morning we sat in the car ready to go, but he paused before starting the engine. He turned to me and spoke.
«Do you remember U.Nu?» he asked.
It was now seven years since I had been a monk in robes, but the events of those joyful days had not faded in my memory.
«Yes of course,» I answered, «I think he was a very special person.»
«Do you remember when he bowed at your feet?» he continued.
I did remember the moment well, but how did Bhante know? We were alone in the Dhamma hall when it happened.
«Yes,» I answered, «but he only bowed at my feet because I was then a Bhikkhu and he is a devoted Buddhist.»
«No, this is not the case,» said Bhante. «He came to my room later to tell me what he had done, and why he had done it. He told me about all the time you had spent together during his stay at the monastery and all the conversations you had. He told me

then that he felt obliged to show his utmost respect to you as he saw a special and rare Dhamma quality within you. That is why he bowed at your feet, not because you were a monk, but because of this special quality. I also acknowledge this special Dhamma quality and that is why I accepted you as a disciple and monk all those years ago.» He paused for a moment and then continued with, «Good, now, to the station.» He started the engine and pulled away from the kerb gently.

But for me?

I don't know if my mouth was hanging open or not, but I could not be surprised if it was. I was shocked, stunned, unable to speak. 'What? A special quality? What special quality? And now what do I do with this information?'

I felt more comfortable thinking I was just one of many students or disciples, never special but simply serving my teacher and serving the Dhamma the best I could, but special qualities seen by two people for whom I could not have a greater respect? This revelation felt more like a burden than any kind of praise, and in fact only ever encouraged me to work harder to guard my integrity in my practice.

Even if I reveal this intimate moment now it was always a deep secret that I carried in my heart, and rarely shared with anyone. I felt almost embarrassed to speak, even honestly about true events that happened as a matter of course.

I arrived home, spent time with my sons, living back at the house with Fiona almost as a married couple again, and taught at the Buddhist group on the few Friday evenings before I left for the country I had fallen in love with.

Henry arrived in Budh Gaya first as arranged and as he was a naturally gregarious and likable man it did not take long for the town to know him and appreciate his honesty and good humour.

I arrived two weeks after him, by which time he was well established and had been busy promoting the Lotus Tank Vipassana courses.

The first course began on the following Monday and we and a crowd of perhaps fifteen people assembled for my first teachings in India that year. It was up to Henry to make the introduction and mention that the courses were free but a donation would be greatly appreciated. He did a good job and everything went well. Later he told me that during all the time walking to the Lotus Tank that morning he was silently wishing that no one would come so he wouldn't have to speak. After that first introduction, such was his enthusiastic nature, it was difficult to shut him up!

Following two weeks of these introductory courses came the retreats at the International Meditation Centre, this time with many people signing up for the obligatory ten days of silent sitting and walking meditation. Henry was in charge of the money and organization of the retreats and I was in charge of the Dhamma teaching. In all our years together this system worked very well, principally I think because both Henry and I had the same intention to serve those who came to us with the best Dhamma we could.

The Dhamma season continued with retreat after retreat and a rhythm was organically established.

One day a young Israeli woman called Simi arrived in town. She had taken Theravada ordination in Thailand and was now traveling as a Buddhist nun (Bhikkhuni). I don't remember how we met, but intuitively she was attracted to me, or at least my way to present a love based Dhamma and so we became friends. She did not however, like Henry and took many opportunities to mock him. This was unacceptable behavior in my eyes, perhaps established in some kind of jealousy, but naturally I had to stop it. In one moment when she was attempting to ridicule Henry for not knowing the meaning of the Pali word Satipatthana (the original name for the practice we now call Vipassana) I had to step in and support my friend.

«It is true,» I said, «that Henry may not know the meaning of the word Satipatthana, but he is not a Buddhist and so there is no reason for him to know it. However, and much more important, he knows how to practice. He brings awareness into his life and makes his effort to serve others with love and joy.»

It is said that in the many years since the time of the Buddha, many men and women have awakened, but not all have the articulation to share their understanding. These beings are called Pacceka Buddhas, silent Buddhas. If Henry had to fall into a specific category of understanding he would align with the Pacceka Buddhas.

Something about my protection of his dignity and understanding touched him deeply and later that afternoon, when the Lotus Tank meeting had concluded, he mentioned it and asked me to give him a Dhamma name so that our teacher, disciple relationship would be clearer and perhaps more obvious to others.

Many people connected to the popular Buddhist or spiritual world want Dhamma names each for their own reasons and as I had seen in Lucknow during my last visit to India, it seems that you just had to ask and it could be done. Even if my own Dhamma name was Paññādipa, it came only at my ordination without me requesting it.

I told Henry that I did not do that, but he insisted. Again I declined and again he insisted. This battle of wills continued as we walked around the perimeter of the Lotus Tank with almost the comic ending of me fast walking to get away from his persistent demand! Finally I stopped and gave in. «Alright Henry I'll do it,» I sighed. «I'll meet you in Pole Pole later and we'll see what name I can find for you.»

Pole Pole (Swahili term meaning Shanti, or calm or peaceful) was our local and favourite small Indian café directly opposite the Burmese Vihar. It was run mainly by a young man called Pappu and his friend, Jimi.

We had befriended these young men and recommended their café to anyone who was interested. They served large glasses of western style tea, noodles, toast and best of all, pommes frites. This was the place to go alright.

I went to the Bhante at the Burmese Vihar and sought his guidance about a name for Henry. By this time we had become quite close, this being the third year I had stayed in Budh Gaya. I explained the situation and asked him if he could translate the name I had in mind into Pali. He thought for a moment and gave me his answer. Dhamma Chanda.

Loosely translated this means, Fire or Passion for Dhamma, a name that suited Henry perfectly. He was pleased, honored and humbled, perfect for a true disciple of Dhamma.

Retreat followed retreat and Henry learned his part as I learned mine. Both of us took great care with what we were doing and Henry was always honest enough to admit any mistake, and as everything could be easily corrected it was considered only a learning experience.

Simi would come to the retreat centre to offer assistance and she and Henry finally found a way to be together without conflict.

On one of these occasions she asked me a question.

The question was, «Michael, what do you do to people in your room?»

I was surprised and so I replied, «What do you mean?»

«Well,» she continued, «I see them enter your room emotionally low with their heads down and even crying from the retreat, but when they leave they are smiling and energetic again. What do you do?»

«Oh that,» I replied, «I just love them. It seems to be enough.»

Love means to be open hearted, not to judge and not to make conditions around a relationship. Until we have awakened, the world will often seem a dangerous and unpleasant place. After we have awakened, it's just the world with many beautiful things and many not so beautiful things. The difference in our view is the amount of fear or the amount of love we carry.

Pure Dhamma retreats are not for the faint hearted. Here no matter how much we try, we always meet ourselves, the parts that we have invested so much time and energy into avoiding.

With discipline and determination we will recognize that we cannot escape the consequences of our past and that we have to be patient and self loving to transcend the unhappiness of meeting these painful conditions once again.

But that is the practice, to free ourselves from our emotional relationship to our old story. Only by doing this will we be free in life.

Here we need support, not further criticism.

Here we need clear direction, not new vague ideas.

Here we need love, not bullying.

The Master exists to serve the disciple.

When you come to me I have no new theory to offer, only the lineage of Pure Dhamma. To live with love and awareness so that you will bring the beautiful blessings of egolessness to your own life and the life of all the beings you share this planet with.

One day Venerable Rastrapal came excitedly into my room.

«Mr Michael,» he began, «I want you to come and see my bigger Dhamma centre. It's very close and I want to offer it to you and Mr Henry.»

It seemed that he was pleased with our pure presentation of Dhamma, even outside its usual Buddhist format, and was now offering a place five kilometres outside the town for our exclusive use. He would provide the staff and he and Henry would work out the financial calculations between them.

This sounded like a wonderful opportunity, and it was. When the next retreat began it was at the International Meditation Centre, just outside Budh Gaya. This, as Venerable Rastrapal later told us, was the first purpose-built Vipassana centre in India but had stood dormant for several years waiting for the right teacher to appear.

We taught there for the next several years until it was sold to a huge Buddhist organisation for them to build the world's largest statue of Matraiya, the future Buddha, on the grounds. The meditation building would be a hotel and the statue would sit on top.

As previously stated, Venerable Rastrapal was a highly competent businessman and it is sure he received the best price for the land and building.

In the end the statue was never built as opposition was quite fierce. Not to the statue *per se*, but to the amount of money required to do such a thing. It would be hundreds of millions of rupees, and with the same money thousands of people could be cured of the many life threatening illnesses that fall onto poor people.

The project was abandoned and the International Meditation Centre left to decay in the Indian sunshine.

The season wore on and we enjoyed our time and the people who came to us. One particular French woman called Brigitte became important for me some months later, but in Budh Gaya she attended my talks and we got to know each other a little. Henry and I had our local contacts in the town and we were both well liked it seemed partly because I think, of the respect we had for our Indian hosts and so did not quibble over every rupee asked for. I think because of that we were always asked to pay a fair price for whatever we needed. We bought Indian style clothes and became part of the scenery. I never wanted to be a tourist in India, so this life suited me well.

The traveler's season in Budh Gaya is about three months ending at the end of January. After that it becomes too hot and dusty to stay without a good reason. Also of course, the cafés close because there are no longer enough customers, and so it is time for the remaining few travelers to leave.

Puri is known as poor man's Goa but as it is relatively close to Budh Gaya, only an overnight and all day train, Henry and I went there to relax and swim.

Puri is a small town in the Bay of Bengal. The hotels were simple and clean with western beds, such a change in degree of comfort, and good food. It was a good place to regain our energy and it is where Henry learned to swim. During the first days he would stay on the beach, drink coconut water from the many vendors and enjoy the clean air and sunshine. We met fellow westerners, some from Budh Gaya and enjoyed our holiday. At one point Henry was encouraged to try the water and he did. That was it! Now we could hardly get him out.

Truly I loved this man. He was like my son, my best friend and my disciple all rolled into one joyful, great big friendly dog.

Now the two day train journey to New Delhi and home to the Isle of Man or Birmingham. From our recent experience with Afghanistan Airlines we were flying with separate but reputable companies and agreed to meet up again soon and discuss our plans for the next season in Budh Gaya.

When I arrived home again there was a letter waiting for me from Brigitte, the French woman I had met in Budh Gaya. She asked me if I would be interested to come to the south of France and teach a seminar for perhaps seven days. I immediately agreed and arrangements were made. At the same time I also received a letter from another woman, this time English, who had sat with me at the Lotus Tank inviting me to teach in Cornwall. These were important moments in my life as I began to become known outside India or the Isle of Man.

I made my way to the south of France, by boat, bus, ferry, bus and train, finally arriving in Matabiau station in Toulouse. The journey was long but exciting and I had persuaded my current girlfriend to accompany me so that she could offer a yoga session to the group each morning. This does not really express her competence in this area as Grace lived up to her name when it came to demonstrating yoga asanas and sharing her ability. She had trained in meditation with me for many years and we had become close and loving friends. We were met at the station by Brigitte who drove us to the château where the seven day seminar would be held. It was an interesting drive and 'quite French,' according to British established stereotypes as at one point she drove only with her knees on the steering wheel whilst she lit a cigarette and let it hang from her lips. Marvelous.

We arrived safely some time later and met the group. It was small, with only seven people, six women and one man, but this was my first professional teaching outside India and I was enthusiastic as always to give the best of me.

The seminar began with an introductory talk from me and a line by line translation from Brigitte. I had never even imagined a presentation could be like this but after the initial shock and an adjustment to my speaking rhythm, all went well.

Everyone worked hard it seemed to me, but there was one young woman who really impressed me with her determination to sit well, even while enduring great pain, and always conducting herself in an elegant manner.

We did not really have a contact as she could not speak English and I could not speak French, however, in spite of the language barrier, we would meet each other many times over the years becoming closer and closer in our friendship until finally, standing in front of the great Buddha statue in my teacher's new monastery ten years after our first meeting, I asked her to marry me. This woman, Isabelle became my wife, supporter, companion and disciple. A true blessing in an already blessed life.

The seminar was considered a great success and another visit would follow quite soon.

After my return to the Isle of Man I immediately began to plan my visit to Cornwall. I had met Sandra at the Lotus Tank where she had asked me, «How do we get you to teach in our town?»

«You just invite me and we see where we go from there,» I replied.

She did, and I arrived.

Professionally things began to move now, with secondary invitations from France and Cornwall, an article and photograph in the local newspaper on the Isle of Man leading to new people coming close to me and from that invitations to teach again at the university for the adult education evening and Saturday classes. Soon however, India was calling again.

It took me several years to realize that India was extremely generous with her care for me and this time would be no different. As became our format, Henry arrived before me to begin the publicity and organize the beds and the Indian team with Venerable Rastrapal to help at the retreat centre. Then I would arrive two weeks later to almost a hero's welcome in the town and to find Henry with his head shaved. This became a custom with him but as it was India and as people can easily do things in India that they may not do at home, I paid no attention. It was only after his death that his first wife Susanne, whom he was about to meet in the next few weeks at the Lotus Tank, told me that the reason he always had his head shaved when he arrived in Budh Gaya was to show the world that he was my disciple.

I met Henry in the grounds of the Burmese Vihar and he told me that things were going very well and the first Lotus Tank course had attracted a lot of good attention and that the first retreat in about two weeks time was already almost full.

Our retreats at the International Meditation Centre outside the town could accommodate about fifty people per retreat and more if Henry juggled beds and spaces. Because Dhamma was never a business for me, it has always been an important point that we serve the people who come and will always do our best to make space for those who want to come. The discipline is quite exacting and I never wanted to compromise that because of the authentic training I received, and people on the whole were well-behaved. Only on a very rare occasion did we ever have to ask someone to leave.

The first time was when three young Israeli women were found by Henry smoking marijuana on the roof after an afternoon meditation session. The taking of drugs is unacceptable conduct, as was the talking and laughter that followed, especially as the whole purpose of our time together is to illuminate the clarity of the mind and to honour the tradition that we have come to be a part of.

On another occasion we were told that an American man had been secretly using heroin whilst sitting with us. It was only when the retreat had ended and he had returned to the town that we discovered this. He went to the roof of his guest house and under the influence of this particular drug, tested his idea that he could fly. He couldn't and broke his leg. He was lucky to survive in one piece and was airlifted out of Budh Gaya.

Henry always did his best to guard the integrity of our retreats, but often people come with their own fixed ideas of what they can do or not do whilst staying with us.

«There are two women who want to come and I think you should meet them first. They are in Sarnarth right now and will be back in a few days,» he said.

«O.K.» I replied quite uninterested, «No problem. Introduce them to me and I'll be very happy to meet them.»

A few days later Henry came excitedly to me to tell me that, «They are here!»

He took me across the road to the small café of Pole Pole, to be introduced.

Two young women stood there, one quiet and quite shy, and the other not so much. It was a pleasant and easy meeting with Chantal and Saskia.

Once again, India kindly provided my time there with wonderful

women who would later shape my life in a most important way.
The retreat began eventually and was full. Saskia and Chantal were there and were an invisible part of the programme.
On the third day Chantal came to my room and complained. She was a young Belgium woman, slim, attractive and well-educated. She sat in front of me and criticized the accommodation, the retreat structure and me. She was unhappy and disappointed and so it was her intention to leave. I waited until she stopped speaking and then quietly and lovingly asked her a specific question about herself.
Her face turned pale and her mouth fell open in shock just for a second.
«How did you know that?» she asked.
«Everything about you is telling me.» I replied.
In that moment something profound changed between us and we became very close as teacher and disciple. She sat many retreats with me that season, eventually finding her own private time each day to come to my room and tell me about her developing Dhamma understanding. At five o'clock each evening there would be a slight tap on the door and she would be there waiting to share her experience with me.
I liked her very much and at the end of the season she fell in love with another fellow meditator and they went to Thailand together on a post retreat season holiday.
On her way home with Aeroflot her plane crashed and all on board were killed. It is with a sadness that I write these words, but perhaps we could say that each of us were blessed to know the other.
Saskia was a different story. She was an attractive, tall, blonde German woman in her mid twenties and because of her buoyant personality and a love of humour we connected and became friends immediately. That loving friendship exists to this day, and I am able to put my hands together in Anjali and say 'thank you,'

to her for everything she gave me, especially as it was free from intention.

Saskia sat many retreats with us that season, and then in later years would arrive in Budh Gaya to meet Henry and me as close friends and often assist Henry in his duties on retreat. Once when I collapsed from exhaustion in my room, she gave me fresh fruit, compassionate care and nursed me back to full strength.

Many years later when I was at home on the Isle of Man a letter and photographs arrived from her informing me that she had given birth and here is the picture of her new born son.

His name is Aaron, and written underneath the photo of a brand new baby boy were the simple words, 'isn't he cute?'

She invited me to visit and meet him in her home in Germany, and because we were such good friends and because I was free from traveling I was able to do it.

Once there she announced that she had told her friends that I was coming and would I give a Dhamma talk in her sitting room.

Never being someone who needed to be asked twice to share Dhamma I said yes and met four or five other people who came to hear.

Without realizing it, and certainly without intention, this was a key moment in my life and many visits followed and a group began to form around me. Then weekend seminars were asked for and finally organized retreats. Saskia was always an integral part of this development in my life and stayed that way until she left to live in another area of Germany, and we lost her care and enthusiasm for promoting Dhamma. However, this is still my life today, to travel to Germany several times each year and give long retreats, seminars and public talks and always share the gift of Dhamma that I feel I received from my teacher all those years before. In fact it is true to say that Germany is now my Dhamma home.

Even if Saskia and I rarely meet these days, I often thank her in the Dhamma hall and always in my heart, for the opportunity she gave me to present Dhamma in Europe.

The season and the programme of retreats wore on. New people came, each with their own story which in the end was the same as everybody else's story. 'I want to be happy, I don't want to be unhappy, and I don't know how to do it!'
Every person without exception was treated with kindness and love but they must follow the rules. The rules on retreat exist to give the practitioner the best possible environment for the development of deep awareness and open-hearted acceptance of the reality of the moment, culminating in wisdom that stays with that person forever. Wisdom then is not the acquisition of new ideas, but the absolute freedom from the old ones.

If we let go a little, there is a little peace.
If we let go a lot, there is a lot of peace.
and if we let go completely, complete peace.

One morning I met Henry who told me he had fallen in love with Susanne.
«Who?» I asked.
«Susanne,» he continued, «you know, the German woman from the Lotus Tank courses. The attractive one with glasses. We spent the night together.»
After this description I remembered her.
«Susanne,» I cried, «but she's intelligent!»
I couldn't help myself, but Henry was Henry and although never an idiot or stupid he had not received a complete education. Now we would say that he attended the 'school of life,' and it was life's often hard and uncaring experiences that shaped him.
Even now whenever Susanne and I lovingly speak about our dear friend, this moment arises in the conversation and we share the

joy of remembering such a beautiful, loving and compassionate person as I met that morning in the town we loved.
Henry and Susanne became a couple and as a couple or individually, they were always a part of the incredibly small group of very close friends to me. After the retreat season ended they travelled together, made their plans for the rest of their lives and soon Henry moved to and lived in Germany where he stayed until he died.

There were other western and much more famous teachers in Budh Gaya at the same time each year as Henry and me. They made their retreats and we made ours, and we had no contact with each other until a message arrived one day to say that Christopher Titmuss would like me to come for lunch with him.
Christopher was a 'big name' and he would arrive each year to make two very well attended ten day retreats at the large Thai temple in the town. With more than a hundred people he would have a team of assistant teachers to help, but he was the draw.
I realized that I was being invited once again to be checked out, but as my Dhamma pedigree is quite high, I did not feel intimidated.
Actually I did not have lunch with Christopher, he stayed in the background and I was interviewed by one woman assistant teacher about my practice and reasons for teaching Vipassana. I explained that I was instructed by my own teacher, Sayadaw Rewata Dhamma, to do this and there was a pause, and then a question.
«Really?» she said, «your teacher told you to do this?»
«Yes.» I answered, «He wanted me to share Dhamma so that others could benefit.» It was the truth. Even after all these years I still do not know of another teacher who was directly instructed by his own teacher to continue the line of Dhamma from the Buddha himself.
Some years later in December 1996, as I was leading my usual

series of ten day retreats with Henry at the International Meditation Centre in Budh Gaya my lineage was revealed to me. Bhante was traveling with a group of Burmese pilgrims to the four holy places in India as I had done many years earlier when, to much mutual delight, we met.

I had missed my breakfast that morning having spent time with a student who was struggling with his retreat experience and so asked Henry to take care of the morning schedule whilst I cycled the five kilometers into town to have a coffee and cinnamon roll.

As I sat alone in this small café I noticed a monk standing at the gate of the Burmese Vihar. I looked and looked hardly believing my eyes until finally I had to approach. As I stepped into the daylight our eyes met and we both smiled. It was him.

«Ah Michael,» he said, «there you are. I've just sent someone down to the retreat centre to bring you here.»

It was a wonderful meeting for the both of us equally delighted by the other, and later when we were joined by Mar Mar Lwin the trio was complete. How wonderful. However, once again he would speak in a way that would shake me.

We sat together at the Burmese Vihara in the early morning sun quietly speaking in a caring and loving way when I asked, «Bhante, who was your teacher?»

In the past he had mentioned many Burmese teachers to me but never anyone in particular and so simply out of curiosity I asked the question.

He smiled and gestured to a statue of the Buddha standing behind us and answered simply, «The Buddha.»

He then continued, «The Buddha taught his disciples, who then taught their disciples, who then taught their disciples and so on, until my teachers taught me and I taught you. You now continue this line as you teach your disciples. This is the way of Theravada, to maintain the purity of Dhamma by following a direct path from the Buddha.»

These words, like his message from U.Nu did not sit comfortably with me whilst at the same time I was happy that he thought so highly of me. Once again it only increased my integrity to stay true to the path and Dhamma.

It was here also on this special occasion that I was asked by Bhante to lead the very first Vipassana retreat at his new monastery in Birmingham, the Dhamma Talaka Temple. It was such an honor and privilege to be asked by this person I respected so much but I wanted to be clear.

«Ah Bhante,» I said, «I no longer teach Buddhist retreats.»

«No matter,» he answered, «I am asking you to lead the first retreat, a Dhamma retreat at my new temple when it is completed.»

«Thank you,» I said, «I am honored. When will it be ready?»

«Very soon now.» he finished

Seven years later the retreat began.

The assistant teacher and I finished our lunch and I left. I had answered every question as honestly as I could and so went back to our own centre to continue with the day's activity of sitting and walking meditation. I had noticed as I had arrived for my meeting with Christopher that students were able to do almost anything they wanted to do and that there was no real guidance. I also thought that even with more than one hundred people on retreat we would still insist on compliance with the rules of practice and was also fairly sure that Henry could handle the extra responsibility.

Some days later I received another invitation, this time to meet the man himself.

Christopher, as I got to know him later, was an eminently likable man with, as we discovered during my final teaching year in Budh Gaya, a taste for young women who sat with him on retreat.

He was very kind and said publicly many favorable things about me, including his view that I was the hardest working teacher in

Budh Gaya. Perhaps that is true, I don't know, but I felt that I was here to share Dhamma, not be on holiday.
He invited me to teach at Gaia House in England - and that really was a big deal!

Grace and I were still a tenuous couple and so she would often join me in India to sit a retreat and then travel together, or simply travel together. Whichever it was we were usually able to enjoy this beautiful country and each other.
I eventually arrived home and continued to build my reputation. One day I received a telephone call from someone inviting me to lead a retreat at Gaia House and before that, to present a talk at Sharpham college in Devon. This really was the big time for me and so I eagerly said yes.
After this initial introduction I taught many times at Gaia House but always felt like an outsider, and slightly uneasy with the direction of this particular institution. It was a business after all with debts to repay and a constant need of publicity. Christopher, whom I met many times was always kind to me but the Gaia House version of what Dhamma is and how it should be presented differed greatly from mine. I was and am a 'purist.' We come to train, not to indulge the emotions or simply leave with a good feeling. I discovered that other teachers often used notes to support their Dhamma talks. At first I found this so shocking that I could not accept it as being true. I had never seen my teacher use notes and my intuitive feeling was that we should know our subject and share our enthusiasm for it rather than rely on notes and give lectures. It is also my feeling that the Dhamma talk is about an intimate connection with the group, a sharing of our understanding, and this cannot happen if the teacher simply follows their own programme with no regard for the day's events. I was also given the instruction, though not from Christopher, not to speak about sex or death in the Dhamma hall, because people

wouldn't like it. However, as these are the beginning and ending of what we call life I found them to be important subjects for investigation through silent sitting and humour in the evening Dhamma talks.

Eventually after many visits I was no longer invited and someone more fitting took my place. I was not unhappy to be ignored in this way and some years later in Budh Gaya was happy and relieved to be no longer associated with such centers of modern spirituality where pleasing the students seemed to be much more important than a true sharing of Dhamma.

I journeyed more and more to Germany and France where small groups of enthusiastic people would come to me for retreats, or seminars or public talks. I never had a press agent or professional publicity and so everything was word of mouth. My reputation continued to grow and I felt comfortable with my Dhammic direction.

In France I taught Vipassana retreats at Vajjra Yogini, a large Tibetan Buddhist Centre in the south, and these were always well received with a good attendance.

I met Isabelle many times there and on one occasion she gave me the opportunity for an impromptu Dhamma Talk in the afternoon. We had the habit of sitting together on a small bench in the garden after lunch, where we would each smoke a cigarette in silence, a habit still fashionable in those days.

One day a senior Tibetan monk came to me and in his lovely smiling voice pointed to my cigarette and exclaimed, «Ah, so this is your nadhi!»

He then explained that 'nadhi' is a spiritual grounding device, and without it until Awakening, we would simply float up into the universe and disappear. Only when we are ready can we let it go, until then it can be seen as a safety device, to keep us on the earth. I was happy for this and continued to smoke for several years until, as the monk pointed out, the moment arrived and it was no longer necessary.

One day Isabelle, having finished her cigarette, left and headed back to the main house to prepare for the afternoon meditation session.

I waited several minutes and then rose to follow her. I was surprised to find her frozen in a posture in the distance and so I carefully approached her to ask if everything was alright.

«Michael,» she said when I was close enough to hear her whispered voice, «don't come closer. There is a snake.»

In those days she had a very strong fear of snakes and lying there, coiled up in the grass was a large snake.

Now I, for whatever reason, do not feel afraid of these beautiful creatures and so I gently took her arm and carefully led her away.

The first Dhamma talk that afternoon was based upon this experience and was something along these lines:

Imagine you are afraid of mice and a special group of people are able to capture and kill all the mice that live on this planet and send them into outer space.

Do you still have fear?

Of course you do. The fear just transfers to another object, perhaps a snake or an elephant or more subtly, the fear that possibly one mouse survived and is now waiting under your bed to attack you whilst you sleep.

You have to understand that the fear and the mouse are two separate things.

The fear is not the mouse, and the mouse is not the fear. The mouse (in this illustration) is the mouse, and the fear is the fear. We must understand that the mouse is the condition for the arising of fear, but is not the fear itself. This is very important.

So, the work for us is to let go of fear, and not confuse our practice with the objects of the fear.

Fear is fear, that's all. No need to make a fuss. Accept the feeling as much as you can and allow it the space to pass by itself.

This applies to all objects of fear, even the most subtle one like death.

What does it mean when you say 'I have a fear of death?' Reflect. We don't know what death is and so we create an imagination around it. If you say it is the fear of 'not existing' we cannot know what that is really like, and so we compromise our ideas and say that we are 'afraid of the unknown.'

But again reflect, if it's unknown, how can we be afraid of it?

What we are afraid of is losing the known, even if that known is difficult, unpleasant and painful. Because we know it, it is familiar, and that's what we don't want to lose. The familiar!

Don't take my word for it. Look in the world and how people hold on to a life that they think is completely unsatisfactory, but won't change anything of significance. People are afraid to let go, to jump into the abyss of Love. They are afraid they will lose everything.

The truth is that the only thing they really lose is their fear and the millions of objects that condition that fear.

A mouse is just a mouse. A snake is just a snake. Old age, sickness and death, is just old age, sickness and death.

Understanding in this way is called Awakening, and Awakening is true liberation.

However, I do not tell you to live recklessly.

Take care of you. Don't pick up venomous snakes. Respect them and treat them with the wisdom arising from a loving heart, but don't allow fear to dictate your life.

Dhamma is everywhere and in every moment and in every situation we have the possibility to see the truth manifest in front of us.

Back in England I would visit Bhante, often staying for several weeks but then journeying on. My whole life was contained in a backpack and I became known as the 'Dhamma Bum,' a title that

I was unaware of at the time but later felt quite pleased with. Here I was, without any intention wandering like Jesus, Ghandi, the Buddha and especially Kwai Chang Caine as played by David Caradine in the television series Kung Fu.

Naturally we had no social media in those days and so, because I felt so overflowing with Dhamma, I began to write books.

The first book was called 'The Western Lay Buddhist,' and was meant to be a support to those people really looking for what Buddhism could and should be in their life.

I gave it to my teacher to read and waited for his approval. It came and the book was placed in a box where it stayed until many years later it was discovered and published as 'Walking the path.'

However, the first book published and offered to the public was called, 'Higher than Happiness,' and proved to be and is still, quietly successful.

Other books followed but each one with the intention to support people in this practice. My deepest feeling is that if we don't commit fully to the path of Awakening, we may as well stay at home in bed. Dhamma is too beautiful and too important to compromise.

The years rolled on and the routine of Henry and I became second nature and so now when I reflect I have no real idea of individual years, only various meetings and surprises.

One year I met Neusatas.

At the beginning of one season in Budh Gaya I had a fire in my room. I was not there at the time and even now have no idea how it started. There was no damage to the room itself but I lost many things, from clothes to small gifts I had bought to take home with me, and perhaps more importantly, the little bit of money I had saved through donations.

I had already begun teaching our annual outdoor courses of Vipassana at the Lotus Tank before beginning our annual series of ten day intensive retreats.

The news of the fire spread through the small town quickly and the next morning when I was walking to my place at the Lotus Tank a student of mine, a young Spanish woman called Neusatas, arrived by my side.

«Michael,» she said, «I heard that you had a fire in your room and lost many things.»

«Yes,» I said, «It's true.»

«So,» she continued, «I would like to give you $100.00.»

A hundred dollars, this was a fortune to me and certainly very much needed. However, it was here that I bumped into my British cultural upbringing and I immediately refused.

«Thank you very much, it's very kind but not necessary.»

I had lost almost everything – the money would be like medicine for an illness, it was, in fact, completely necessary!

She offered again but still I refused.

This was my cultural past arising and memories of my grandmother and her sisters after a Sunday afternoon of tea and scones in a small café on the Isle of Man, arguing about who would pay the bill.

These arguments became quite heated and even physical as each insisted that they would pay and the others should 'put their money away!'

Allowing generosity from another, even a sister was not considered good manners.

Finally for the third time Neusatas offered the gift of $100.

This was the moment when I saw.

By continually refusing her kindness I was taking something away from her. The moment was passing and she was standing next to me with her heart and her kindness in her hands offering something to me.

Finally I accepted her gift and thanked her.

She received something and I received something – a double

giving.

In our life we all know this beauty of the heart when it wants to share, and we all know that feeling of rejection, however well-intentioned, when it is refused.

By not accepting her generosity I was taking away the moment of true 'dana' (unconditional generosity).

All happiness in life is ultimately about balance. To flow, and so be in harmony with this balance, is already a gift for ourselves. When we are in balance we will be able to give and serve others as well as making the space for them to give and serve us.

Without the giver there can be no receiver, without the receiver there can be no giver. The harmony of these two things manifesting in life is always something beautiful.

This is an important Dhamma teaching, to provide the space where others can be kind. To give the opportunity for generosity. Others may take it or not, that is their choice, but without the opportunity for giving perhaps they will never see and know the kindness of their own heart.

And as contrary as this may sound, giving this space is a true gift. Generosity is not only giving, it is also making available the conditions to receive.

In the same year Isabelle, the young woman I had met in France came to Budh Gaya to sit three ten day retreats with me. I was delighted to meet her again and the retreat began. She was always a dedicated student and surrendered to the rules without complaint. This is not always the way even today and perhaps especially in Europe with students arriving for retreat with their own agenda of what they will do and what they will not do. The loving and caring voice of the Master goes unheard as people look for the easiest and most comfortable way to pass ten days. They miss the opportunity to train, to surrender ego to the moment and see and experience perhaps for the first time the nature of mind.

In this way Dhamma is diminished in the world and all that is left is a presence of training with teachers comfortable with compromising that which has real value. It is a fact that when Dhamma becomes a business, integrity is the first thing to leave the Dhamma hall.

At the end of the first ten days Isabelle came to me and told me she was leaving.

«I have to see more of India,» she said, and I agreed.

To arrive in this country and sit a ten day retreat in Budh Gaya, the home of Vipassana meditation is something very special, but often simply being in and traveling through this country is retreat enough. Culturally there is no preparation for India, and you can speak with people recently returned, look at photographs and videos and read books, but the moment we step off the plane we are in a different world and this world should be explored and appreciated.

I understood completely and wished her well. We would meet again many times in the future, eventually spending the rest of our lives together.

At the end of 1997 I received an invitation from the Vipassana group in Israel to conduct a retreat there in the early spring of the next year. It would be a big event in Tel Aviv with more than a hundred people attending and once again opened a door in my life that I had not anticipated.

I arrived to lead the retreat and was met by the now disrobed Buddhist nun, Simi.

She welcomed me to her house and I passed the night there in preparation for the next day, the first day of the retreat.

«What would you like for breakfast?» she asked the next morning.

«Oh, as you like,» I replied.

She went to the garden and returned with two avocados straight from the tree. This was fantastic. Avocado on toast, with coffee. Can life be better than this?

Maybe Israel would be yet another country that would be a beautiful blessing for me? It was.

The retreat began and I connected with the group. Lots of stories, lots of jokes, but more importantly, lots of sitting and walking meditation. I gave the best of me and I feel it was reciprocated. One evening during the walking meditation I went outside to breathe a little fresh air. It was already dark and I was gazing at the starlit sky when a voice called me.

«Hello Michael,» it said. I looked into the gloom and could see an outline of someone but nothing distinct, so I merely acknowledged the greeting with my own 'hello.'

There was a pause until the voice said, «Do you not recognize me?»

It was true that I didn't but mostly because they were only a shadow in the darkness.

He stepped forward and suddenly became familiar. I recognized the person but as yet could not put a name to him. Again they spoke, this time laughing.

«It's me, Oved from Budh Gaya.» Of course it was, now I knew him.

We greeted each other with affection and he told me that he had just seen my name on some publicity and come to say hello. It was a wonderful meeting.

We arranged to get together and share old times and this is what we did. At the end he said, «You should come here to teach for more than one retreat. People love you, and the worst thing that will happen is that we will spend the summer on the beach in Tel Aviv.»

It sounded like a good idea and if that really was the worst thing that could happen, what did I have to lose?

Also I was tired of a particular aspect of my Dhamma life.

Living as the 'Dhamma Bum,' was an important part of my ongoing training but there were times when having no money and sleeping on the floor in other people's homes was tiresome.

I had been invited on several occasions to present talks and give workshops at the famous ten day Mind, Body, Spirit festival in London. On several occasions Grace and I went there and took an exhibition stand to sell my book, Higher than Happiness and many pre recorded Dhamma talks on audio cassette.

This was a new and strange world for me and certainly one I didn't belong in, but if I didn't take it or anything in it seriously it was highly educational. Anything that could be construed by the mind could now be called spiritual and sold for an excessively high price, from healing to the magical 'happiness spray,' to purification of the soul and exciting business opportunities, everything was available.

One of the highlights for me on one occasion was meeting Donovan,' the singer songwriter from the 'sixties and 'seventies. We spoke together for about twenty minutes and he was kind and considerate even inviting me to his home in Ireland. I had assumed it was just politeness and so never went.

However, it was here that I was seen as a potential business asset by two women who had their own promotion company called Manna Management. They told me that they would make me famous with posters in London thirty feet high. Now, I have no interest in fame whatsoever, but I feel my life almost as a mission in the midst of what I see as a callous and misdirected spiritual world, where my place is to bring the purity of Dhamma training to benefit the disciple and then by extension, all beings.

We began a relationship which was in the end disastrous. It seems I knew more about my work and the promotion of it than they did, and although once again the universe provided a wonderful learning opportunity, it was obvious that we could not last together. Now I had been invited to return to Israel by someone that I liked and respected and teach Dhamma. I finished the retreat to thunderous applause, very unusual in the Dhamma hall, and said

goodbye.
Even if I was asked to return I forgot completely to mention Oved's invitation, but never mind, I would be back.

I returned to Israel two months later and was met at Ben Gurion airport by Oved. The security for arriving or departing was extremely tight for very good reasons I suppose, but what I noticed was that it was carried out by the most beautiful Israeli women in tight fitting uniforms. Obviously being a security guard was not considered a reason not to be desirable, or perhaps that was part of an overall plan to seduce terrorists into confessing?
At the other side of the barrier Oved and I embraced as friends and he asked if I would like to take a coffee before we set off for his parent's apartment. I said yes and sat alone at a table as he collected our order.
Just a moment later a very beautiful young blonde woman, dressed elegantly and smelling of expensive perfume came to where I sat and began to speak to me. She was engaging and very friendly, and I thought, 'well, this is wonderful. What a fabulous welcome to Israel.' Just then Oved returned and spoke some very harsh sounding words in Hebrew to which the young lady replied 'in kind,' and angrily walked away.
«Russian prostitute,» he explained. «Lucky for you I was here. They will take everything from you and then leave you beaten in the street.»
I was not perturbed by this possibility and only thought, 'wow, a real prostitute! This is the first time I ever knowingly met a person such as this. Brilliant.'
I had arrived in Israel with all the money I had in the world, £50.00, and so was anxious to begin teaching. Oved on the other hand didn't seem to mind a bit. He had his Tai Chi classes in the evening and spent the day time taking me to visit his parents, his four sisters and their families and eating lunch on the beach.

On Shabbat after giving free open air Dhamma talks in the park in Tel Aviv, we would go to eat with his parents who had almost adopted me as another son. They were a big loving Jewish family from Iraq, generous with their time and care. They were not vegetarian of course, but the amount of delicious dishes prepared especially for me was humbling. The father knew four words of English which he would be happy to share with me whenever I arrived, «Hello,» he would say offering his large hand, «how are you?» I would smile and say hello, with no need to go further than that.

Often his four sisters and their families would also be there and the atmosphere was always warm, loving and humourously Jewish, and incredibly crowded. I could not have felt more welcomed into this huge loving family.

On occasion Oved and I would visit the younger sister at her home to drink a coffee, eat cake and just pass the time of day. The conversation was the same with all his sisters who never hesitated to ask if he had met the right girl yet, and when would they become aunties to even more babies?

Oved would not get caught in a trap of conversation directed at family life and answer simply, «Not yet,» and «there's plenty of time.»

It was this younger sister who gave me the nickname, 'the Shadow Man.'

Oved and I were sitting together in the salon whilst she was in the kitchen preparing a tray of cake and coffee. When she entered the room she looked around and said, «Where's Michael?»

«I'm here,» I replied. She turned to face me and said, «Oh, I didn't see you. You're just like a shadow man!»

I actually felt quite flattered by this name because it reminded me of an experience with my teacher many years before.

We were sitting next to each other on the sofa in the small anteroom at the monastery. It was perhaps four o'clock on a

Sunday afternoon when a retreat had ended and everyone else had left. We were talking about who knows what, when we both fell into silence. I took a sip of the tea I had brought with me and just for a moment looked out of the window opposite into the deserted street.

Then I turned to say something to my teacher, but he was gone.

How had that happened? I didn't notice him walking past me. He hadn't said anything. He had just disappeared.

I looked again to my right, and there he was exactly as he had been a few moments ago. He had vanished right before me, but hadn't gone anywhere.

I did not mention this to him, but took some time to try to understand what had happened. Finally I arrived at an understanding that is comfortable for me.

Our conversation had naturally ended and so when I turned my attention to my cup of tea and the window, he allowed himself to fall into a deep mental silence. The vibration from his physical form immediately became very subtle and so there was nothing for me to register when I next looked at him, and so did not see him.

Moments later when he returned to 'normal consciousness' and his mind energy appeared in his body, he reappeared.

It sounds a little bit like magic, but actually we have all had a similar experience where we walk into a room thinking that we are alone, until suddenly we see someone sitting in plain view. This is when we exclaim, «Oh, I'm sorry, I didn't see you there.» This is only what had happened with the sister of Oved. In the silence and environment of friendship and love I had fallen silent, and just for a moment, become invisible.

Now, to the family I was known as the Shadow Man.

«Oved,» his family would call, «you must come for dinner next week, and bring the Shadow Man with you.»

How I loved this family.

However, as the time passed I began to feel frustrated and helpless, at least at home I could be earning a little bit of money, but here I was on a never ending holiday. At this time we were sharing a house in a small town about half an hour outside Tel Aviv, called Hod Sharon. It was very pleasant but ultimately monotonous until eventually one late afternoon Oved arrived home and said in an almost military manner, «Put on your teaching clothes, you're giving a talk to my Tai Chi group tonight.»

Finally, the day or rather evening, had arrived!

We drove to the sports club, which was the venue for the regular Tai Chi class and waited for the large group to assemble. When everyone was in place Oved asked me to wait outside while he made his introduction. It was a special moment for me as I stood outside and listened to his words.

«I know that you all think I'm wonderful and I'm happy for that, but tonight I want to introduce you to my teacher. We met in India many years ago and he is in Israel now to share Dhamma.»

I entered the room and sat on the seat especially prepared for me. I gave my talk and offered Anjali. Actually it was a familiar talk for me as I had refined my teaching into a format suitable for exactly this kind of thing. A particular talk for the first meeting, another for the second and so on. This formula had always worked well and I had the ability to hit certain points along the way.

This talk was extremely well received and was the beginning of the development of a large sangha in Israel that would last until I left. But there was something else about that evening that changed my life.

When the class was finished Oved and I went for coffee. We sat together outside, both of us very happy with what had transpired. «That was a very good, well-rehearsed talk,» he said, and then continued speaking.

But I had already stopped listening after the words, 'well-rehearsed.'

This was a shock, but it was true, it was a talk I had given many, many times before, and in that moment I spontaneously threw everything away. I decided intuitively that I would no longer prepare and rehearse Dhamma talks, but only speak from the heart and my own understanding. After all, I either know what I'm speaking about or not, and if my intention is to share the most important thing in my life so others can be helped, I need to be at all times authentic.

So that was it, and from that moment to this, I have never rehearsed my Dhamma talks or comments before sharing them with the group I am in front of. Of course I have a general feeling based upon the day, private interviews and Dhamma hall feeling etc, and I usually have the story I want to tell, but beyond that, it is an intimate relationship based in sharing, and not in lecturing.

Israel was a wonderful experience for me and for the first time I began to have some money. I was teaching four evenings a week and all day Saturday outside in our large garden. No incense was necessary as the perfume of the wild flowers filled the air.

Many people would come and I think these were some of the happiest days of my life.

The large group meant that I could pay my share for the house and food and so feel fully integrated into the country and the relationship between Oved and me.

We lived well together and our friendship was what would now be called a 'bromance.' We are both heterosexual men but one time whilst in a café I went to use the toilet and when I returned Oved was talking with two young women, who seeing us together had asked if we were gay. Oved's beautiful response was a smiling, «Not yet.»

Time and visas expired and I left to go home. I returned some months later but the momentum had been lost. I realized then that people need constant contact with the teacher, or they drift away. The spiritual world is a huge supermarket, and the next big thing is only just around the corner. This, plus our general short attention span, means that students are often just waiting for the newest 'quick fix' to arrive in their life.

I stayed for some weeks with Avivit, an incredibly kind and generous woman who had been an instrumental part of the original meditation group, in Tel Aviv until Oved was available in a new house.

I taught courses and retreats, met wonderful people but in the end had to go home.

What was that sound I heard in my head? Oh yes, it was India calling again.

More teachings in Budh Gaya followed this time by an invitation to teach three short retreats on Koh Phangan, one of the beautiful islands of the coast of Thailand. Henry and I arrived and brought with us our partners to enjoy the wonder of this tropical island. Grace with me and Susanne with Henry. Our time there, at a place known as the Sanctuary, was considered a great success and resulted in an invitation for the next year, but it had been so difficult to arrive that as much as we had enjoyed it, we declined.

We all arrived in Bangkok, rested and eventually put our partners on their respective flights and waited for our own, a few days later.

Henry told me that he wanted to buy new clothes, and would I accompany him. I said of course and off we went.

Obviously Henry and I had similar taste in fashion and it was a pleasure to support him as he tried on a variety of trousers and jackets. Finally he made his choices, encouraged by me, and bought everything he wanted.

That done, it was time for him to return to Germany and me to the Isle of Man.

The very next time I met Susanne she took me to one side and told me quite strongly that I should never go clothes shopping with Henry again.

«He stepped off the plane looking like a throwback to the 1980's,» she said.
Who knew that corduroy and flared trousers would go out of fashion?

Sometime later my relationship with Grace ended. Kindly and lovingly, but there was nothing left to do. My priority in every moment was Dhamma and a non compromising attitude to my practice, my teacher and of course the Buddha. How can anyone ever compete with that? It is like trying to hold onto a wisp of smoke.
I met Henry in India later that year, had new experiences and as always met wonderful people, but things were about to change again.
It was the introduction to the year 2000 and big celebrations were held everywhere in the world it seems with the sky lit up with fireworks, the sound of bells and people shouting 'Happy New Year.'
For me there was a melancholy with the deep sense of the emptiness that underlies all things.

The new century brought with it the opportunity to teach in the United States of America. This was unexpected but very welcome and seen initially as a dream come true.
America was the home of wide open spaces, freedom and infinite possibility, after all that is what I had seen on television since my earliest childhood days. From the Lone Ranger, The Streets of San Francisco, to Hill Street Blues and Seinfeld, everything exciting and wonderful lived in America. This was an opportunity not to be missed.
The invitation came from a student of mine, a young American woman named D'vorah who had sat retreats with me in Budh Gaya.

Although as teacher and student we had spent many hours together, the most noticeable event was once on retreat when I was awakened at two o' clock in the morning by someone hammering frantically on my door. I stumbled out of bed, pulled on some trousers and opened the door to find D'vorah standing there in distress.
She stumbled into my room and began to pace backwards and forwards mumbling to herself. I lit a cigarette, took a seat and waited for her to calm down a little so we could talk.
Finally she stopped pacing and said to me, «I think I'm hallucinating. I'm seeing rats in the dormitory.»
«You can relax,» I replied, «they're not hallucinations, they're real. Go back to bed. Tuck in your mosquito net and rest. The rats won't harm you. They live here with the rest of us.»
We became close friends after that and finally, some years later, she came to visit me on the Isle of Man where she asked if I would teach Dhamma in Portland, Oregon. It sounded wonderful so I agreed.
Christopher Titmuss had already told me that if I really wanted to make some money I should go to the U.S.A. and as I was so tired now of having so little in terms of financial security, the timing was perfect.
First however was the matter of a visa, an important requirement for my legitimate employment as a Dhamma teacher at the Sanctuary, a modern spiritual centre in Portland.
I applied for a religious teacher's visa which was granted primarily I think from the necessary reference from my teacher.

Here is the letter he wrote to the authorities:

THE BIRMINGHAM BUDDHIST VIHARA.
Ven. Dr. Rewata Dhamma.
M.A. Ph.D. Dhammachariya - Spiritual Director.
September 13. 2000
To whom it may concern.

This is to certify that Michael Kewley has been a devoted and dedicated disciple of mine for over twenty years both as a layman and ordained monk. He teaches Vipassana (Insight) and Metta Bhavana (Development of Loving Kindness) meditations over the years on my specific instructions in the East and the West. Many people benefited by his teachings, and he is held in the highest regard by his students throughout the world. His devotion and dedication to the Buddha Dhamma is beyond reproach and his presence in any community can only be seen as an asset.
I will be most grateful if you could help him in this matter.
Yours in the Dhamma
Ven Dr Rewata Dhamma.

Dates were agreed with D'vorah and the Sanctuary, flights booked and goodbyes said. The visa was for five years so I would have the time to make my mark in the Dhamma world, earn some real money and become a famous teacher.
The days passed and with them the excitement I had originally felt began to fall away. Now in its place came the arising of dread. Something didn't feel right. I couldn't quite understand it but more and more I just didn't want to go.
However, finally the day of departure dawned and it was time to go. I arrived at Heathrow airport and waited for my flight. I had just enough time to telephone Grace to say a last goodbye. It was a touching conversation where in a moment of honesty I was able to say that I really didn't want to go.
Her simple answer helped me a lot. «Never mind, you can come

home if you don't like it.» She was right. Now I knew that I was free to change my mind, I could go. It sounds strange, but we build prisons for ourselves by the terms and conditions we place upon our own lives.

The flight was long and uneventful except for the suspicion I had that one of the female cabin crew who was serving us was slightly drunk.

I eventually arrived in Portland and was met by D'vorah and some friends and given a hot meal and warm welcome.

The days passed and I explored the town and surrounding area which was wonderful and exhilarating. Having only really experienced Summerhill Glen as a forest until then it was incredible to be in a place where the trees were so huge. The Washington Gorge was inspiring as was the daily view of the snow capped Mount Hood in the distance.

I met the lady who was so proud to tell me that she had invented blue chocolate for Walt Disney, and I drank coffee whilst walking in the street as I had seen in the movies. I ate Mexican re-fried beans and corn bread and had dollars in my pocket. This was the American Dream as seen on T.V.

I began teaching in the evenings at the Sanctuary and was quite popular even during the first few days, but still something did not feel comfortable inside me.

Then it happened.

One night I had a dream where a voice spoke to me and asked a simple question; «Why did you come here?»

I answered, «To become rich and famous.»

There was a pause and the voice now compassionate and loving responded, «Is that a real reason to leave your home and family?»

Of course it wasn't!

I awoke and it was clear. I shouldn't be here. This is not my place and my reasons for coming had no value at all. I need to go home. Immediately.

It was difficult to explain what had happened to the people who wanted me to stay, but our personal motivations are important and fame and riches were never a part of my Dhamma Path. In the end, integrity is everything.
I changed the date for my return flight and some days later found myself saying yet another goodbye.
Everyone had been so kind, but in truth I had never felt so far away from home, in every sense of the word. In India I was always comfortable, but here I really felt alone and out of place.
My flight left early in the morning on the last Thursday of October - American Thanksgiving Day. As we flew over part of the magnificent three thousand mile long Rocky Mountains the lady passenger next to me saw me looking in awe out of the small window. She smiled and said, «Aren't they cute?»
Next stop Chicago, then London then the Isle of Man.

I returned home quietly and waited for the universe to reveal itself. On the Isle of Man I spent more and more time in my forest in Summer Hill Glen with Sam, the lovely dog of Fiona. I was a single man now, happy to be alone to sit and travel and share this beautiful Dhamma with whom ever would listen. I spent time in Germany with the ever growing sangha making public talks and intensive retreats. I heard from Henry that Venerable Rastrapal had by now sold the International Meditation Center to the large Tibetan group at Vajjra Yogini in France where I had taught so many Vipassana retreats in earlier times.
This was disappointing, but gave me an idea.
I had been teaching in Budh Gaya for almost ten seasons, I loved this place but perhaps the time had passed and I should move on, after all the town was changing and growing and had lost some of the magic I had felt when I first arrived.

So I would return one last time and make three special retreats, mostly to say 'thank you,' and offer Anjali to India for all the wonderful gifts she had given me during these years. Yes, that was it, a month of 'thank you retreats,' and I would let it be known to as many people as possible in the hope that they would join me for this special time.

By now it was 2001 and globally things were about to happen.

September 11th is a special day for several reasons. Personally it is the birthday of my father, so it was always a time of happy memories, but of course now there is something different to remember.

The planes crashed into the Twin Towers time and time again as the footage was replayed so often on television. I watched the news with my sons, all of us I think with broken hearts.

How could this be? How is it possible for human beings to behave in this way? There was a huge space in my comprehension of the behavior of others and it troubled me.

Of course I spoke about it at the different groups I was invited to, always making the same point, that nothing just happens, and that however terrible this thing was, it had a cause, and that the consequence of such action cannot be good.

Perhaps it helped people understand, but I felt that I was now in a place of spiritual isolation. I wanted to speak with my teacher, but felt foolish with my feelings and more, didn't want to disturb him with such stuff.

Henry and Susanne came to visit me and of course we had a lovely time but there was an incident that once again changed something inside me.

One foggy Isle of Man evening we visited a friend of mine who had a very nice bookshop, selling my books and C.D's also.

I introduced my friends to each other and as I was speaking to Margaret, my lovely bookshop friend, Henry and Susanne browsed the spiritual section. They both found new books by two very famous American teachers and were excited to share their finds with me.

I opened the first book and read a small section. 'That is not correct,' I thought as I turned the page. The next book, by someone equally famous brought the same internal comment from me. Once again came that feeling of spiritual isolation. These two teachers were million selling authors belonging to a select group of famous names in America, yet what they had written as a Dhamma explanation to life was to my understanding, completely wrong and pandered to the spiritual market and self promotion. This now was too much. First the horror of the Twin Towers and now the corruption of Dhamma. I had to take a deep breath and contact my teacher.

Henry and Susanne ended their stay and I said goodbye to them at Ronaldsway Airport, with the parting words, «See you in Budh Gaya.»

That evening at home I telephoned my teacher in Birmingham. He was not very good at pleasantries so I had to get straight to the point.

«Bhante, I'm having some difficulty with what happened in America recently,» I began. Then I tried my best to explain the sorrow I had felt when I saw the extent of human unkindness and that I felt now that I really wanted to live away from people and in a way, not be corrupted by society.

He gave his little laugh which was a known signal now that I had not said something completely foolish. «Michael,» he said, «this is how it is for all the Masters. They want to serve the world with Dhamma, but not be too close to it. This is natural, so do not struggle with these feelings.»

Suddenly I felt much better, lighter and more joyful. Perhaps it was just his voice, but the words were like a soothing balm to my pain. Now slightly more confident I took the opportunity to mention the second thing that was on my mind - the books!

I knew I should be careful not only from a professional stance of not criticizing other teachers, but more, I knew that he knew them personally.
Once again I explained what had happened and mentioning the names of the authors of these two books, I said simply that I thought their view of Dhamma was not correct.
I wondered if I would be rebuked for saying such a thing but actually what I received was the little laugh and then another heavy burden from my teacher.
«These people Michael,» he said, «they're just hippies. They do not have the understanding that you have!» Another Dhamma bombshell, and until this writing now, an event shared with only a few very close disciples.
So now I felt better. My understanding and my feelings were approved by my teacher, so I could relax.
Michael, my eldest son wanted to come to India with me, make the retreat and then stay on and travel whilst my youngest son would stay at home with his grandmother and travel later, and this is exactly what happened.
I celebrated my fiftieth birthday in an Indian restaurant with a small group of students on the Isle of Man and left for India before Christmas.
Michael and I arrived in New Delhi tired but happy, and then continued on to Budh Gaya. For reasons that I cannot remember now, it was not possible to make three retreats so one big one would have to do. I did not see this as a problem and in fact as happens so many times, the cancellation became a blessing. We began as always with the preliminary five day Lotus Tank course and then the formal ten days silent sitting and walking meditation practice.
Students and disciples from other countries, including the Isle of Man, had arrived to join what was advertised and promoted as 'the very last Vipassana retreat' with me in Budh Gaya.

One very special person that I met on my first day there was Isabelle.

We had become close friends by now and she had made yet another retreat with me in the mountains in France just a few months earlier. I was sitting in my friend the tailor's shop where they had given me a bottle of 'Thumbs Up' in those days, the Indian equivalent of Coca Cola. I didn't like it when I was a monk and nothing had changed during the intervening years, however not to seem impolite I accepted and drank it from the bottle.

Just then Isabelle walked past. It was the first time I had seen her since I arrived and the shock, and the excitement and the 'Thumbs Up,' combined, gave rise to an incredibly strong case of hiccups as I chased down the street after her. Not very elegant, I admit, but I didn't want to miss the moment.

The retreat went ahead as planned and all worked well.

Michael, my son, sat perfectly for the ten days, as did everyone else, and no problems were encountered.

One afternoon I found a small piece of chocolate wrapped and balancing on the handle of my door. I didn't know who had left it there, but later discovered that it was a small gift from Isabelle. Our flirtation had begun in the town before we started the retreat, but as I was still so naive I had not realized, and still did not realise what was happening. Clarity was still some days away!

The retreat finished and we all entered town life again only to discover that scandal was rife. Christopher Titmuss had been accused of seducing young women in his room whilst on retreat. Actually Henry and I had heard these rumors many times in the past but I had always dismissed them as untrue. How could someone involved in Dhamma ever exploit other beings? I saw then just how deep my naivety ran. It seems to me that it is an expression of the pure heart, and so corruption of Dhamma is almost unbearable to accept.

When we live without the desire to influence, persuade or

exploit others we show something beautiful - we show Dhamma. A young woman in my room one time on retreat told me that she had fallen in love with me. This happens occasionally and as always, compassion and integrity are the qualities needed, for ourselves, for the other and for the reputation of Dhamma. When someone makes themselves vulnerable in front of us it is our responsibility to take care of them, not exploit the situation. When I responded to her words she continued, «How could I not be in love with someone who listens to all the terrible things I say about myself, but never judges?» This is how Dhamma manifests. Not by judging or telling others how they should be, what they should wear or how they should think, but being peacefully with the moment as it is, and then responding wisely. Love is always an expression of wisdom.

Christopher had answered this first single accusation by standing in his Dhamma hall in front of the whole retreat community of more than one hundred people, and announced that such a thing had happened only once and that he had been lead by his heart. All the men groaned at such a feeble excuse. If we cannot wait for ten days to be with someone in an intimate way, it is not our heart that is leading us!

However, other young women immediately banded together and told the same story about his seduction techniques, even to the point of establishing a website for solidarity. So first came the fall from purity, and then the lie. I have already said that I liked Christopher very much, but even without personal judgement, this was hard for me to accept.

I had trained in the purity of Dhamma, with a Master who told me that my responsibility was to serve the world with love and wisdom, and that none of it was about me.

I sat alone in Pole Pole one morning a few days later when one of Christopher's retreat managers came along. He was a young American man who had sat two or three retreats with me at Gaia

House and who joined me at my table.
«Did you hear the news?» he said. I answered that I had.
«What do you think?» he continued.
I told him that so great was my love for Dhamma that such a story had broken my heart and I am now so pleased not to have any connection whatsoever to Gaia House or other spiritual institutions.
«Without integrity we are lost,» I concluded.
He paused for a moment and said, «But you must notice beautiful women in your Dhamma hall that you would like to sleep with?»
My honest answer, then and still now is this: of course I know that my Dhamma hall contains men and women. Of course I know that some are younger, taller, shorter, fatter than others, but truly in my eyes, they are fellow human beings and no more. It is my responsibility to take care of them and more than that, serve them with truth.
My Dhamma name is Paññadipa. During my ordination I was told that this means 'Island of Wisdom,' implying that I am alone in my practice and life, and my integrity. However, years later my teacher told me that the word 'Dipa' also means 'light' as in the light of a candle to illuminate the darkness. Therefore Paññadipa also means 'Light of Wisdom,' and wisdom is the manifestation of purity.
After this incident there was a meeting of the famous American and British spiritual teachers to decide and then agree upon when it is acceptable for a teacher to sleep with a student. In my mind, simply to have such a meeting reveals the lack of depth in modern spirituality. Meditation teachers abound, but Dhamma Masters are as rare as hairs in the palm of your hand.
Christopher continued to teach and his reputation did not seem to be tarnished. I wondered then, what wisdom he could possibly be sharing with others now?
Henry and I wanted to go to Puri for one last time and so we

invited Brigitte and my personal favorite choice, Isabelle.

We booked our tickets and took the overnight train from Gaya. Because of many delays the journey was even longer than usual but traveling with Henry was alway a joy as he too loved India and was not afraid to try many new snacks on board.

We also bought food from the vendors at the different stations, drank lots of chai and coffee and laughed so hard when poor Isabelle, finally persuaded to try a simple pakora, found that the one she had chosen contained only a very hot chili!

Isabelle loves India too, but not being British, spicy food is not always so easy for her.

We finally arrived almost at the station but the train was too long for our coach to reach the platform, and so we had to scramble down with the other passengers and walk the last hundred meters with our bags.

A rickshaw followed to my regular hotel named the Holiday Inn, of course, no connection whatsoever with the huge hotel chain known throughout the world. I enjoyed staying here after my usual months in Budh Gaya because it was simple, clean and comfortable with western beds and toilets. It was slightly more expensive than the more familiar guest houses, but I enjoyed the comfort and the cleanliness. I was greeted as a familiar friend and chose my room. Isabelle, for the same reasons as me took the room next to mine. Henry and Brigitte took rooms in a guest house further along the road, but we all agreed to meet every morning and late afternoon in my room for meditation and any Dhamma questions. I was happy enough for this and the rest of the day would be ours to swim in the Indian Ocean and eat delicious food at the famous 'Peace restaurant.'

Russell and Shelley the long time students of mine from the Isle of Man joined us a few days later and we became a small Vipassana group in the beautiful coastal town of Puri.

Isabelle and I became a couple on 18th January 2002, and I was

certain from the first moment that this was the woman I wanted to marry, even if like many divorced people, I had vowed never to do that again.
Each evening our small group would walk along the beach before a communal dinner. It was here that the term 'Pure Dhamma,' was originally coined for my presentation of the teachings of love and awareness. I had already freely expressed my concern and disappointment over what I considered to be the corruption of Dhamma and what I wanted was to only be connected to the pure Dhamma.
«That's it!» shouted Henry in a 'eureka' moment, «let's call it Pure Dhamma.»
So that was that. The name and the philosophy stuck and although it was some years before it became public, it was then and always has been my guiding principle.

Isabelle and I were now a couple but she lived in France and I stayed on the Isle of Man. At this point we were both relaxed enough to let nature take its course as to where we should live as a couple. In my mind I always thought that the Isle of Man would be a good choice for us, but a better option was waiting.
On one of my still regular visits to my teacher he gave me the date for the first retreat in the now finished Dhamma Talaka Monastery in Birmingham. Although I had shared in its construction and ground breaking ceremony it was nevertheless quite impressive as a completed structure.
Everything was agreed and I began to notify people with the date and the address.
In all there were about ten people who came and sat this first retreat, one of whom of course was Isabelle.
We met at the airport and I brought her to the monastery and introduced her to my teacher, a special moment for me.
Then I took her to the peace pagoda especially constructed

according to my teacher's specifications where the retreat should be held. It was a large temple and Dhamma hall with the central point for the eye being the huge Buddha statue, smiling and looking benignly at the beings that presented themselves in front of him.

It was here I asked Isabelle to marry me. She said yes without hesitation, so that was that. One less thing to worry about, as Forest Gump would say.

The retreat passed without incident although everybody met themselves, which is not always a comfortable experience, but everyone survived. At the end in the early spring sunshine were the photographs of us all, some with monks and even Mar Mar Lwin joined in. Special!

We eventually left the monastery and spent the last night in a small hotel close-by. In the morning I went alone to say a private goodbye to my teacher and speak about the Buddha statue that he had brought for our first retreat on the Isle of Man so many years before.

Some weeks later I was alone at home on the Isle of Man when the telephone rang. I answered and was surprised to hear the husky voice of my teacher saying my name.

It was unusual that he would call me, the only other significant times were about the creation of the Manusa Dipa Vihara, now completely defunct, and the death of his great friend and my first Buddhist teacher, Hamalawa Saddhatissa.

Once again pleasantries were discarded and we arrived straight at the point.

«Michael, I want you to come to the Buddha Day celebrations this year in Birmingham.»

Buddha day, or Vesaka Puja is the celebration of the birth, enlightenment and final passing of Siddhartha Gotama, the Buddha. Each event is said to have taken place on the full moon of May during his lifetime and so are commemorated as closely

as possible to the present full moon in modern times, usually on the most convenient Sunday in the month.
I almost let out an audible groan. I had attended many of these celebrations in the past and they have a resemblance to me of Easter when I was a child.
I quickly thought of reasons why I could not come. It was expensive to travel (true), I was busy (not true), I just didn't want to come (absolutely true).
He must have noticed the pause because he quickly interjected, «Michael, I want you to be the guest of honor and give the special afternoon Dhamma talk.»
I was truly taken aback. Me, the guest of honor? Obviously he couldn't find anyone else.
Now everything was different, certainly not from a position of arrogance, but rather a position of service. My teacher has asked something of me, and it is my privilege to serve. I did not know what he truly had in mind, but I agreed immediately and our arrangements were made.
I would arrive in Birmingham, Saturday 25th May, stay with my teacher, give the Dhamma talk the following day and return home on an evening flight.
Good, that is simple and clear, and mostly what happened.

I arrived in Birmingham and went straight to the monastery to be met by Mar Mar Lwin and Bhante and was treated in a loving and affectionate manner, offered tea and biscuits and asked about my life.
I had decided to stay in the same small hotel as before so as not to be a nuisance in the monastery and so after this social and almost familial interlude we agreed that we would meet in the monastery grounds the next morning at ten o'clock, as the ceremonies would begin with a Dana lunch offering for the monks at eleven o'clock. In all the intervening weeks between the invitation and my

arrival I had not planned a talk in any way. I wanted to say to the community only that I felt honored and privileged to be a disciple of the Buddha and my teacher. This was a pure thought and did not give rise to further comments. 'Right,' I thought, 'that will have to do, now let's see what can happen.'

I met Bhante in the grounds of the monastery as planned and he took me with him to welcome the many Burmese and British families coming for this once a year special Buddhist ceremony. What I had not, and could never have anticipated was Bhante's presentation of me to each family.

We were standing together and each new arrival would offer Anjali to him and say a few words of greeting. Then he would introduce me not only as his disciple, but now a famous Dhamma teacher presenting courses in many countries in the world. These families then would look at me with different eyes and offer a humble and respectful Anjali. I felt like I could be my grandfather's favourite grandson being presented after winning an award.

This went on for what seemed like a long time with me inwardly squirming at each introduction until finally it was time for him to leave me as the guest monks were arriving. Even then it was not so easy for me as I was passed over to Mar Mar Lwin whose job it was to welcome the guest monks and in doing that, also present me.

«This is Michael,» she would say, «he was one of my monks.»

Eventually everything was ready and I was left standing outside with the local sangha.

Even if we had met briefly at the retreat and Dhamma talks some months earlier and even if today I was the guest of honor, not one person came to me to say hello or make me feel welcome.

It was a surprising thing, but in reality there is as much jealousy and competition in the so-called spiritual life as everywhere else. However, such behavior is cold and cannot be called a practice of loving kindness.

Finally the monks had eaten everything that was offered to them and I was ushered into the huge peace pagoda in preparation for my two sentence Dhamma talk. The room was full with more than six hundred people present, mostly sitting on the floor and already shuffling either from boredom or anticipation. The monks themselves, including my teacher, were settling down to sleep as is their custom after lunch, and I was given a place at the back of the room.

A friend of mine, a man named Yann Lovelock, a long time supporter of Bhante and the monastery, made the customary welcoming speech and introduced the first speaker. I hadn't expected this as usually I am a 'one man show,' but I sat still and waited. The speaker was a young man from Venerable Sanghrakshitas community, the 'Friends of the Western Buddhist Order.'

I thought he spoke very well and said everything necessary for such an occasion, but as I looked around the room I saw that his words did not connect in any real way with his audience. Now, as I say, I am always a 'one man show,' so it was interesting for me to see how other teachers present the Dhamma to the world.

He finished and sat down.

Yann took the microphone again and began my introduction. Like everything Buddhist it was joyful and he took the opportunity to give me a long 'rock and roll' style introduction, calling me Bhante's favourite and most famous disciple, as well as an international teacher, etc, etc...

I felt I had to stop him and so I stood up and walked to him and took the microphone.

I took my place slightly to one side of the great Buddha statue where, on the other side, my teacher sat cross legged in a very ornate large chair completely asleep. Next were all the guest monks sitting in a straight line with their heads nodding as they found themselves in between sleep and wakefulness.

I looked out at the gathered crowd and said what I had come to say.

Two sentences. It was a privilege to be a disciple of my teacher. It was a privilege to be a disciple of the Buddha. Just then a thought came. I will just say this next thing, then I will sit down.

Modern television is filled with what is known in America and the United Kingdom as 'soap operas,' half hour stories of particular communities of people who should simply not live together! One famous one in England is called, 'Eastenders'. The continuing story is shown many times a week with a special long edition on Sunday afternoon.

I stood in front of the six or seven hundred people and made one small point to emphasize the importance of the Buddha.

«This man,» I said gesturing at the beautiful statue, «brought something wonderful to the world, and its presence is still felt today. Actually, if it wasn't for this man living in India two thousand six hundred years ago, none of us would be here right now, we'd all be at home watching the omnibus edition of Eastenders.»

The room exploded with laughter. My teacher woke up. The monks sat up and I knew in that moment that I had connected with the room. The Dhamma talk fell out of my mouth and it became a celebration of the teachings.

I spoke for forty five minutes, said thank you and took my place at the back of the room again.

Following this moment I was given the title Dhammachariya, meaning Master. I spoke to Nagasami, a monk and authority in Pali language who explained the significance to me after which I told my teacher I could not be a Dhammachariya because I was not a monk.

«It is true that it is usually a title for monks but when we feel someone truly understands Dhamma, it can be given,» he said.

I never understood and did not have the occasion to ask if this whole Buddha Day celebration was just a subterfuge to bring me to the monastery for this incredible honor, but an honor it was, and the final gift of my teacher.

He took my arm as we stood for photographs and said quietly, «That was a very good talk.»

I was happy with everything especially the opportunity to be of service to my teacher, but then something happened that I did not feel so comfortable with.

I had been ignored earlier in the day by the Birmingham sangha, but now I was seen as a celebrity and they surrounded me, calling me Dhammachariya and asking me to contribute to the monastery newsletter.

I was not impressed, and my only thought was, 'You didn't want to know me when I was a stranger standing alone in the grass, now you all want to be my friends.'

Such hypocrisy is not unusual in the world but my feeling is as always, that given enough time and opportunity, we will always show our true selves - Buddhist or not!

I said a grateful goodbye to Mar Mar Lwin, bowed to my teacher and left.

I never saw him again and he died exactly two years later on this very day.

- PART 3 -

MY LIFE AS A KOAN.

A journey to Awakening

The year passed and in between teaching and traveling I was preparing to leave the Isle of Man permanently and live in France. Isabelle had already spent some time with me on the island and had always enjoyed its beauty, but as the weather had been so awful each time she was there, the decision to live in a country known for its good weather and fresh summer fruit and vegetables, made itself.

I had already introduced her to Eileen and was happy for that. It was a good, friendly and respectful meeting, and in a strange way I felt proud to put these two special women together. I always feel that Isabelle and my father would have been good friends also and the four of us could have spent happy and joyful times together.

On 18th January 2003, thanks in part to the kindness of a British Airways desk clerk, I arrived in Toulouse airport with the last of my belongings, including the big Buddha statue that my teacher had given me all those years before. My bags were really overweight, but this particular lady helped me and with some expert weight juggling and the turning of a blind eye, she sent me on my way without having to pay excess baggage fees.

Isabelle and I took an apartment in Foix, the capital town of Ariege and I began my French life.

I took French language lessons at home with a lovely young woman teacher called Sophie.

Like Henry and the Lotus Tank, for our first meeting I was hoping that she wouldn't come, but she did and she was wonderful, inspiring me to go past the idea of sounding stupid. If I have any skills at all in French now I give all credit to Sophie and her way of sharing this beautiful language with me, perhaps also supported by Mr Sneath at The John Hamilton grammar school for boys in Liverpool.

After only a few months in Foix we had the possibility to rent a house in the small village of Pradieres, close by. We counted our money, reflected on the cost and took a chance. It was a good decision. The house was simple, the two other families in the village were very friendly and helpful and actually took me under their wing. By this time we had our two cats, a brother and sister called Bimbo and Frenchy. They were still kittens when we arrived and so grew up in nature and a sense of freedom.

One of my greatest pleasures and something completely new to me in our little village was the garden. It was quite large and although I would like to take credit for the vegetables we were able to grow, I have to say that the soil was so rich almost nothing else was necessary after the planting. Everything natural of course, and no chemicals ever in contact with our food.

One time on the Isle of Man I had given Isabelle a salad with tomatoes. She tasted it and said, «Not enough sun.» Now I understood. The tomatoes here depending on the variety were enormous and full of flavor. I would spend many hours in the garden talking to the plants, honoring nature and being alone.

From a teaching perspective we made several retreats in the mountains in the south of France, and even private retreats for close French disciples at our home. Of course I was still journeying to Germany which was rapidly becoming the gift of my professional life, and the Isle of Man to teach the group there and also one week courses at the university and so life was comfortably busy.

In our private life we both felt that we had been a couple now for long enough and it was time to get married. It was our original intention after all, and Isabelle was impatient to change her name to Kewley.

She worked hard with the incredibly difficult French bureaucracy, organized everything necessary and we married in the simplest way possible on 18th January 2005. Two close friends were our required witnesses and when it was my turn to say 'oui' Isabelle kindly nudged me in the ribs. So that was it and we were married. We went home, toasted each other with champagne, exchanged rings and continued with our life.

Like the Buddha, three of the significant moments in my life arrived on the same date. I think that it mostly happened by chance but it does make remembering special moments (and forgetting them) them easier!

Our simple routine continued until one year later I received a message from my niece on the Isle of Man saying that Eileen, my father's wife of twenty five years had died.

I had not seen her since my last teaching visit there some months before, but her decline had been rapid and she died of natural causes in hospital on 28th January 2006. She was seventy six.

Naturally I went to the funeral and took my place as the oldest surviving male in the Kewley family. I was happy that I could say goodbye to her in this formal way as we had always shared a good relationship and I truly feel that since my father's death some years before she would awaken each morning with a sense of disappointment that she herself had not passed away in the night.

At home once again in France some months later I received a letter from Eileen's solicitors informing me that I would receive an inheritance quite soon. Naturally this was wonderful news and although the amount was not colossal, it certainly was more money than I had ever had in my possession before. The will was divided between my two sons, Joyce, the sister of Eileen, my sister and myself.

One day the bank transfer took place and suddenly by our meager standards, we were wealthy people. Now, what to do with all this money?

Neither my lovely new wife nor myself held a fascination for money, but we didn't want to see it simply sitting in the bank and so we decided to buy a house. After all we had to live somewhere and provided no banks were involved, it seemed like a good idea. Of course it wasn't a lot of money so whatever property we bought would probably need some renovation.

Once again Isabelle did the work, this time on the computer and finally found three or four houses within our price range in the department of Les Landes, about two hours driving, north of Toulouse.

We went to visit the houses with the agent, and were disappointed by each one until finally, hot, tired and bored we arrived seemingly in the middle of nowhere. This was a house in a forest clearing, certainly big enough for two people and two cats, but it would need a lot of work. Isabelle jumped at it and said, «This is it, this is the one.»

I was more reluctant but also thought that if she wanted it, it was certain we could make it work. My father had shown me many things based in an old philosophy that a man must have many skills, and working in and on the family home should be high on the list.

We were driven back to Nerac, the nearest town, took a coffee and talked seriously about the house. If I'm traveling would she feel comfortable by herself? The nearest neighbours are a kilometer away in each direction, and there is so much work to do, can we do it?

We reached our decision and made an offer for this house. It was accepted and many months and legal procedures later, it became ours.

There was a lot of work to do, both inside the house and outside on the huge piece of land that we could never call a garden, but did belong to us. Upon reflection, I think that this was one of the happiest times of my life. The work was demanding and often difficult for both of us, but we were a good team and slept well at night after many hard days labour.

I now lived in a forest. It had been my dream since I was a young parent on the Isle of Man taking my sons to Summer Hill Glen on Sundays whilst Fiona slept, and Isabelle had made it happen. The chain of cause and effect was long and complex, but here I was, living the life of a forest dwelling monk, even better than I had ever imagined.

In the early morning I would take my coffee outside to the terrace and sit in my meditation posture with Bimbo on one side of me and Frenchy on the other. Then, wonderfully, the deer would arrive and come within touching distance and eat the grass. We would all be together sharing our mutual space. The wild pigs would stay further away but they too were welcome. Bimbo found and honed his hunting skills and would often bring gifts of mice and other small rodents into our bedroom in the middle of the night, then sit back and watch with amusement it seems as we dashed around half asleep trying to capture these small creatures and return them to the wild. Frenchy meanwhile enjoyed her life of being the lady of the house and would take her place at night sleeping squarely in the middle of my chest.

It was a wonderful part of my life and offered many lessons.

One day I was walking alone in the forest when I heard a strange sound. At first I thought it was a bird and so I looked into the branches of the trees, but saw nothing. Then, just as the small path turned I saw one of the most beautiful sights I had ever seen in my life.

Trotting towards me in a quite nonchalant manner was a baby deer, a fawn. He was unaware of me until we almost bumped into each other.

We both stopped and I spoke gently like a parent might.

«Hello,» I said, «what are you doing here? Where is your mother? Don't come too close to me, I'm a human, and the humans that live close to this forest like to hunt and kill little babies like you.»

I looked to my left and standing perfectly still just a few meters away was his mother and a brother or sister.

I gently clapped my hands and ushered him away.

«Go, go to your family. Go.» He hesitated for a moment and then joined his family and the three of them gamboled away into the forest.

It was one of the most beautiful moments of my life, and arising from that was a great Dhamma teaching.

A deep and profound insight arose in my heart that this incident had not 'just happened,' because nothing 'just happens.' It had taken from the beginning of all time and every aspect of human, animal and geographical evolution to arrive in this place where two separate species could meet and share a moment. But as the reflection opened there was also the subtle deepening of understanding and the recognition that Isabelle and I had to have become a couple for me to be in this place, to be in France, to be alone in a forest.

For that to happen every moment of our lives and all the people we have each met and known and fallen in love with had to be exactly like the way it was, for better or worse, and then reaching further back to the lives of our parents, grandparents and great grandparents.

Nothing just happens and each moment is never an accident but a series of tiny events each dependent on the one that preceded it. There are no accidents, only cause and effect and things do not happen for a reason, they happen as a consequence. Each moment is a new moment and can never be repeated and so, not understanding this simple yet incredibly profound teaching, leads us back with no deviation to the First Noble Truth of the Buddha, that life as we experience it has the quality of being unsatisfactory. This moment and this realization flowed into my personal universe and influenced every moment from that time on. It was an immense feeling of interconnectedness, the deepening of an insight I had experienced when I was a monk whilst cleaning out the small pool in the garden of the monastery.

So we settled into our country life and the time passed and because the time passed I got older. Now I was approaching sixty years of age, but still fit and strong and I heard India calling again.

This, we decided would be a good time to return to Budh Gaya and once again offer my thanks for everything she had given me over all those years, from a new life to a new wife. It had been ten years since I was there last and I knew everything would be different and I supposed that no one would remember me and that I would be a stranger again. Our retreats there had finished but they had continued in Europe and brought many wonderful things with them. Our annual New Year Retreat in Germany became more and more popular and because of such good organization and generosity from the students and disciples, brought enough money to finance a three week holiday to India.

We arranged our dates and flights for after this first retreat of the year, applied and were granted our tourist visas, and organized ourselves in preparation for our big day.

Two friends decided they wanted to come with us, and although slightly reluctant, we agreed. The reluctance was based on the feeling that both Isabelle and I love India and accept it for the generous country it is. However, not all tourists or travelers feel that way and this proved to be the case with our friends. Whilst we saw the wonder and beauty of this country they in the end, saw only the dirt on the street.

It's a long journey to New Delhi from Toulouse, but we made it and arrived filled with excitement. I was so happy to be back. It's true that many things were different, but it was still India.

We all took a taxi into town and then to the station to reserve our seats on the first available train to Gaya. Of course we were all exhausted from the long flight but at the same time eager to get to our first real destination.

I took the passports from the others and sat at the desk when it was our turn to be served.

Everything was in order until finally the man looked at my passport.

«This is you sir?» he asked.

«Yes,» I replied.

«And you are sixty years old?» he continued.

«Yes,» again I replied, wondering why he should ask such questions. Maybe he was about to tell me that I look ten years younger, and ask me how I did it? But no, he simply told me that as I was sixty years old I would receive a reduction on the price of my ticket.

The train was the next afternoon and so we took a small hotel in the Paharganj area and rested. Isabelle and I ate in a small Indian café whilst our friends searched for and found a Macdonalds.

The train was on time as far as I remember, and I ordered the usual evening meal. For me this is a favourite part of being in this country and in all the years I have been a guest there, I have never been truly sick. The simple rule is 'don't drink the water,' and in my personal experience, everything else is fine.

We arrived at Gaya junction about four o'clock in the morning and stepped over many sleeping Indian bodies waiting for their own trains. It is an ability that Indian people have and that I have always admired, the ability to find a place to lie down and sleep. We westerners pace up and down, drink chai and continually look at our watches.

Waiting is always suffering.

We took an auto rickshaw the thirteen kilometers to the outskirts of Budh Gaya and got out just before the Burmese Vihar. We had all agreed that we would find a good hotel for our first day, to shower, rest and refresh ourselves, so we began to walk the long single street towards the stupa.

It was now perhaps six o'clock and the town seemed to be deserted. Isabelle and I were like excited children to be here again, pointing to the various shops and market stands.

«That was my tailor,» I said as we passed the place where I had first seen Isabelle and out of shock and delight developed the hiccups ten years before.

«This is where I had my meditation cushions made,» said Isabelle as we passed the stand further along the road.
I'm sure our friends hated us then for not sharing in their disappointment of this country. Suddenly we heard a voice shouting and a figure waving at us.
«Guruji, Guruji.»
To say I was surprised would be an understatement. I had truly thought that no one would remember me after so many years, but this would not be the case. I received a hero's welcome to this town I loved so much and it began here with Gautam, the owner of Lassie corner.
To quote my father in such situations, «Well Michael, it's not often you're right, but wrong again!»

I had known Lassie corner well and it became a popular meeting place being so close to the entrance of the stupa, and one of my favourite cafés to take a special cooked breakfast of poori and sabji, a sort of fried chapatti with spicy vegetables.
On one occasion when I was there sitting and drinking a chai, a very famous western Tibetan Buddhist monk walked straight to my table and sat opposite me.
«You're Michael Kewley?» he said.
«Yes,» I replied.
«You are my favourite guru in Budh Gaya,» he continued.
«But I'm not a guru,» I answered.
He pointed his fat finger at me and laughed, «And that's why you're my favourite!» he finished.
I felt this to be a good compliment, especially from such a well known figure. The modern spiritual world is filled with people presenting themselves as awakened and enlightened, and to reinforce that idea in others they behave in a way that is not completely natural.
The soft almost whispering voice, the inability to complete even

a simple sentence without slipping back into bliss. The enigmatic laugh as they show their understanding of something that you as the student, have not yet realised.
An oscar winning performance of a presentation of enlightenment. But Awakening is as natural as breathing. It is not outside our ordinary human experience and those who make a show of something special in this dream-like way only present something that is known in Vipassana training as 'Soft Mind'. The mind without any real energy.
If this had been the Buddha's realisation, his teaching could not have continued and survived for almost two thousand six hundred years. All the beautiful teachers I have lived and trained with, were quiet, gentle, loving people with tremendous energy and vitality. Their Dhamma talks did not send me to sleep, but inspired me to practice. To come fully into my own life and to make an even greater effort for my own liberation.

Gautam came running over, presented Anjali to me and offered chai to welcome us to his town. The five of us sat together in the cold Budh Gaya morning waiting for the sun to arrive to warm us. We asked about a 'good' hotel and Gautam, like all Indian men, told us that it would be very difficult at such a time of year, but he could arrange it for us and get the best price. I think he had forgotten that both Isabelle and I knew how India worked, but nevertheless were grateful for his assistance.
The hotel we took was expensive by Indian standards, but was comfortable, clean, offered breakfast and had a shower. What more could we need. We freshened up, ate and Isabelle went to rest.
For myself, I did not wish to miss a single moment as in my mind we would stay here for only two days, so I went to explore. I met so many people who recognized me and offered Anjali whilst welcoming me back.

I made my way to the Burmese Vihar to meet Neusatas, the Spanish lady who had given me the $100.00 at the Lotus Tank after the fire in my room and arrived at the gate.

Chulu, the reservation manager was there and greeted me and told me where to find Neusatas. She was still a regular visitor and kept her room year after year. As I walked through the grounds I met the abbot, Sayadaw U Nyaneinda, who met me with a broad smile and the simple words, «Ah Michael, so you came back.»

It was a special moment for me, so touching to be greeted this way by this man, and I remembered all the assistance he had offered during the years I was teaching here, first in his Dhamma hall and later at the International Meditation Center. We spoke together reflecting upon who had died and the changes to the town until his duties called him and I went to see my friend. Venerable Rastrapal had died some years earlier but was well remembered in the town both as a good monk but perhaps a better businessman.

Next it was time for lunch and the only possibility on our first day back was Mohammad's restaurant. I had known Mohammad since he was a fourteen year old boy running a simple restaurant while his two older brothers cooked and got stoned in the kitchen. Whatever people may think, Bob Marley is as much the sound of India as any Hindi film music.

In those early days I was eating there one evening and had ordered thukpa. This is a mixture of spaghetti in a soup of vegetables and spices which you can order with or without meat. Mine was vegetarian naturally but to my horror I found a piece of meat in the bowl. I picked it out with my chopsticks and held it up as the young Mohammad was walking past.

«Mohammad,» I said, indicating the offending morsel of meat with my eyes.

He looked, he saw and without slowing down in any way, picked the meat off my chopsticks, said, «Sorry sir,» and continued to the kitchen where he presumably added it to the pot of non vegetarian thukpa.

Later, he chased his brothers out and became a well-respected and well-loved business man, taking care of not only his own family, but almost anyone else who needed it.

When the modern western media continually reinforce the nonsense idea that all Muslims are murderers and rapists they really need to stop corrupting the world with such poison and meet people like Mohammad and the millions of others like him. Once again I received a hero's welcome as we stepped into the tented restaurant and were shown all the improvements.

Now he had a new guest house and tomorrow he could offer us two double rooms.

We ate a wonderful Indian meal and he took us to see his guest house in the old Indian village of Budh Gaya.

He and I walked together like old friends, which in a way we were, and Isabelle and our western friends followed behind. We arrived at his guest house that really was wonderful. He showed us the first double room, designated for our friends and opened the door. It was clean, spacious and simple with a shower and two single beds.

Next came our room on the ground floor. Again clean, spacious and simple with a shower and two single beds, but also a sofa and extra space.

«Michael,» he said, gesturing with his arm, «this is for you and madam.»

I thanked him as I heard a mumble from behind me.

It was from our woman friend who was disappointed that we had been offered the larger room rather than them.

Isabelle, now perhaps a little tired of this attitude spoke a truth relevant to the situation.

«You know,» she said, «you have to be loved in this town to receive such kindness. This is the place of Michael.»

The next day we moved in and were grateful for such hospitality.

We would often go to the flat roof to be in the sunshine and look at life in the Indian village it overlooked. It was very pleasing perhaps especially the young married couple below and the love and attention they bestowed upon their small son.

Each morning we would rise early and go to the meditation garden next to the stupa and sit together with the sun rising and daylight hitting our faces. At the end I would chant, smile at my wife and we would go for breakfast.

Our friends left after two days and went to Goa, to be in more familiar western surroundings, but we stayed. The days passed and I would ask Isabelle if she was ready to leave, her answer was always the same, «No, not everyone has met you yet!»

In the end we were there for seven days and received kindness and generosity from many people.

«Sir, sir,» they would cry, «do you remember me?» and mostly I did, but even when I didn't I would say yes, and stop and speak with them.

The familiar places of ten years earlier were changed or no longer there, but it was still Budh Gaya and our last evening was special for us.

For the final time, perhaps in this lifetime we walked together around the candlelit Stupa, offering thanks to the Buddha and the Dhamma, and the people of Budh Gaya. Tomorrow we take a train to Varanasi, to stay for some days before traveling on, at least that was the plan.

The journey to Varanasi was not so easy with our train from Gaya already three hours late and we had to get off at a station half an hour outside the town and take a taxi. Of course we knew this when we booked our tickets, but what we didn't know was how difficult it would be.

Finally we arrived and found a comfortable guest house and installed ourselves.

Varanasi, a favourite destination for both of us.

The next morning we rose early and went to the river. It is so beautiful there in the pre-dawn darkness with the boatmen waiting for tourists, both Indian and western to hire their boat and glide along the water. First we were offered small candles in leaves to place in the water as a blessing. We, as people who have visited this country many times, know this is really for tourists and a way to make money, but this is Varanasi, and this is the great river Ganges, and the whole presentation is beautiful, so we did it and enjoyed it.

Then we set off. Exactly the same route as I had taken the first time twenty years before, first down the river watching the devout men and women purifying themselves in the holy waters, and then up the river to the burning ghats, and a brief rest for the boatman. It was cold, but we were happy to be in this special place that we loved so much.

Finally we returned to the ghat and sought out breakfast.

German Bakeries are commonplace now in many towns in India and Varanasi is certainly no exception. Here you can go and sit on the roof in the early morning sunshine, eat almost western bread and jam with good coffee and look out over the rooftops back to the river.

Then back to our guest house for a shower and a rest.

Later in the afternoon a walk along the riverbank trying to avoid as much as possible the aggressive touts selling postcards and anything else they can find.

The next day we went to Sarnarth to see the stupa that marks the place where the Buddha gave his first sermon.

This was more the idea of Isabelle who wanted to make a photo shoot for the Pure Dhamma website. This was not my best day as I inexplicably felt exhausted and the long, dusty and noisy auto rickshaw ride had not helped. I put on my teaching shirt, posed in the sunshine, and Isabelle clicked away.

So my desire to serve Dhamma but my insistence in being left alone becomes my koan.

It is true that I am a recluse.

I venture into the greater world only to share Dhamma and I am pleased to do it, but I do not crave celebrity or fame. My Master sent me to this place from the peace of the monastery for the sake of others so they too can hear and meet Dhamma. It was never about me, but only to make available the teachings of Love and Awareness.

In these modern times the spiritual world is enormous and filled with guru celebrities, and so many books and courses available, but I only reflect that even if I sat in front of a crowd of one thousand people, how many could honestly say that they are true disciples of Dhamma? I have never been interested in spiritual fashion and new age ideas. I trained with a Master who trusted me to guard my own integrity and serve others, and I, although I have met many who did, cannot compromise what I have understood. I am pleased that I am not connected to any associations or spiritual centres and I stay true to the highest and purest sharing of Dhamma, to honor the Buddha, my own teachers and the Dhamma itself. This is why I am an outsider and this is why we called our movement, Pure Dhamma on the beach in Puri all those years before. The highest and simplest Dhamma training is based in awareness and love. It is a true and generous sharing from heart to heart.

We sit together in the silence of meditation, and I will tell stories and jokes to open your heart and to inspire you to further training so that your life will become a blessing to you and all the beings that you share the planet with. But this responsibility always rests with you.

I offer no badges or marks of progression, only the opportunity to be in the service of those who are also brave enough to put down what they carry and realise full spiritual Awakening for themselves. I will always endeavor to be available for others, as my Master was for me, but in truth, without seeking or desiring celebrity, I search for those who want Dhamma in their life as much as the Buddha did. As much as my Master did. As much as I did.

We spent our days in Varanasi listening to sitar music at night in a small café and reading and meditating in our room.

We looked towards our next destination, planning our journey to Rajasthan, neither of us realizing what was about to arrive in our lives.

The following evening we decided to take our dinner at the German Bakery. It was close, convenient and so far had not disappointed. We ordered and ate the delicious food and took a drink. Orange juice for me and mango juice for Isabelle. Soon we wandered home and went to our beds.

I was awakened in the middle of the night to a strange sound which took a few seconds to recognize. It was Isabelle, in the bathroom vomiting for all she was worth.

I went to help, and took her back to bed, but this was just the beginning.

Over the next few hours a slight tummy upset turned to diarrhea which in the end manifested as dysentery.

The advancement was rapid and she fell in and out of consciousness. She had brought some western medicine which seemed to help a little and I sat with her for three days and helped her to drink a little water and clean her when necessary.

Perhaps it was strange but I never felt overly disturbed by the situation and I was certain that I could do whatever I needed to do when the time was right.

On the fourth morning she awoke with brighter eyes and said she would like some toast. That was it, the recovery had begun.

In reality it took many months for her health to be fully restored,

but with gentle loving care everything found its balance again.
Upon reflection we think the mango juice from the German Bakery was the culprit as it probably had water added to it. To repeat the simple rule of traveling in India: don't drink the water! That evening she ate a meal in bed especially prepared for her by the very helpful and kind staff at the guest house.
Now we sat together, she in her bed and I on mine and she began to speak about her experience. It was a debriefing and I listened as she explained the process she had encountered.
«It was not particularly unpleasant,» she said, «as there was no pain, but the interesting thing was that I had the feeling that I would not have minded if I had died.»

The Dhamma journey is a process of cause and consequence like everything else in life, and so if we face the right direction we cannot be surprised to arrive at our destination, even if we have already forgotten that it was a journey at all.
I had been an ardent disciple of Dhamma for more than forty years and had given myself completely to the discipline and integrity of practice. Without realising it my journey was almost completed, it needed only one more key to open the door of liberation.
I sat on the bed next to her and heard these words, 'I would not have minded if I had died,' and immediately in my mind my own peaceful loving voice answered, 'me neither.'
It was the moment of complete and absolute acceptance of the world and universe that we do not control, a surrendering without remainder into the universe.
Then came the deepest understanding and my release from the world.
I can only speak now with cumbersome conventional language to point to that which is far beyond language. I do not speak about the experience of full Awakening, that was only a timeless moment that seemed to last for hours, but the complete freedom

from fear and desire, the attributes of 'self'.

Twenty years earlier I had sat alone at the burning ghat with my hand trailing in the holy waters of the Ganges. This image was strong and I imagined all the fear I carried in my life flowing down my arm and into the water, to be carried away forever.

Now it had happened and my life and everything in it would never be the same.

I turned my head to face Isabelle but she was completely unaware of the enormous passage of time that had elapsed since she spoke and that I had been sitting almost trance like and without moving for such a long time, but in a moment I realized that she was simply continuing the sentence she had begun about not dying. It was a moment, but inside that moment was the intuitive understanding of all things.

I sat with her until she was ready to rest again and I took her dishes back to the kitchen. Everything was different now and I had to tell someone.

I had never understood why in all the Dhamma stories, the disciple at the point of Awakening must share the reality of that experience. Now I understood. It's just too big, too huge, we have to take it out of ourselves.

I felt I could not tell Isabelle what had happened.

Even if she was a true disciple of Dhamma, that her husband had to all intents and purposes, died in Varanasi that evening, never to return in the same form, might be too much to bear.

For two years it was a secret between us, although many times I suspected she knew. There was always something subtle in her comments about my behaviour. 'You are you, but not you,' she would say. We persisted in this way until one morning as we shared a simple breakfast together I could no longer avoid her questions, and admitted everything.

It may sound romantic but we were and are, a true love story, a couple connected beyond the conventional relationship of man and woman, and as she heard the words she already knew to be true, her heart broke and a single tear rolled down her cheek. We sat in a shared, loving and peaceful silence but knew our life together could never be the same.

Upon Awakening, when all the misunderstandings of 'self' are completely dissolved and all the desires and fears associated with it fall away, the only thing that is left is a convenient illusion of a person, a compassionate smile from the heart, but nothing tangible to hold on to.

To be with such a being is a beautiful but often frustrating blessing and is known as 'living with a cloud.' This is the end of the path to Awakening.

But that was many months in the future. Right now I had to release this enormous pressure of love, compassion, joy and oneness. It was not an excitement, it was a pain, but who could I share this death and rebirth with?

I went to the Internet room that adjoined the guest house and sent a message. There was only one person I could trust with this information, and that was my own closest friend and disciple Henry, Dhammachanda.

Here is the actual message I sent:

Dear Henry.

Sometime during these first few days of February 2012, whilst staying in the Indian holy city of Varanasi, this being, carrying the name Michael Kewley, awakened.

All fear and attachment dissolved and the space left manifested only as universal love, compassion and joy. I look for someone to call 'me', but find only a smile.

You know that I trust you completely to accept this honest revelation and my only feeling is to share it with you, based upon our relationship of friendship and Dhamma. It is for you to do with as you like.

It is said that in every instance enlightenment must proclaim itself once to others, and after forty years of sincere and dedicated practice to Dhamma we cannot be surprised to arrive finally at the place of liberation.

Life is short and uncertain and I want only to share my love and joy and final release with you.

May you be well and happy always.

Michael

Isabelle continued to recover and as her strength returned we walked a little bit and sat in the gentle Varanasi sun. Whatever had happened, I was still her caring loving husband and she my delicate wife.

Eventually we met our friends again at the airport, took our flight and made our way home, back to our forest and our simple life.

Now everything was different, but nothing had changed.

Full liberation is a life-affirming, life-enhancing experience. Releasing the last remnants of fear and the attachment to an always limiting self identity. In this place there is energy and vitality as any notion of who and what you are simply falls away. Here there is the beautiful completion of 'oneness' with life, with the universe and with all beings. A dissolving into emptiness.

I slept, I cooked, I walked in the forest. I shared my time with the beings close to me and offered my love to the universe. Having completely put down the notion of 'self' my life was now experienced without desire or fear, expectation or anxiety, only love, compassion and an intuitive flowing from moment to moment.

Where there is fear, there is self. Where there is desire, there is self. Where there is self, there are difficulties.

This is what the Buddha and all the great Masters pointed to, that freedom from suffering only comes with freedom from self because only self can suffer.

In the most beautiful way, each day is the same day. Life is expressed only as Dhamma and so is the living presence of a being who does not feel himself to be outside the universe judging and commenting, but completely one with all things.

Sleeping, waking, laughing, sharing the loving yet desireless heart, everything is Dhamma. This is my life, which is not mine, but the experience of liberation.

As the snow slides gently off the leaf in springtime, the last vestiges of self fell away that evening in Varanasi and I put my hands together in Anjali to every being I have ever had contact with who, simply by their presence in my life, brought me to this place.

It is my passion now more than ever, to share the purity of Dhamma and I make myself available for anyone who is truly interested, but I cannot be part of the selling of integrity.

I will offer everything, but what will you bring as part of our relationship?

I am only a simple Dhamma Bhikkhu, beyond fear and desire and sharing only the contents of my heart.

I travel to where I am invited and share the truth and beauty of Pure Dhamma to the best of my ability. I live from the kindness

and generosity of others and feel always that my life is blessed.
I have no political, social or religious views of inequality to expound, I have only Dhamma. Live with love and be aware. Only in this way will you truly bring happiness to your own life and the life of all the beings we share this beautiful planet with.
This was my journey. A gentle, loving but consistent step by step path of liberation.
It was not magic, not even spiritual, but practical, personal and founded only in the determination to no longer be a victim to my fear.
Even the longest journey begins with a simple intention.
All these words are offered with humility.

Epilogue.

In my Dhamma life I am happy to be a simple Master, taking care of that which was entrusted to me. I offer no ceremony, no certificate, no initiation, no ladder to climb in front of others. I give no reward, no badge of office for your effort in meditation. I share only my love and enthusiasm for pure Dhamma, the teaching of Gotama before religion was born. I encourage only honesty and integrity in practice - such a difficult path to walk when the spiritual business world offers so much. In the temples and monasteries I see people with their hands together in Anjali all the while pushing for their place in front of others. I hear people speaking of love and compassion all the while happily eating the flesh of fellow beings. I hear people speaking of mystical experiences all the while pursuing the lowest aspects of human behavior. For me, I have nothing to offer but the silence of meditation and the elegance of Pure Dhamma practice. Not seeking to be someone, but aspiring to be no-one is the way of Pure Dhamma, and those who arrive with humility and right intention will always find a place next to me.

May all beings be happy.

Michael Kewley.
France
December 2016

A journey to Awakening

Acknowledgements.

This is the first time I have been asked to write a book that had a consistent story and time line running through it from beginning to end.

Usually I present short teachings about Dhamma in daily life or singular subjects such as Vipassana teachings or Kamma, to support students and disciples in their daily practice, and so this book was a true challenge.

The memories came thick and fast and although I tried to keep them in a chronological order I would have been completely unable to do this without the invaluable help, support and direction of Vera Steckel.

Her expertise guided me through the Dhamma journey of my life and although I have made every effort to present this as a story rather than a historical document, it would have been a very different and much more confused tale without her patient and caring help.

The second person to acknowledge for their invaluable and patient assistance is Leonie Gschwendtberger. She, like Vera took time and care to share my story with others, correcting sentences and idioms to make it available to all.

Finally, my wife Isabelle, friend, disciple and protector of Dhamma and it's practice in the world.

Organizing the format of the book you are holding, checking and double checking that the presentation is not only pleasing to the eye but correct as far as we can make it.

To this triple gem of women I offer my utmost thanks.

Without your place in my life it is certain to me that this book would not have materialized and so I bow to your efforts and offer my Anjali to you.

May you and all beings be happy.

Also by Michael Kewley

1994: Higher than Happiness (Revised edition: 2014)
Mehr als nur glücklich sein (German version)

1996: Vipassana, the way to an awakened life (Revised edition: 2013)
Vipassana, der Weg in ein erwachtes Leben (German version)

1999: Not This (Revised edition: 2013)

1999: Life Changing Magic (Revised edition: 2009)

2006: Walking the Path (Second Edition: 2007)

2007: The Other Shore

2009: Life is not Personal
Nimm das Leben nicht persönlich (German version)

2007: The Reality of Kamma

2011: Buttons in the Dana Box
Knöpfe in der Dana Box (German version)

2011: The Dhammapada

2015: Loving Awareness

About the author

Michael Kewley is the former Buddhist monk Paññadipa, who is now an internationally acclaimed Master of Dhamma, presenting courses and meditation retreats throughout the world. For many years he was the guiding teacher at the International Meditation Centre, Budh Gaya, India and is the founder of the Pure Dhamma tradition of spiritual Awakening.
A disciple of the late Sayadaw Rewata Dhamma, he teaches solely on the instruction of his own Master; to share the Dhamma, in the spirit of the Buddha, so that all beings might benefit. On 26th May 2002, during a special ceremony at the Dhamma Talaka Temple in England, he was awarded the title of Dhammachariya.

More information about Michael Kewley, including videos and Dhamma talk extracts, can be found at:

www.puredhamma.org

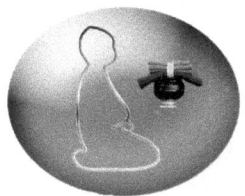

A journey to Awakening

www.ingramcontent.com/pod-product-compliance
Lightning Source LLC
Chambersburg PA
CBHW071328190426
43193CB00041B/964